Topiary, Knots and Parterres

PIMPERNEL PRESS LTD

www.pimpernelpress.com

IN ASSOCIATION WITH THE EUROPEAN
BOXWOOD AND TOPIARY SOCIETY

Topiary, Knots and Parterres

Caroline Foley

Pimpernel Press Limited
www.pimpernelpress.com

Topiary, Knots and Parterres
© Pimpernel Press Limited 2017
Text © Caroline Foley 2017
For copyright in the illustrations see page 288.

A catalogue record for this book is available from the British Library.

Designed by Anne Wilson
Typeset in Garamond

ISBN 978-1-910258-18-7
Printed and bound in China
by C&C Offset Printing Company Limited

9 8 7 6 5 4 3 2 1

ENDPAPERS Parterre designs by Claude Mollet included
in *Le Théâtre d'agriculture et mésnage des champs* by
Olivier de Serres, published in 1600.
HALF-TITLE PAGE Gardeners demonstrating their first
electric clippers on the topiary at Levens, in the early
1950s.
TITLE PAGE The venerable Jacobean topiary garden at
Levens Hall, Cumbria, as it is today.
RIGHT Elegant topiary at the Château de Veyrignac in
the Dordogne, France.

Contents

Introduction

THIS BOOK is a celebration of the delights of topiary, which – according to the *Oxford Companion to Gardens* – is quite simply the 'art of shaping and training trees and shrubs'. My aim is to knock it off its perch as the grandee of garden techniques and to explode any false mystique surrounding it as an exclusive type of gardening. Topiary is a medium that deserves to be in every gardener's box of tricks, and the techniques should be at the disposal of every horticultural student. It can make a splendid alternative to expensive architecture and sculpture. It lends itself to folksy humour as much as to clipped perfection – covering the full gamut from the ridiculous to the sublime.

At the sublime end is the green architecture which the seventeenth-century English diarist John Evelyn described as *hortulan*, where gardens became part of the grand scheme along with the building, with a key palette of stone, water and evergreens. The clipped evergreens contrast and soften stone and marble. As a dark living backdrop they set off and enhance them.

Topiary makes plain or fancy hedges, which can be decorated by clipping topiary extravaganzas – balls, vases, birds or myriad other characters – along the top or on the piers or finials.

It can be carved into sheer walls (*palissades*) of great height or make an entire garden room (*cabinet de verdure*) with elegant windows or arches (*berceaux*).

Other techniques include pleaching to make aerial hedges; grafting and training as espaliers, cordons, Belgian fences, *drapeaux marchands*, *palmettes obliques*, heart shapes and other fancies, for improved fruiting.

BELOW Sublime Versailles: a detail from *L'Orangerie et la Pièce d'Eau des Suisses*, by Jean Cotelle, 1693.
OPPOSITE, CLOCKWISE FROM TOP LEFT The faintly ridiculous: *Sir John Saxy upon his Yew-Tree*, by James Wigley, 1729; figurative hedge topiary in Kent; *palissades* from *La Théorie et la practique du jardinage*, by Antoine-Joseph Dezallier d'Argenville, 1709; a Victorian illustration demonstrating ways of training fruit trees; an Italianate palette of clipped evergreens, water and stone at Hatfield House, Hertfordshire.

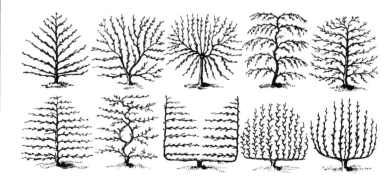

Decorative effects can be achieved by plaiting the young shoots, tying them down or weaving them together. Topiary pieces can be grandiose, or kitsch, or abstract and formal.

'Parterres', says the *Oxford Companion*, 'are flower gardens, particularly in the area adjoining the house, laid out in a regular ornamental manner.' In fact, they were often designs traced out on beds without flowers but filled with inert material to show off the pattern – ground brick, marble, even coal dust. From the time of the Italian Renaissance, when gardens became part of the architect's brief, they were designed to be viewed from above. They were on geometric lines, and usually comprised equal numbers of beds with different patterns. In Italy these were known as *compartimenti*, while the French called them *compartiments*.

In seventeenth-century France, the *compartiments* had become *parterres*. Instead of being numerous regular squares with patterns based on squares and circles, they were now one large overall flowing pattern, like a Turkish carpet laid before the palace or château in grand style. Categorized by type, they ranged from the elegant *parterre de broderie* (embroidery parterre of swirling patterns), to the *parterre de pièces coupées* (where the patterns were cut into the turf on simpler

lines) and the much plainer *parterre à l'anglaise*, which the English called a 'plat'.

Though in practice the words have often been used interchangeably, the distinction between knots and parterres is that knots (in French *entrelacs*) form an actual knot without beginning or end, so represent infinity. The symbolism goes back to third-century BC Sumerian carvings of intertwined snakes. The eternal 'lovers' knot' was the height of fashion in England at the time of the Tudors (who had a passion for puzzles).

The arrangement of the patterns on the ground, whether knots, compartments or parterres, often sprang from practical considerations. The simplest of patterns is the four-square garden intersected by a cross – *charhar bagh*, from *charhar* (four) and *bagh* (river). This was dictated by the need for water, irrigation frequently being achieved by means of a grid system with water drawn from a central source. Later it came to represent the Cosmic Cross, which symbolizes all of creation (there are four points of the compass, four seasons, four corners of the earth and four winds of heaven).

With the rise of Christianity the Cosmic Cross became the Holy Cross. The fountain in the centre now represented baptism and possibly the Holy Spirit.

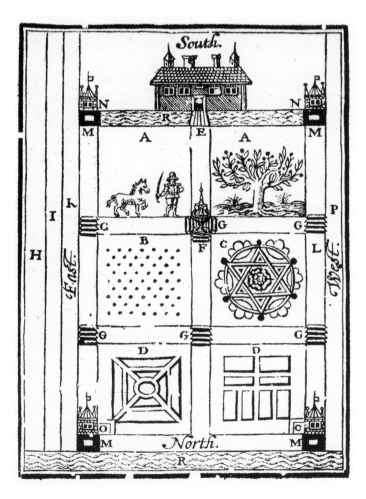

OPPOSITE LEFT A bay tree with a trained heart-shaped stem.

OPPOSITE RIGHT Grandiose topiary at the Tulcan Cemetary, Ecuador.

ABOVE LEFT Kitsch rabbits.

ABOVE RIGHT Formal topiary patterns, from *Erlustierende Augenweide in Vorstellung herrlicher Garten und Lustgebuade*, by Mathias Diesel, Augsberg, 1717–22.

LEFT A garden plan designed on the cross, showing a knot and the quincunx pattern. From *A New Orchard and Garden*, by William Lawson, 1618.

BELOW A design for a knot by Thomas Hill (alias Didymus Mountain) in *The Gardener's Labyrinth*, 1577.

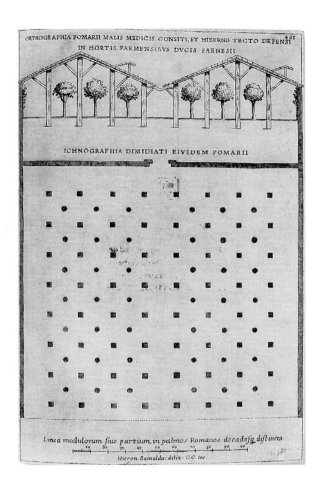

The number four (or multiples of it) has appeared over and over again in garden design and parterre patterns, and still does.

The quincunx is an arrangement of five objects in a square or rectangle, with one in the centre and the other four at each corner. It allows maximum sun to fruit trees but was also commonly used for formal plantings of topiary, as it offers diagonal vistas through, as well as vertical and horizontal ones, with opportunities for focal points in all directions.

The labyrinth pattern has variously been seen as a trap for evil spirits, a path to good fortune, a pilgrimage, a meditation tool and a place for courtship and dalliance. It is a matter of wonderment that the pattern has appeared in places around the world as diverse as on rock engravings in Goa and in the White Sea, in Iron Age Galicia and on Cretan and Roman coins. The Greek historian Herodotus (484–425 BC) in his *Histories* (Book II) spoke of a labyrinth at the palace of King Amenemhet in the nineteenth century BC, in Hawara, Egypt, as 'surpassing description'.

However, it is the Cretan legend of the Minoan labyrinth of 1600 BC that resounds through garden history. According to the myth, in the reign of King Minos there lived on the island of Crete the half-man half-bull Minotaur, the offspring of Pasiphae, Minos' queen, and a divine bull from the sea. At the command of Minos, the architect/inventor Daedalus constructed at the king's palace at Knossos a labyrinth in which the Minotaur was imprisoned. Every year (or every nine years – the stories vary) the Minotaur was fed the tribute of seven young men and girls from Athens. Theseus, the son of the King of Athens, volunteered to be part of the tribute, with the intention of killing

LEFT ABOVE Quincunx pattern by Giovanni Battista Ferrari in *Hesperides*, 1646.
LEFT BELOW Two knots and a labyrinth by Thomas Trevelyan, seventeenth century.
OPPOSITE A seventeenth-century hedge maze at Villa Pisani, near Venice.

the Minotaur. Ariadne, daughter of King Minos, fell in love with Theseus and gave him a ball of golden thread to unwind as he went into the labyrinth, so that, having killed the Minotaur, he could find his way back.

Meanwhile, Daedalus, the labyrinth-maker, and his son and assistant, Icarus, were also imprisoned in the labyrinth. To escape, Daedalus constructed wings of wax and feathers for them both. In his elation at flying, Icarus forgot his father's warning not to go too near the sun. The wax melted and he fell to his death in the sea.

The labyrinth, or the 'House of Daedalus', has been a central theme in gardens since the Middle Ages. The topiarized hedge labyrinth appeared around 1600, at much the same time as the boxwood parterre (boxwood having been previously ostracized for its unpleasant smell). In time, the 'unicursal' (single path) labyrinth turned into the maze – not a journey but a 'multicursal' puzzle with dead ends designed to confuse and entertain.

Other patterns for parterres came from embroidery (as in the *parterre de broderie*), lacework, floor tiles and ceiling motifs and the carved bosses on roofs. While the Italian Renaissance designers tended to prefer simple geometric patterns, the French Renaissance made parterre patterns of flowers, birds and feathers reflected in their china and fabrics. Heraldry also appeared in the parterres, especially as a celebration of victories. The Germans particularly favoured figurative topiary on top of clipped hedges.

A reaction came as the finest royal gardens, glittering Versailles their figurehead, came to be seen as suffocating showpieces. All had become too tight-laced, too predictably geometric, too symmetrical. As, in 1731, Alexander Pope was provoked to remark in *Moral Essays*:

. . . Each alley has a brother,
And half the platform just reflects the other.

Anti-topiary rumblings had started a century earlier. In his *Essay of Gardens* in 1625 the English philosopher Francis Bacon commented, somewhat acidly, 'As for the making of knots, or figures . . . they be but toys.'

RIGHT Victorian-style bedding out in Wales. OPPOSITE Sculptural curves at Château de La Ballue, Brittany.

With the Grand Tour, interest in classical antiquity and the romantic, idealized landscapes of Poussin and Claude put paid to topiary, certainly in England and also widely on the Continent. Horace Walpole, Whig politician and man of letters, aptly said of William Kent, the earliest English landscaper, 'He leapt the fence, and saw that all nature was a garden.' The fashion for the Palladian landscapes of the English landscape movement resulted in many beautiful landscape gardens. The irreplaceable cost was the demise of the venerable formal gardens and their topiary.

Revival did not come until Victorian times, when bedding out in parks and gardens was invented to display the plants introduced by the great plant hunters scouting untrodden corners of the globe.

The devotees of the Arts and Crafts movement in England at the turn of the twentieth century enjoyed using topiary as furnishings for their gardens. After a lapse through and after the war years, topiary (always irrepressible) surfaced again. The Japanese influence, expressing venerable age in 'cloud' topiary, is a strong theme among modern designers today, as is a free-hand sculptural style.

Until the nineteenth century, this history necessarily follows the major trends set by the privileged few – the emperors, kings and queens, cardinals and great landowners who were in a position to employ the most skilled architects, artists and artisans of their day. Only these gardens have records and plans, the written accounts of the garden architects as well as of horticultural and agricultural authors.

While the chapters pick up the main trends from the Roman patrician garden to the French baroque and the landscape movement, lines of influence twist and overlap throughout the history of garden design. The Romans were influenced by the gardens of ancient Greece. Later, both Greeks and Romans were impressed by the Islamic Paradise gardens. Into the obscurity of the European Dark Ages the Crusaders carried back from the East the words of Aristotle and Vitruvius (and hitherto unknown seeds) to be grown in the monasteries. Medieval Christian gardens bore a strong resemblance to Islamic Paradise gardens. Renaissance gardens harked back to ancient Rome. And, although the eighteenth-century landscapers deplored topiary, they were as much inspired by the

great Renaissance architects as were seventeenth-century French formal gardens. The influence of the greatest French garden designer, Le Nôtre, spread as far as the radiating avenues of nineteenth-century Washington, DC. And it echoes still.

While it cannot be doubted that topiary must have existed in the earliest civilizations, no actual remnants survive. All we have are tantalizing fragments in literature, fables, poetry and art, and some clues from archaeological excavations. We read that the Spanish conquistadors were amazed by the richness and magnificence of the gardens of pre-Columbian America (dating from 2500 BC), which had 'parterres' filled 'with artificial plants made of gold and silver'.

Cortés described the gardens of modern-day Texcoco in Mexico as 'the largest, freshest and most beautiful that ever were seen'. His fellow conquistador Bernal Díaz del Castillo (c.1495–1584) wrote in *The Conquest of New Spain* that 'no future discoveries will ever be so wonderful. Alas! All is overthrown and lost, nothing left standing.'

In 800 BC, in the *Odyssey*, Homer writes of King Alcinous, ruler of the Phaeacians, in whose island in the Ionian Sea tall trees of pears, pomegranates and apples 'full of fruit' flourish along with 'sweet figs and bounteous olives . . . and well-laid garden plots full of flowers'. He speaks of regularly spaced trees, pools and fountains, and rustic trellises for vines.

The Greek envoy Lysander (d. 395 BC), was hugely impressed by the beauty of the trees in the Persian garden of Cyrus the Younger and with 'the accuracy of their spacing, the straightness of the rows, the regularity of the angles and the multitude of sweet scents'.

However, it is in ancient Rome that we finally get the first mention of topiary as we know it. Buried under the ash of Vesuvius, Herculaneum lay hidden for sixteen centuries until some workmen digging a well came across it in 1709. From the breathtaking wall paintings we can see a dreamlike world of azure blue skies, elaborate trellises, urns, exotic birds and flowers. There is no topiary depicted but we know it was there. This is because, by strange coincidence, Pliny the Elder – who died while trying to mount a rescue during the eruption of Vesuvius – made the first known mention of it in his great encyclopedia of natural history, *Historia Naturalis* of AD 77–79.

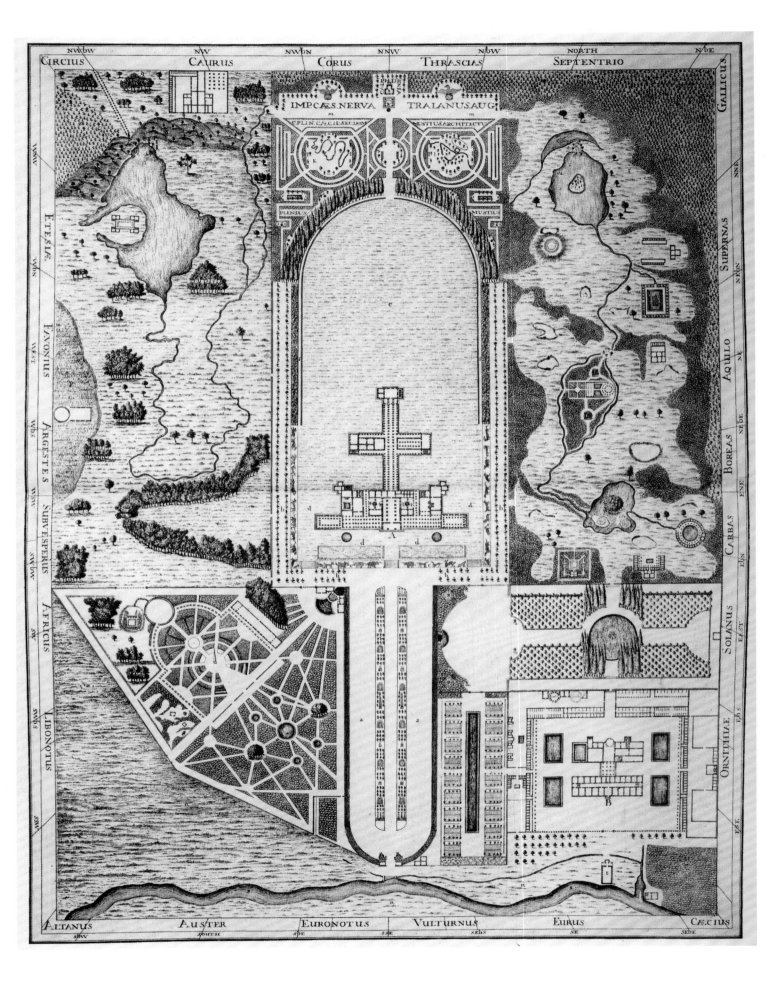

The Patrician Gardens of Rome

AD 79–476

THE ROMAN SCHOLAR and naturalist Pliny the Elder (AD 23–79) mentions topiary when weighing up the pros and cons of the Mediterranean cypress. In his *Historia Naturalis* (AD 77–79), he remarks that that the slim Mediterranean cypress comes into its own in the topiarist's horticultural works of art ('in pictoras operis topiarii') because its 'fine short, evergreen leaf retains the outlines of hunting scenes, fleets of ships and imitations of real objects'. 'Nemora tonsilla', or 'barbered groves', he claims, were invented by a certain Gaius Matius, 'during the reign of Augustus', a period of comparative peace and prosperity at the turn of the first century AD.

Little is known of Matius other than that he was described by Cicero as *doctissimus*, so we can assume that he was learned. It was recorded that he had been a close friend of Caesar's, sharing camp with him on the military campaigns in the savage wilds of Gaul and Britain.

OPPOSITE An eighteenth-century reconstruction (employing some poetic licence) of Pliny the Younger's villa in Tuscany. Published by Robert Castell in *Villas of the Ancients Illustrated*, 1728. The hippodrome is flanked by parkland and fishponds. In the formal gardens at the bottom of the plan are colonnades, fountains and pools, with clipped topiary. In the roundels at the top, rocks, cascading water, trees and classical ruins are in romantic disorder.

LEFT Pliny the Elder working on his *Historia Naturalis*, using dividers and an astrolabe. From the frontispiece of a fifteenth-century Venetian manuscript of the book.

However, it is Pliny's nephew, Pliny the Younger (AD 61–112), a Roman consul, and valued in posterity for his descriptive letter writing, who gives the most vivid account of Roman topiary. Until the discovery of Hadrian's Villa in the fourteenth century and then of Herculaneum in the eighteenth, Pliny the Younger's colourful letters were the main source of information on Roman villas and their gardens.

He was seventeen when his uncle died leaving him a string of villas and gardens. He describes the boxwood at Laurentinum, his garden close to the sea near Rome, where 'all round the drive runs a hedge of box, or rosemary to fill any gaps, for box will flourish extensively where it is sheltered by the buildings, but dries up if exposed in the open to the wind and salt spray.' However, if the boxwood did not survive well there, it certainly did in in his villa, Tusci, in the cooler hills of Tuscany, where he had an extensive topiary garden.

In a letter to his friend the consul Domitius Apollinaris,[1] he describes how, in front of the colonnade of his house, there is a terrace laid out with box hedges which are 'clipped into different shapes, from which the bank slopes down, also with figures of animals cut out in box facing each other on either side . . . All round is a path hedged by bushes which are trained and cut into different shapes, and then the *gestatio* [a hippodrome, probably no longer used for horse-racing but as place to take exercise] inside which are various box figures and clipped dwarf shrubs. The whole garden is enclosed by a dry stone wall which is hidden from sight by a box hedge planted in tiers.'

Subjects for topiary

We gather hints about the Mediterranean cypress, the favoured subject among the Roman beau monde for topiary, from another great scholar, Columella (Lucius Junius Moderatus Columella, AD 4–70). His books, *De Re Rustica* and *De Arboribus,* which had citations from Cato the Elder, Varro and others, were the definitive Roman agricultural encyclopedias.

Columella's take on the Mediterranean cypress is that it is difficult to grow, bears no fruit, has a pungent smell and does not provide agreeable shade; and its weedy timber is little better than that of a shrub. In fact, it is such a failure as a plant that it is consecrated to *Dis Pater*, the god of the infernal regions (or hell) and is placed by house doors as a sign of mourning.

Pliny the Elder, meanwhile, claimed that there were two types of Mediterranean cypress – the female pyramidal type and the spreading male. These were the slim Italian cypress (*Cupressus sempervirens* 'Stricta')

[1] Pliny the Younger, *Letters*, V
[2] Pliny the Elder, *Historia Naturalis*, XXI
[3] Horace, *Odes*, II, 15, 5–6
[4] *Historia Naturalis*, XVI, 20
[5] *Historia Naturalis*, XVI, 28

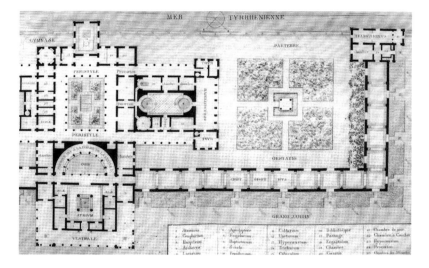

A nineteenth-century reconstruction and plan of Pliny's seaside villa at Laurentinum. From *Le Laurentin, maison de campagne de Pline le Jeune*, by Louis Pierre Haudebourt, 1838. Haudebourt imagines being taken on a tour of house and garden by Pliny the Younger himself and talking to his architect.

as opposed to the stone pine (*Pinus pinea*) or possibly the spreading Mediterranean cypress (*Cupressus sempervirens* var. *horizontalis*).

Also mentioned by Pliny the Elder, for clipping into a 'round bushy shape', is 'Jupiter's Beard'.[2] This most likely is *Anthyllis barba Jovis*, which bears the same popular name today. Bay laurel and myrtle were also favoured for topiary, especially as they have the added attraction of scented foliage.[3] Yew, being poisonous, was not considered suitable. Pliny claims that it contains 'so active a poison, that those who sleep beneath it, or even take food there, are sure to meet their death from it'.[4]

Boxwood, *Buxus sempervirens,* was the main subject for topiary in Roman times, as it still is today. Pliny noted in *Historia Naturalis* that it was 'esteemed for a certain toughness and hardness and for its pale colour, while the tree itself is valued in ornamental gardening (*topiario opera*)'.[5]

He defines three types of boxwood – the *Gallicum* or 'Gallic box' (*Buxus sempervirens*), which is trained 'to shoot up into conical pillars and

Boxwood-edged bays in the
reconstructed Roman palace of
Fishbourne, Sussex.

attain a considerable height'. There is also oleaster (*Elaeagnus*), which, he
says, is 'condemned for all purposes and gives off an unpleasant smell'.
The third sort is 'a cultivated variety of the wild box which spreads more
than the others and forms a thick hedge and will stand clipping'.

Topiary in Roman Britain

In the remains of the great palace of Fishbourne in Sussex, archaeologists
have reconstructed the garden from the first-century planting trenches
where the soil, clearly enriched, was darker than the surrounding poor,
gravelly subsoil. This contrast in the colour of the soil revealed a pattern

of a double strip of convex curves (making alcoves suitable for statuary or seats). The darker soil was the right depth and width for a box hedge. Though here there were no traces of pollen left, apart from that of common weeds, there is clear evidence of boxwood pollen in other Roman sites in Britain – in Frocester, Silchester, Winterton and Farmoor.

[6] Cicero, *Paradoxa Stoicorum*, 5,2
[7] Pliny the Younger, *Letters*, LII

The Roman gardener

The Roman gardener was generally known by his particular function. The *arborator* worked on trees, the *vinitor* cared for the vines, the *olitorius* tended the olive groves, while the *aquarius* saw to the fountains and waterworks. The gardener in charge of the ornamental gardens was the *topiarius* – derived from *topia*, which the *Oxford Latin Dictionary* describes as 'contrived effects of natural scenery'. This originated from the Greek *topia*, which was a painting of the idealized garden in the portico of a real garden. The *topiarius*, therefore, was the skilled head gardener who would work alongside the architect to create the *opus topiarium*, or the ornamental landscape. His job would also entail *nemoria tonsilia* or clipping hedges, as well as root pruning.

Rome depended on slave labour and generally slaves were treated no better than livestock. They could be killed or punished at the whim of the master, or sold off for a likely public death as gladiators. Yet, while most laboured in the mines or quarries or on the roads, some had high positions as the tutors of patrician children, as accountants or physicians.

Or as gardeners. The most educated gardeners in Roman times were Greek slaves. Though there is no actual record of topiary in Greece, it is generally assumed that it was Greek gardeners who introduced topiary to ancient Rome. The Roman orator Cicero, whose secretary, Tiro, was a slave (freed before his master's death), described the *topiarius* as being among the 'higher classes of slave'.[6] An educated *topiarius,* could, with luck and a fair master, earn money, buy his freedom and even become a Roman citizen.

A further indication of the high status of the *topiarius* was that he was allowed to clip out his name in the boxwood in bas-relief alongside that of his master. Pliny the Younger records that, in his hippodrome in Tusci, 'there are box shrubs clipped into innumerable shapes, some being the letters which spell the gardener's name or his master's.'[7]

The pruning tool of the Roman gardener was the *falx*, which, according to *A Dictionary of Greek and Roman Antiquities*, was a term that covered the sickle, the scythe, the billhook and various war weapons as well as the pruning knife or pruning hook. The *falx* differed from the straight-edged knife, or *culter*, in being curved. Different shapes and sizes of *falx* were

Three images from a coin, showing an Egyptian king, a man cutting corn and, at the bottom, the billhook-shaped *falx*, taken from Columella's *De Re Rustica*, IV. The *falx* in its various forms was the main pruning and topiary tool in Roman times and for centuries after.

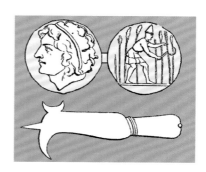

[8] Columella, *De Arboribus*, 10
[9] Pliny the Elder, *Historia Naturalis*, XVIII, 67
[10] *Historia Naturalis*, XVII, 24

used for specific tasks, including reaping, hacking down (thorns, butcher's broom or bracken), as well – of course – as pruning (vines). Sometimes the cutting edge was serrated or toothed. For trees and topiary there was the *falx putatoria* or *falx arboraria*, which is much like today's billhook.

Columella tells us in *De Arboribus* that after a branch had been cut off with the *falx*, the cut would be smoothed with a chisel.[8] The Elder Pliny notes in *Historia Naturalis* that *falces* were sharpened with whetstones 'from Crete and other distant places', with the addition of oil or water which the 'mower' carried in a horn upon his thigh.[9]

Pliny implies that grafting was already a well-known skill. He expresses the opinion that the scion – the detached shoot that will be joined on to the rootstock – should not be cut while the wind is blowing. 'A graft should not be used that is too full of sap, no by Hercules! No more than one that is dry and parched . . . it is a point most religiously observed to insert the graft during the moon's increase.'[10]

The names of individual topiarists have been found carved on tombstones. 'Lucrio, a *topiarius* from around Naples' was one such. 'Fortunati' was a *topiarius* from the Como region, whose stone also commemorated his wife and his 'pupil', or apprentice. They may have been freemen. Some inscriptions were on communal tombs, possibly for estate staff or members of a *fratres*, a 'brotherhood' burial club, set up by the poor to share their funeral expenses.

Augustus and after

The period from the first to the third centuries AD was a golden age in the Roman Empire. The reign of Augustus (27 BC–AD 14), first Roman emperor and successor to the murdered Julius Caesar, brought relative peace, *Pax Romana*. During this time, magnificent public pleasure gardens sprang up around the imperial city of Rome. They were on formal lines, with pavilions, colonnades, statuary, fountains, pools and topiary. There were beds edged with box and stocked with flowers. Trees and shrubs for shade would have included stone pine, chestnut, plane, bay, walnut, acacia and cypress.

The statesman Cato the Elder (234–149 BC) recommended in his *De Agricultura* (160 BC) that gardens, especially if near the city, should be planted with 'all sorts of ornamental trees including myrtle on *palissades*, both black and white'. Water was abundant, as it flowed through the aqueducts designed by Rome's engineers, sourced from distant mountains to feed the Roman baths and fountains.

Vitruvius, writing in the first century BC, laid down the principles of classical Roman architecture in *De Architectura*, the *Ten Books of*

A highly decorated Corinthian capital from the Coliseum, Rome. A drawing of the Italian School, 1535–7.

Architecture, dedicated to Augustus. Though referred to by Pliny the Elder as 'Vitruvius the architect', he saw himself first and foremost as a *ballista*, or artilleryman, a master builder and an engineer.

Buildings should have the three 'Vitruvian virtues', *firmitas, utilitas et venustas*, expressed through symmetry and balance, order, proportion and 'decorum'. They should be solid, useful and beautiful. Architecture should be inspired by nature and reflect the natural inherent order and harmony. As birds and bees build their nests from natural materials, so should humans. The proportions of buildings should correspond to those of the human body, as do the Greek proportions for the Doric, Ionic and Corinthian columns.

The columns, with their capitals on top, were designed to resemble the human figure. The monumental Doric column, found in the Parthenon, was the earliest model. It is the heaviest and shortest of the three forms and has no base. A more graceful shape comes with the Ionic column, which was calculated to represent the proportions of a man's foot in comparison to his height, to show the beauty of the male body. The Corinthian column, similar to the Ionic column but slimmer and lighter, is said to evoke the slenderness of a maiden. It is more elaborate, decorated with acanthus leaves in accordance with an old legend of love. In three-tier buildings, the Doric columns would be on the base, the Ionic on the next floor and the Corinthian columns at the top. Vitruvius was to devise a module of half the width of the diameter

TOPIARY, KNOTS AND PARTERRES

from which all proportions of the three classic columns would be taken in multiples or fractions.

The eighteenth-century English landscape garden was inspired by the Vitruvian virtues and by the letters of Pliny the Younger. There was one exception – they did not share the Roman enjoyment of topiary figures. Horace Walpole, in the *History of Modern Taste in Gardening* (1750s–60s), expressed astonishment that Pliny the Younger, in an age 'when architecture displayed all its grandeur, all its purity, and all its taste; when arose Vespasian's amphitheatre, the Temple of Peace, Trajan's forum, Domitian's baths, and Hadrian's villa, the ruins and vestiges of which still excite our astonishment and curiosity; a Roman consul, a polished emperor's friend, and a man of elegant literature and taste, delighted in what the mob now scarce admires in a college garden.'

While the Roman poor lived in multi-storey, barrack-like slums on the outskirts of the city, wealthy citizens, like Pliny, would own several properties. They would have the *domus* in town and would enjoy the *villeggiatura* – escape from the city to the peace of the villa. The exodus might be to the *villa maritima* (by the sea), the *villa rustica* (in the country) or the *villa suburbana* (outside the city). The villa, which continued to be a key element in life in the Renaissance, represented a retreat to simple living and relaxation, and opportunities to study, to entertain friends, to go hunting or to pursue other forms of open air sport. Pliny the Younger writes with relief that in his villas 'there is no need to put on your toga . . . everything is calm and quiet.'

Though the villas represented the country life away from the stress of the city, those Romans rich enough to have two homes would have in both underfloor heating supplied by hot air flowing through hollow bricks. Their villas would be filled with fabulous Greek art. Their libraries would be stacked with volumes of poetry and literature in Latin and Greek and their cellars stocked with wine.

Pliny the Younger describes how, when dining out in the Hippodrome at Tusci, water tumbled from under a marble seat into a stone cistern in which was a marble basin. On the rim of this were the heaviest dishes of a feast, while floating in toy-sized boats and birds would be the lighter accompaniments. Hero of Alexandria had invented the steam turbine – the aeolipile – the wind wheel and the slot machine in the first century AD and he describes

The reconstructed Roman garden, based on the Villa dei Papiri, Herculaneum, at the Getty Villa, Malibu, Los Angeles.

[11] Pliny the Younger, *Letters*, XXIII

in *Pneumatica* how to make a bird sing by trick waterworks. Such novelties were much enjoyed in the gardens of the Roman rich.

Pliny the Younger rejoiced in wide-open views, something that would disappear for hundreds of years after the fall of Rome, when gardens became enclosed and secretive. He writes rapturously about the character of the countryside round Tusci. 'Picture to yourself an immense amphitheatre, such as could only be a work of nature; the great spreading plain is ringed round by mountains, their summits crowned by ancients wood of tall trees . . . Below them the vineyards spreading down every slope weave their uniform pattern far and wide . . . Then come the meadows and cornfields . . . The meadows are bright with flowers . . . It is a great pleasure to look down on the countryside from the mountain.' Meanwhile, on the second floor in Laurentinum, the dining room commanded 'the whole expanse of sea and stretch of shore with all its lovely houses'.[11]

The classic layout of the house would include an atrium – an open courtyard space within the house (and later without) – with a peristyle, or roofed colonnade, around the edge, like a cloister. In the garden there would be a hippodrome for horse-racing or other sports, divided by box hedges and topiary work. There would also be a *xystos*, or garden walk, with flower beds edged with box or rosemary. Nearby would be a

BELOW LEFT A four-square Roman 'Troy Town' labyrinth with fortifications, from a Roman villa in Orbe, Switzerland.
BELOW RIGHT A Roman 'meander' labyrinth of AD 250. In the centre is Bacchus, the god of wine, with a follower.

TOPIARY, KNOTS AND PARTERRES

fruit and vegetable garden (arranged quincuncially), a rose garden and a labyrinth.

The mosaic labyrinth was a Roman invention. It was usually square, divided into quarters and was known as a *Roma quadrata*, possibly referring to Rome's four gates. As it was only three or four metres square, the paths were too narrow to walk. The mosaics often included depictions of battlements, towers, weapons and fortifications, along with the portraits of Ariadne or the Minotaur from the Cretan legend. On the central spot would stand Theseus, or sometimes Romulus, founder of Rome.

Pictured as being surrounded by walls, the labyrinths represented a fortified city. A seventh-century BC Etruscan wine jar from Tragliatella, Italy, portrayed solders on horseback racing away from a labyrinth with the word 'TRUIA' – possibly meaning Troy – on the rim. This might be why Pliny the Elder records that the labyrinth pattern was marked out on the ground and was known as *Lusus Troiae* – the 'Game of Troy'. This was performed in the Circus Maximus on state occasions by youths demonstrating their horsemanship.

The fall of Rome

As Rome fell into decline, Christianity slowly surfaced. In AD 313, the Edict of Milan legalized Christianity throughout the Roman Empire. Constantine, the first Christian emperor, who was baptized shortly before his death, set up an eastern capital in the ancient Greek city of Byzantium, and changed the name to Constantinople.

In AD 395 the empire was split in two. The western half met its death blow in AD 476 when Romulus Augustulus, the last Roman emperor, was deposed by the German warrior chieftain Odoacer.

But while Europe sank into the Dark Ages, the Byzantine Empire flourished for the next thousand years.

Byzantium and the Paradise Garden

AD 395–1453

THE EARLY GARDENS OF BYZANTIUM were modelled on the style of Rome. Luxurious villas had enclosed formal gardens, containing temples, groves and elaborate mosaics and water in many forms. Practical advice on matters such as irrigation came from the *Geoponica* or *Agricultural Pursuits*, compiled in Constantinople. Widely read, this was a collection of agricultural lore drawn from multiple ancient sources, including Pliny the Elder's *Historia Naturalis*.

Plants in patterns

The Byzantine gardens were set out In the old way, between grids of water channels with straight paths in between. The beds would be sunk below the paths so that they could be flooded for maximum irrigation in a hot climate. A characteristic of the Byzantine gardens was that plants were organized in patterns. They were meticulously arranged in rows or in concentric circles by type – evergreens, fruit trees, shrubs and flowers in descending order. Flowering plants would be placed in straight lines and only rarely mixed.

Byzantine romance

Byzantine romance overflows with rapturous descriptions of the Paradise garden. There would be abundant flowers, shrubs, trees, fountains and exotic animals and birds. A fourteenth-century Byzantine allegorical poem, 'Sophrosyne', by Theodore Meliteniotes, describes what seems to be a popular planting plan with a 'pleasing symmetry and order'. In an imaginary hippodrome garden, the trees are planted in concentric circles.

All around, nearest the wall, non-fruit-bearing trees stand in rows, as if they were a 'first chorus'. A 'second chorus', of evergreen trees, stands within this first circle. The fruit-bearing trees stand as the 'third chorus',

Detail from a mosaic of the sixth century AD at Sant'Apollinare in Classe, Ravenna – last outpost of Byzantium.

＋SCS BALTHASSAR ＋SCS MELCHIOR ＋SCS GASPAR .

Detail of the Three Kings from another mosaic at Sant'Apollinare in Classe.

having all the branches leaning towards the earth, and all of them nodding downward because of the weight of the fruit.

'A sweet Zephyr' is blowing. A pool in the centre has animals and birds on its edge, with water pouring from their mouths, and the garden is reflected in the pool. It is likened to the Garden of Eden. Trees and shrubs include cypress, palm, willow, poplar, oak, elm, ash and box. Some have been chosen for the sound of their rustling leaves. Water is enjoyed for its sound as well as its coolness. Tactile, soft-leaved plants, like velvety sage, planted at the edges of paths, brush your clothes as you walk by.

The gardens aimed to delight every sense. Few would be without the scent of roses, lilies, violets, narcissus or myrtle – each of which had a symbolic value. For taste and their blossom there would be fruit – apple, pear, pomegranate, orange, lemon, fig and different types of nut. Birds always played a large role.

Topiary

Topiary is mentioned by Theodore Hyrtakenos, superintendent of 'public teachers of rhetoric and *belles lettres*' in the time of Emperor Andronikos II Palaiologos (r.1282–1328). Among Hyrtakenos' ninety-three surviving letters is the 'Description of the Garden of St Anna'.

This opens with St Anna's lament at her childless state and ends with the annunciation that she will be the mother of the Virgin Mary. It is not known if the garden was taken from life, imagined or inspired by earlier literature, or a mixture of the three. A repeated reference to lush fruit is obviously allegorical, intended to highlight St Anna's fruitlessness. Apart from this, it might have been a description of a real garden.

Hyrtakenos owned a grove and we know from his letters that he grew pomegranates to give to the emperor. In his position as a court official, he would have been familiar with the great gardens of Byzantine's high society. He is not being entirely poetic when he speaks with some authority about the hydraulics for an automaton fountain, the spacing of trees and topiary.

First he sets the scene. The garden has a surrounding wall in the shape of a ring (circular, of course). A double frieze has been raised upon the wall, soaring aloft high in the air. Wall and frieze are beautiful ornaments each for the other, and encircle the garden in safety. The wall was put together with the stonecutter's craft, so that 'the clever thief could not indulge in theft, nor could the one who enslaves his eyes to love burn into carnal fire because of curious looks'. This seclusion gives the mistress of the garden freedom to converse with God when she desires, raising her mind without distraction.

As an extra layer for complete seclusion, there is an inner circle of topiarized trees – a 'chorus of cypress trees' – which have been clipped or 'configured through man-made artifice'. He describes the trunks of the trees as 'stripped bare and shaped in a cone-like foliage'.

Topiary appears again in another Byzantine romance, *Belthandros and Chrysantza,* written by an anonymous author in the thirteenth or fourteenth century. We read that in the garden Belthandros, saw 'both banks of the river variously set with white vines and flowers of narcissus and with a covering of trees. He threw a glance up at them and saw their beauty, their pleasing symmetry and the graceful rise of their trunks.' These were clearly clipped to shape, as he adds that you would 'certainly have said that a carpenter had turned them smooth on a lathe, set them upright and planted them'.

An account of a real garden with a topiary tree comes from John Geometres, a tenth-century Byzantine soldier, poet and monk. He writes about his own small garden in Constantinople, which, he says, gives him pleasure all year round. A great feature is a 'beautifully shaped bay tree' that protrudes over the wall and is, one imagines, admired by passers-by.

The Paradise gardens of Islam

Islam was born at Mecca with Muhammad in the seventh century AD and sparked a renewed love of gardens. The Koran promises that for the faithful 'the Gardens of Paradise shall be their hospitality, therein to dwell for ever.'

Like the gardens of Byzantium, the Islamic gardens were based on the Persian desert gardens that preceded them. The Persian *Pairidaēza*, which originally just meant an enclosure or park, later became the Greek *Paradeisos*, which described large royal gardens and hunting grounds stocked with wild beasts.

These were peaceful enclosed oases, offering shade for physical and spiritual refreshment for mind and body in hot climates. Water – source of life and symbol of purity – would flow through channels into the courtyards. Usually there would be a fountain, a pool in the centre or a pavilion. These gardens were rectangular in shape, geometric, abstract and kept to the pattern of four quadrants, the *chahar bagh,* divided by the four rivers of Paradise. Shrubs, trees and flowers were carefully placed to add to all the pleasures of the senses. Many of the courtyard gardens were covered in exquisite tiles, mosaics or painting. Sometimes clipped specimens were used to punctuate a border.

Wondrous Islamic gardens blossomed in the Ottoman Empire, the Middle East, Africa, Spain, southern Italy and later in Mughal India. *A Book of Plants*, written by Abu Hanifah (820–895) was taken along with medical drugs and living plants to Cordoba, a great cultural and scientific centre. Seeds and plants were brought from Africa, India and Syria. Medina Azahara, 'City of the Flower', capital of Muslim Spain on

the outskirts of Cordoba, was built in the tenth century. In the thirteenth century, the Alhambra in Granada was created as a holiday palace for the Moorish Sultans in an area that had so many glorious gardens it was described as a 'goblet full of emeralds'.

In 1453 Constantinople fell to the Ottoman Turks under Mehmed II. Little is now known of the gardens of the great palace complex built by Emperor Constantine from which the Eastern Roman Empire was ruled for eight hundred years, because what is left of it lies beneath the sacred Blue Mosque.

SERENISSIMO PRINCIPI, AC IL-
LVSTRISSIMO DÑO.D. GVILIELMO V.
COMITI PALAT. RHE. VTRIVSQ.
BAVARIÆ DVCI. &c.
Vt medio Pretius se transformabat in vndis,
Formosæ cupido Femonæ captus amore:
Sic varia PRINCEPS TIBI nunc se Goltzius arte
Conmutat, sculptor mirabilis, atque repertor.

Medieval Europe
and the *Hortus Conclusus*

5th–15th centuries

Following the fall of Rome, Europe sank into the obscurity of the Dark Ages. No trace would be left of the Roman villa gardens or the magnificent pleasure grounds. For the next five hundred years, constant warfare raged between feudal kingdoms. Urban life almost disappeared as the people fled to the countryside to avoid starvation and outbreaks of plague.

Despite this, gardening carried on quietly in the monasteries, where medical and horticultural knowledge was catalogued and preserved. Like the *chahar bagh*, the Christian cloister garden would be cut by a cross.

Water now represented the Holy Spirit and the fountain symbolized baptism. In Genesis the earth is created out of water, the sky is in the midst of waters and living creatures are called out of water. And we read that 'a river went out of Eden to water the garden; and from thence it was parted and formed four heads.'[1] In the New Testament a distinction is made between water and *living* water. Jesus says, 'From his innermost being will flow rivers of living water' – for living water represents the Holy Spirit.[2] 'If you only knew the gift God has for you and who you are speaking to, you would ask me, and I would give you living water.'[3]

In Solomon's *Song of Songs* the *hortus conclusus*, a locked secret garden within a garden, symbolizes the virgin bride: 'A garden enclosed is my sister, my spouse, a spring shut up, a fountain sealed.'[4] The locked cloister garth ('cloister' from the Latin *claustrum*, meaning enclosure) was adopted by monasteries for a life of contemplation. Later monastery gardens were divided into the *herbularis* for medical plants and the *hortus*, or pleasure garden.

Devotion to the Virgin Mary – Marian worship – was of prime importance. The flowers within the garden represented the virtues of Mary. A popular theme in paintings of the Annunciation was an enclosed garden with the Angel Gabriel offering Mary a Madonna lily, symbol of her purity.

The Archangel Gabriel offers the Virgin Mary a lily, symbol of purity. Engraving by Hendrick Goltzius, 1594.

[1] Genesis 2:10
[2] John 7:37–39
[3] John 4:10
[4] Song of Solomon 4:12

An enclosed, walled Marian garden in a flowery mead (note the braided tree on the left). By the Master of Oberrheinischer, fifteenth century.

The rose was the flower of love, passion and resurrection and the red rose represented the blood of the martyrs. The word 'rosary' came from the devotional rose garden. The humble violet symbolized Mary's humility. An evergreen tree represented the tree of life.

The reign of Charlemagne

A chink of light illuminated the Dark Ages during the reign of Charlemagne (r.768–814). As King of the Franks and Holy Roman Emperor, he expanded the Roman Empire greatly, introduced political and administrative reforms, and promoted education, agriculture and the arts. He had scribes write down the ancient songs and myths and works of antiquity translated from the Arabic.

He took a keen interest in plants and in gardens and produced an edict, *Capitulare de Villis*, stating that seventy-three fruit trees and edible plants and a few ornamentals (including the rose, the lily and the flag iris) were to be grown in the royal gardens of his empire. Despite hard times, he, the nobility and some of the more important monasteries enjoyed fabulous pleasure gardens and great parks stocked with exotic animals and birds.

The mission of Charlemagne (often described as the 'Father of Europe') was to restore the might and the glory of the old Roman Empire, to unite the warring tribes into one nation – Christendom. To this end he kept up relations with the all-powerful Harun al-Rashid (the legendary Caliph of the *Thousand and One Nights*), who sent him rare gifts – including an elephant and a water clock – and even permitted Christian pilgrims to visit Christ's tomb in Jerusalem.

One unfulfilled monastery garden plan, drawn up during the reign of Charlemagne, was discovered in the library of the Abbey of St Gall, near Lake Constance in Switzerland. It is a symmetrical plan, along the lines of a Roman *villa rustica*. There is a cemetery for the monks, and there are medicinal gardens and a pleasure garden at the eastern and western ends of the church. (The plan shows the gardens at the western end.)

The Frankish monk Walafrid Strabo (808–849), who wrote the life of St Gall, *Vita Sancti Galli*, also wrote a poem entitled *The Little Garden*. Though mostly concerned with the medicinal properties of herbs, this practical and charming poem is full of sound advice, good humour and gardening lore (describing, for example, such procedures as how to attack matted weed roots with 'the tooth of Saturn'). It gives the strongest impression that there was plenty of fine gardening work going on behind the scenes in the great houses as well as in the monasteries.

The Crusades

In the eleventh century the Crusaders set forth to wrest Jerusalem from Muslim rule. Bribed by the Pope with promises of salvation, great armies of mounted knights, infantry and barefoot peasants marched some two thousand miles to Jerusalem via Constantinople, opening up trade across Europe and the East as they went.

The Crusaders brought back great treasures – not just loot (of which there was plenty), but also knowledge. In Europe, Arabic and Greek texts were eagerly translated into medieval Latin. Exotic seeds and plants, never seen before, were brought to the monasteries and Roman treatises on medical science were copied and preserved. As the seats of learning and education, the monasteries ministered to their communities and to wayfarers. And in the eleventh century great medical schools were established in Montpelier and Salerno to train elite physicians for the court and the aristocracy.

Medieval green architecture

A medieval specialty was garden architecture made from trees and shrubs, dead or alive. A popular style was woven or braided osier willow shoots held between upright stakes or woven over frames. Propagation by taking cuttings of vigorous plants, such as willow, was well known to the medieval gardener. The cuttings would be lined up and clipped back or tied in to the framework as they grew. They also used boards supported by wooden pegs, and balustrading painted in bright colours.

Trelliswork, which had been practised in Rome and became known in England as 'carpenter's work', was a signature feature of the medieval garden. The ground was also often divided into several small gardens, which would be fenced off with trelliswork in diamond or square patterns, covered in climbers for privacy or for scent.

The square motif continued in the ground layout, often with alternate chequers of turf and flower bed. The beds might contain a standard clipped fruit tree, a single piece of topiary or a single species of flowering plant.

In the fourteenth century plant edgings began to appear, with compact plants or those that could be kept clipped – thrift, cotton lavender and box. Wall germander (*Teucrium chamaedrys*) became a favoured edging in

Illustration of an arbour fashioned from living trees. Frontispiece of *The Gardener's Labyrinth*, by Thomas Hill.

TOPIARY, KNOTS AND PARTERRES

Germany and England. Low rails topped with wooden or stone heraldic beasts made an appearance in noble gardens – a theme that would be taken up in Tudor knots.

Liber Ruralium Commodorum

Pietro de' Crescenzi (*c.*1233–*c.*1320) was a Bolognese lawyer and judge, and author of a highly influential book, *Liber Ruralium Commodorum* (*The Book of Rural Benefits*). This was an agricultural thesis, largely drawn from Columella's *De Re Rustica* and the works of other Roman writers, but also including science and learning gleaned from the Arab scholars. The work was translated into French, German and Polish, copied and later printed multiple times in both Latin and Italian. Though the focus is mainly on agricultural matters, chapter eight focuses on pleasure gardens. Crescenzi divides these into three categories – small herb gardens, gardens for people of moderate means and gardens fit for kings and 'illustrious lords'.

Enclosure, Crescenzi writes, should be by done with 'ditches and hedges made from thorns and roses'. For hot places a pomegranate hedge is recommended, and for cold ones a hedge of nut, plum and quince. To avoid the annoyance of spiders' webs, trees should not be planted in the

This fifteenth-century illustration shows a fountain of three tiers – a pattern copied in topiary as the *estrade* tree representing the Trinity – within a fence of woven willow shoots braided between uprights.

Chequerboard beds in a walled town garden, from *Livre des profits ruraux* by Pietro de' Crescenzi. Fifteenth century.

middle of a lawn. In the most suitable places, 'he [the gardener] must make trelliswork and tunnels in the shape of houses, tents or pavilions.'

In royal gardens, Crescenzi recommends making a whole palace with rooms and pavilions with towers entirely from live trees. The trees should be 'trained and clipped' in advance. 'The spaces and room may be measured out and where there would be walls there plant fruit-bearing trees which can easily be interlaced, such as cherries, and apple trees; or else olives, or poplars which will grow quickly. The trees may be grafted with divers fruit by the diligent gardener.'

The arbours and bowers would be turned into verdant walks covered in vines to make sheltered walkways. The trees should be arranged in such a manner as to radiate away from the palace so that 'the birds could be observed flitting from tree to tree.' Recommended trees for the purpose are apple, cherry, willow, white poplar and elm. In Germany, lime trees (*geleitete Linden*) were commonly trained by country people into rustic constructions of several storeys for use at fairs and festivals and for village courts.

A monk is shown enjoying some peace and quiet, in an illustration of the fifteenth-century Italian School.

reputati
dotes: to
hoūm:
Sed tam
lia inue
te: aut
tio ad n
liquarǐ
ab rerſ
cā gignu
tibꝰ herb

aliǭs ex
bꝫdam
aliaſ al
rū foem
& ſarm
ſimile p
uocatur

riſꝗ toto corpore oblite: quiꝫdā inſaes

Earthly paradise

In 1250, Henry III commanded his bailiff at Woodstock to make a good enclosed 'herbary' where the queen could 'disport herself'. The 'herbary' was probably a herbar, or arbour, rather than a herb garden, or perhaps a decorative pavilion constructed of living trees, pleached and with interwoven branches. Later turf was ordered for 'the great herbary'.

As in Byzantium, the fruit tree was seen as beautiful and bounteous. The orchard was a pleasure garden and was often depicted in a 'flowery mead' (meadow).

The *Roman de la Rose*, written by Guillaume de Lorris in around 1230 and partly translated by Chaucer a century later, describes the medieval idyll. The paths are strewn with fragrant herbs and the trees, which come from the Land of the Saracens, are laden with figs, pomegranates, nutmegs and almonds. In short, the garden is 'so fair and spiritual' that it is a 'paradyse erthly'.

Grafting was a medieval passion. An ancient art, it is mentioned by St Paul in his *Epistle to the Romans*, where he says, 'You, though a wild olive shoot, have been grafted in among the others and now share in the nourishing sap from the olive root.'[5] Presumably this is a reference to a desirable 'sport' being grafted on to a strong root system to get the best from both. The twelfth-century French poet Chrétien de Troyes (the inventor of the knight Lancelot) writes about a family tree that fills most of a walled pleasure garden and bears both flowers and fruit, 'including pears'.

In *De Vegetabilibus et Plantis,* a botanical study by a German Dominican friar, Albertus Magnus, grafting and pruning are recommended, as it is 'a great beauty and pleasure to have in one's garden trees variously and marvelously grafted, and many different fruit growing on a single tree'. Moreover, they should be planted for 'delight rather than fruit'.

By the fifteenth century, with new wealth, came the secular enclosed garden and the luxury of the *locus amoenus* or the garden purely for hedonistic pleasure. The patrician gardens of prosperous householders provided a setting for courtly romance. Water now symbolized the fountain of youth. In gardens dedicated to Eros, there are bathers of both sexes cavorting in the company of ladies with their troubadours.

Topiary

The most popular topiary came in the form of *estrade* trees, so called after the French for a 'platform' or 'tier'. An *estrade* shrub or tree would be clipped and trained into three tiers narrowing towards the top, to represent the Holy Trinity. This training could be done with or without the use of a frame of hoops or 'cartwheels' attached to a pole.

Topiarized trees, including the *estrade*, in the fifteenth-century interpretation of Pliny's *Historia Naturalis* (Book XXII) by Giuliano Amadei.

[5] Romans 11:24

The early knot

By the end of the fifteenth century, knots were well established. There is a description of one such at Richmond Palace, where 'under the King's windows, Queen's, and other estates, most fair and pleasant gardens, with royal knots alleyed and herbed; many marvellous beasts, as lions, dragons, and such other of divers kind, properly fashioned and carved into the ground, right well sanded, and compassed with lead; with many vines, seeds and strange fruit, right goodly beset.'

John Leland, 'father of English local history and bibliography', describes two mounts liberally covered in topiary in his book of notes, *Itinerary* (1535–43).

At the Castle of Wressel in the East Riding of Yorkshire there were *opere topiarie* (topiary works) 'writhen about with degrees like turnings of cockilshelles'.

The medieval labyrinth

The fascination with labyrinths continued unabated during the medieval period. At first they were heavy with Christian symbolism but later they became somewhat more light-hearted. By the sixteenth century, the hedge maze had become a regular feature in the garden.

There is a rare inventory for the garden of King Charles V (r.1364–80) at Hôtel St. Pol, in the Quartier de l'Arsenal in Paris in the 1370s. It had *palissades*, tunnel arbours, trelliswork and a labyrinth, known as the *Maison de Dédale* (House of Daedalus), and a collection of bay trees.

The medieval Christian labyrinth was derived from the Roman pattern but took on new meaning as a pilgrimage. Eleven rings, the paths crossing back on themselves to make the unmistakable image of a cross, replaced the seven-ring classical pattern.

Floor mosaics were made to this design, most famously in the pavement labyrinth at Chartres (1235), south-west of Paris, but also at Rheims in 1240 and Amiens in 1288. At Chartres Cathedral there is a U-turn towards the centre. Scholars say that this represents death through which the wayfarer must pass. He will then travel through three semicircles symbolizing the three days between the Crucifixion and the Resurrection. In the rose window above is the same pattern representing the promise of spiritual life after death. It is widely believed – though there is little proof – that the monks would trace the path on their knees at Pentecost as a penance. Sadly, most of these labyrinths were destroyed in the seventeenth and eighteenth centuries.

Before it was banned as unsuitable for a place of Christian worship, the 'game of the labyrinth' was played in some places during the Easter

The labyrinth pattern at Chartres, which includes an interlude of death and resurrection.

Sunday service. It was recorded that at Auxerre from 1396 to 1538 the cathedral canons and chaplains would perform a liturgical dance around the labyrinth (*circa Daedalum*), throwing a ball to and fro and chanting 'praises to the Easter victim' (*Victimae paschali laudes*).

A famous labyrinth legend was that of Fair Rosamund, Rosamund Clifford, mistress of Henry II (r.1154–1189), who was locked away in a labyrinth, or 'Rosamund's Bower', in Everswell, a royal house near Oxford. Though popularly believed to be a hedge labyrinth, in fact it was built 'most curiously of stone and timber strong'. It had 150 doors and was 'so intricate' that no one could find their way without 'a clue of thread'. The king filled the walled park with exotic and dangerous beasts – lions, leopards, lynxes, camels and even a porcupine – and kept the one and only key. As the story goes, Henry's queen, Eleanor of Aquitaine, managed to find her way in, despite all precautions, to present Fair Rosamund with a choice between two ways out – the dagger or poison.

A 'House of Daedalus' was a feature of Hesdin, in Pas de Calais, near Paris, a remarkable garden full of automata and elaborate water jokes, created by Count Robert II of Artois on his return from the Crusades in 1270. Another was in the Hôtel des Tournelles in Paris in 1431 when it was occupied by the Duke of Bedford as English Regent of France.

In England, turf labyrinths were made at sacred sites. The Stations of the Cross were placed at intervals along the path. Later, for a more demanding challenge, the Stations of the Cross with carved figures in wood were displayed along the slopes of 'Calvary mountains' in imitation of a real pilgrimage to Jerusalem.

The first of these was designed by a Franciscan monk, Bernardino Caimi (d.1499). Jerusalem being occupied by the Turks, he wanted to

Projet d'aménagement de Mont-Valérien (Plan for the Development of Mount Valerien). A watercolour of the nineteenth-century French School.

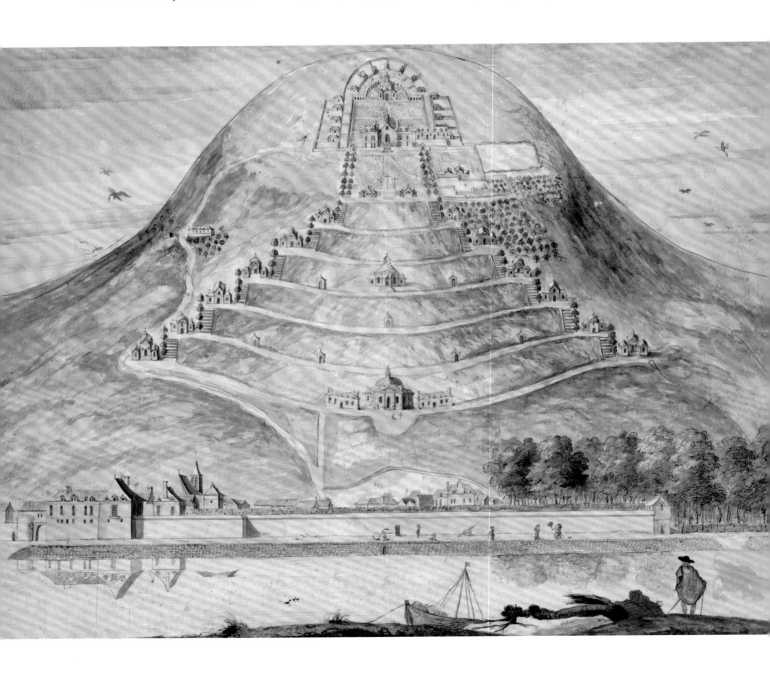

A copperplate engraving from Giovanni Ferro's *Teatro d'imprese*, 1623. 'Ducit Idem Deducitique' ('the same leads and misleads'). The depiction of the labyrinth is merely an impression but the tree in the centre implies that it is a labyrinth of love. Ariadne's thread hangs invitingly from the door.

create a pilgrimage route to evoke the life and passion of Christ in Italy. Forty-five chapels were built along the route in Varallo in the northern Alps. Various others followed this example. At Mont-Valérien in France there were fifteen Stations of the Cross along a path which wound its way back and forth up to the peak.

In 1426 a young Italian, the twenty-two-year-old Leon Battista Alberti, visited Palazzo della Zisa outside Palermo, Sicily. He is said to have been greatly impressed by the Islamic garden pavilion and the pools surrounded by orange and lemon groves. One cannot help but wonder if he was not already gathering his thoughts to fire the greatest revolution in the entire history of garden design – the Italian Renaissance.

The Italian Renaissance
Humanism, the High Renaissance and Mannerism

15th–17th centuries

N 1452, the year when Leon Battista Alberti finished *De Re Aedificatoria*, the ten-volume set *On the Art of Building* based on the works of Vitruvius, Italy was splintered into small warring city states. Milan, Venice and Florence were the main contenders for supremacy. Relative calm descended with the Peace of Lodi in 1454, brokered by the richest banker in Europe, the de facto Florentine ruler, Cosimo de' Medici (1389–1464).

It was in Cosimo's Florence that Renaissance gardens embracing the classical principles of harmony, order and balance were first created. Rationality, the application of mathematics and a sense of theatre would impact on the great secular Italian gardens of the quattrocento and on gardens in the rest of Europe over the next two centuries. The element that would lift the Italian Renaissance garden into an entirely new sphere was Alberti's dictum that the garden should be designed by the architect as a single concept with the house.

Petrarch

Francesco Petrarca, known in English as Petrarch (1304–1374), having researched ancient Greek and Roman tracts on his travels as a Church envoy, reintroduced Humanism to Europe. In his *Vita Solitaria* Petrarch promoted reason, science and mathematics for a new and enlightened age, along with the concept that the intellectual and creative potential of mankind must be used to the full.

He also brought back the Roman idea of the *villeggiatura* – withdrawal to the country villa. He prescribed 'abandoning the haunts of men and crowded cities' in favour of a simple, contemplative life. He inspired the poet Boccaccio (1313–1375), whose *Decameron* extolled Humanism. Boccaccio anticipated aspects of Renaissance gardens when he spoke of villas standing on the heights of Fiesole, outside Florence, describing 'broad straight walks flanked with vines' and 'white marble' fountains.

A painting of the eighteenth-century Italian School showing the Villa Aldobrandini, Frascati. The garden of the villa, originally built in 1550, was known as the Belvedere, because of its open view over the valley towards Rome. This presented a strong contrast with the enclosed medieval garden.

The Italian ruling classes began to follow Petrarch's advice and abandon their fortified castles – if not their luxuries – in favour of the villa. Giovanni Villani, a Florentine banker and chronicler, remarked that 'there was no ordinary or great citizen who had not built, or was not in process of building, in the country a grand and rich estate with an expensive layout and handsome buildings, and much better than in town.' These villas made up a band three miles from the city, built in the style of ancient Rome.

At this time, it was not unusual to be a Petrarchan polymath. No division was made between the hands-on builder and the architect, or the artist and the architect. An architect should be an engineer as well, and have studied music and the arts. Even Leonardo da Vinci (1452–1519) described himself as an engineer first and foremost. Raphael designed the loggia for Villa Madama, while both he and Michelangelo worked as architects on the basilica of St Peter's. Michelangelo redesigned the monumental civic plaza of the Roman citadel, the Capitoline Hill.

Brunelleschi, a goldsmith by trade, studied the dome of the Pantheon before coming up with an ingenious solution for the seemingly impossible construction of the dome of Florence's cathedral. He and the sculptor Donatello travelled to Rome to take measurements of the proportions of columns and arches from ancient sites for future reference.

As engineering took giant leaps forward, stone bridges were thrown up to span vast rivers and airy Gothic church spires stretched ever higher towards the heavens. Huge cannons were cast. Seemingly magical carnival floats for feast days moved without visible means, to the delight of the crowds.

The Humanist Renaissance garden was followed by the gardens of the High Renaissance, where the architectural elements were taken to their logical conclusion. The final phase was the allegorical Mannerist garden, altogether a more playful place, planned for lavish entertainments and *fêtes galantes*.

Alberti

Leon Battista Alberti was born in Genoa in 1404, the illegitimate son of an aristocratic Florentine, whose family shunned him after his father's death. Perhaps spurred by this, he was driven to prove himself the ultimate Renaissance polymath. He was an author, artist, architect, poet, priest, linguist, cryptographer, philosopher and athlete. It is said that he was a fearless horseman and could jump over a man's head from standing.[1]

The intention behind Alberti's proposal in *De Re Aedificatoria* that the garden should be designed by the architect was in part to achieve a harmony between house and garden by using the same patterns and proportions, or

[1] Jacob Burckhardt, *The Civilization of Renaissance Italy*, 1860
[2] *De Re Aedificatoria*, Book IV
[3] *De Re Aedificatoria*, Book X

multiples of each. For the garden to be 'well disposed' it should be planned to echo 'those Figures that are most commended in the Plans of Houses, Circles, Semi-circles and the like'.[2]

Symmetry is another Albertian keystone. 'So agreeable is it to Nature that the Members on the right Side should exactly answer the left . . . that every Part . . . lie duly to the Level and Plumb line, and be disposed with an exact Correspondence as to the Number, Form and Appearance; so that the Right may answer to the Left, the High to the Low, the Similar to the Similar, so as to form a correspondent Ornament in that Body whereof they are Parts.'[3] Trees should be planted 'in Rows exactly even, and answering to one another exactly upon straight Lines'. He recommends planting them in a quincunx pattern or in triads.

Fra Luca Pacioli and Vitruvian Man

The Vitruvian idea that the proportions of buildings and gardens should be taken from relationships found in music, nature and the human body was eagerly adopted. The Renaissance painters of the late fifteenth century were fascinated by mathematics and developed Vitruvius' theories further. The mathematician Fra Luca Pacioli (1445–1517) worked closely with Leonardo da Vinci on the Divine Proportion and the Golden Ratio.

Mathematician Fra Luca Pacioli demonstrates a Euclidean theorem to an unknown companion. Painting attributed to Jacopo de' Barbari, 1495.

Pacioli writes in *De Divina Proportione* (*The Divine Proportion*) of 1509 that 'the Ancients, having taken into consideration the rigorous construction of the human body, elaborated all their works, as especially their holy temples, according to these proportions; for they found here the two principal figures without which no project is possible: the perfection of the circle, the principle of all regular bodies, and the equilateral square.'

Alberti proposes that the garden should be a place of pleasure, with shady walks against the hot sun provided by pergolas and loggias and

Vitruvian Man, also known as *The Proportions of Man*. Drawing attributed to Leonardo da Vinci, 1490.

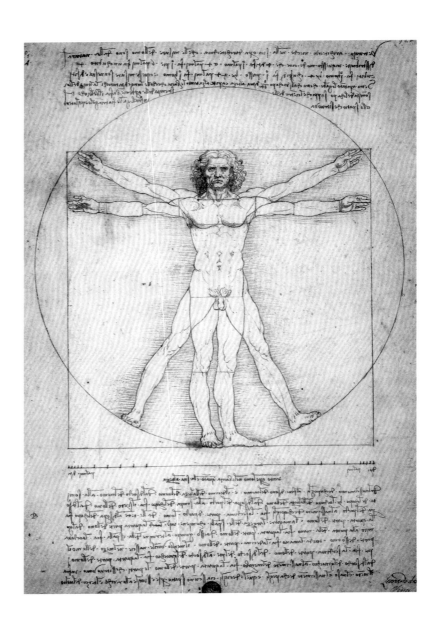

Woodcut of a perspective diagram by Vitruvius. From *De Architectura* (*Ten Books of Architecture*), 1521 edition.

cool nymphaeums, which 'the Ancients used to dress with all manner of Rough work and daub over with green in imitation of the mossy slime that we always see in moist Grottoes.'

Water in every form was a key feature and would become ever more sophisticated. Water staircases, cascades, rivulets, fountains and *giochi di acqua*, or water jokes, were essential ingredients. In the later Mannerist gardens there were ever more remarkable and ingenious musical fountains.

There should be an area for sport (along the lines of the Roman hippodrome) outside the house, and amphorae filled with flowers. An enclosed 'secret' garden was still part of the plan. The *giardino segreto*, for the family, would be separate from the main garden close to the house.

A Humanist garden: Villa Quaracchi

A garden that Alberti may actually have designed, for his friend and client Giovanni Rucellai, is that of the Villa Quaracchi, near Florence. It has a long central axis framed by vine-clad pergolas for shady walks, breast-high box hedges and an avenue of tall trees. A new and charming idea was to prolong the axis so that it crossed a public road to the

This 1549 plan of the Villa Quaracchi, near Florence, is attributed to Alberti, as it contains many features from *De Re Aedificatoria* (*The Art of Building*), especially the symmetrical layout, geometric compartments, and mount. In the road at the bottom a hospitable hut is provided where passers-by can rest and enjoy the garden.

village of Pistoia at the end of the garden and continued down to the river Arno. It was designed so that the master, sitting at the head of his table, could see the boats sailing by in the Arno some two hundred metres away.

A complete departure from the locked and intensely private medieval garden, Villa Quaracchi is hospitable. On the Pistoia road, at the end of the garden between the river and the gate, was a little 'games' hut with seats for passers-by to view the flower gardens and the elaborate collection of topiary. Later designers were to extend this idea so that the central axis would include the 'borrowed' landscape reaching beyond the garden into the distance.

The outlook

Alberti's great joy in the Italian landscape, expressed in his earlier book *Del Governo della Famiglia,* is wonderfully liberating. Gardens look outwards and are designed to have a view. Whenever possible, the garden should be positioned on top of a hill, or have a mount, to add an element of discovery and surprise. It should be 'pretty high, but upon so easy an Ascent that it should hardly be perceptible to those that go to it, till they find themselves at the Top, and a large Prospect opens to view'.

From there would be revealed 'all the Pleasures and conveniences of Air, Sun, and fine prospects . . . a view of some City, Towns, the Sea, an open Plain, and the tops of some known Hills and Mountains'. They should also overlook the garden, where can be seen 'the delights of the Garden and diversions of Fishing and Hunting', and 'enjoy clear brilliant days and beautiful prospects over wooded hills and sunlit plains, and listen to the murmuring of fountains and of running streams that flow through the tufted grass'.

The French philosopher Michel de Montaigne commented astutely in his *Journal de voyage en Italie par la Suisse et l'Allemagne* (1580–81) that on visiting Rome in 1581 he learnt 'to what extent art is aided by a hilly, steep and irregular site, for they derive advantages from this that cannot be matched in our level gardens'.

Where there was no hill, a mount was made to provide a prospect. The seventeenth-century diarist John Evelyn, when visiting the Villa Medici in Rome, described the cool fountains and 'murmuring rivulets trickling down the declining Walkes', the head- and breast-high ('and some double that') hedges that surrounded the flower beds. He commented on a

The Villa Medici in Rome, as John Evelyn would have seen it in the seventeenth century. The Albertian moment of surprise came at the top of the mount in the background, where a view of the skyline of Rome opens up. An engraving by Giovanni Battista Falda (1643–1678).

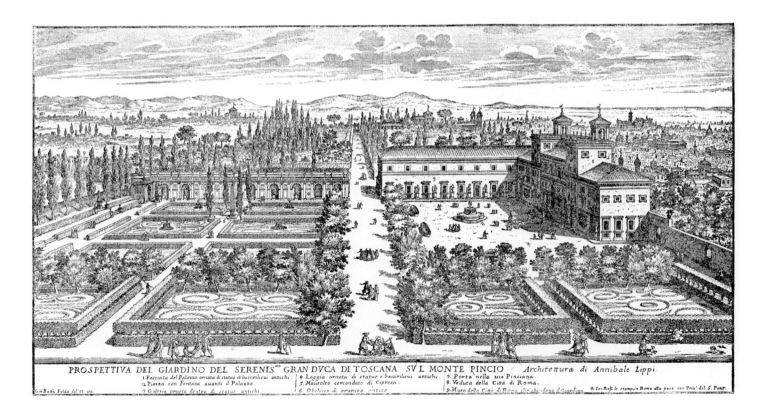

PROSPETTIVA DEL GIARDINO DEL SERENIS.^{mo} GRAN DVCA DI TOSCANA SVL MONTE PINCIO   *Architettura di Annibale Lippi*

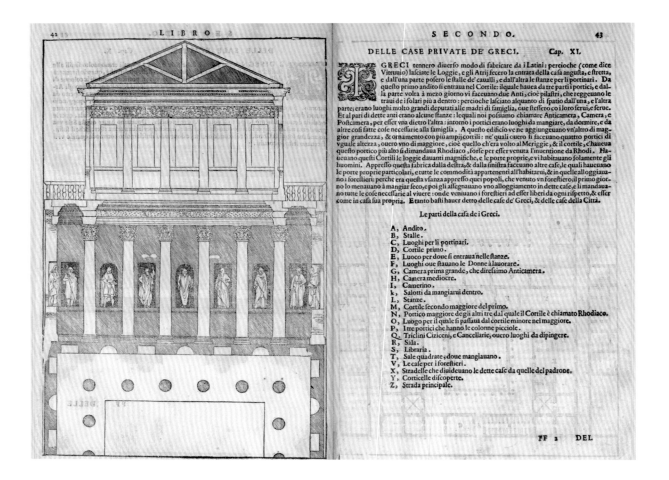

A page from Palladio's *Quattro libri dell'architettura* (*Four Books of Architecture*), 1570, showing the placing of the Corinthian pillars and the symmetry and proportion of the Vitruvian ideal.

steep mount, or *montagnola,* which he described as 'a mount planted with cypresses, representing a fortress'. A dark spiral path brings you to a gazebo on the summit which unexpectedly opens up to a glorious surprise – the view of the rooftops, domes and turrets of Rome.

Palladio

By the mid-sixteenth century Italian architects were set for the High Renaissance. The most influential of all was Andrea Palladio (1508–1580).

The son of a Venetian miller, Palladio was taken up as a protégé by the scholar and poet Gian Giorgio Trissino. He went on to design many palaces, churches and – above all – villas. He followed the teachings of Vitruvius, emphasizing the virtues of utility, solidity and beauty, symmetry, balance and 'decorum', and used the proportions of the classical orders of the Doric, Ionic and Corinthian columns. His *Quattro libri dell' architettura* (*Four Books of Architecture*), published in 1570, inspired architects for centuries to come, including Inigo Jones, Christopher Wren and many architects and designers of the eighteenth-century English landscape movement. Even the Capitol in Washington, built in 1800, was Palladian in style.

Niccolò Tribolo

Architects and artists got out their set squares and drew up plans to scale and made models for gardens – techniques previously only used on buildings. In 1536 Cosimo de' Medici instructed Niccolò Tribolo (1500–1550) to begin working on the ornamentation of the Villa di Castello 'according to the drawings and models he had previously shown him'.

Castello is said to be the first garden to carry a political message – a theme of power and persuasion. This was advertising – a novel idea for gardens, and one that would be copied in courts throughout Europe and beyond.

With this message in mind, Tribolo placed a prominent statue of Hercules defeating Antaeus – a feat achieved by brain, not brawn – to represent Cosimo's own victory in defeating Florence's anti-Medici faction. The Fountain of Venus, a symbol of Florence, stood within a circular labyrinth, promising future peace and prosperity.

Cosimo de' Medici's Villa di Castello, Florence. The garden carried a political message of power and persuasion, a form of advertising that would be widely adopted across Europe. A lunette by Giusto Utens, 1599.

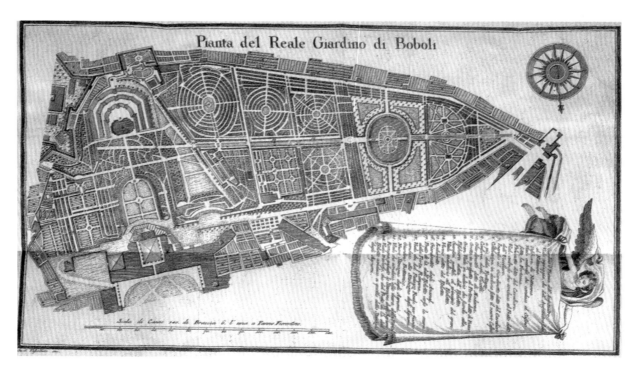

Within the villa, the message was endorsed by Botticelli's *Birth of Venus*, while bright hope for a future under Medici rule was symbolized in his *Primavera*. Outside, in the 'Sacred Wood', a statue of Appennino symbolized the mountains of Tuscany. Further self-aggrandisement came in the form of busts of former Medici rulers, wearing Roman togas, lined up on the steps. Unfulfilled plans included statues representing the self-claimed Medici virtues of justice, compassion, courage, nobility and wisdom.

The Boboli Gardens

Il Tribolo's next commission (though he died before it was completed) was for the even grander Boboli Gardens for the Pitti Palace in Florence, which would become the main seat of the Medici grand dukes. Evelyn recorded in 1644 that he could not 'sufficiently express the pleasure' that this 'sweet retirement' gave him. He told how the parterre – which was laid out in box – had a 'wonderful effect as seen from the castle', that he saw 'a rose grafted on an orange-tree' and 'there was much topiary-work and columns in architecture about the hedges'. The flowers had 'been banished to a special walled part, a small garden on which the Duke spends many thousands of pistoles'.

OPPOSITE ABOVE The High Renaissance Boboli Gardens which provide the setting for Palazzo Pitti are filled with theatrical grottoes, nymphaeums, classical statuary and fountains. The central axis cuts through an amphitheatre and leads to the fountain of Neptune at the top of the Boboli Hill and a view of Florence. A lunette by Giusto Utens, *c*.1599.

OPPOSITE BELOW An eighteenth-century plan of the Boboli Gardens.

BELOW The Belvedere Court at the Vatican was designed by Donato Bramante for Pope Julius II. It is a vast architectural garden, with formal areas to house a sculpture museum, viewing platforms and a stage for theatre and pageantry. An engraving by Claude Duchet, 1579.

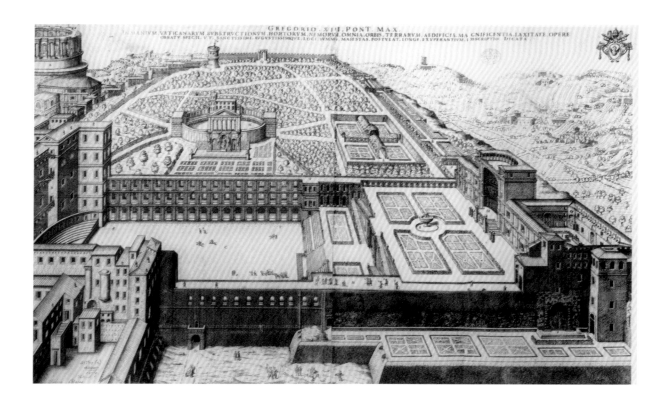

Donato Bramante and the Belvedere Court

A masterpiece of architectural garden design in the High Renaissance style, the Belvedere Court was designed for Pope Julius II (r.1503–1513) by Donato Bramante (the original architect of the Renaissance St Peter's). The brief was to link the Vatican Palace with the Villa Belvedere on the top of the hill. Bramante divided the hilly ground into three levels linked by a set of terraces which were supported by retaining walls. He put in a central axis, monumental staircases and balconies, and created a superb garden theatre.

On the top level were the formal gardens and the papal collection of Roman statuary, incorporated into the design in ornamental niches or as part of the fountains.

The second tier was designed as a viewing platform for the grand papal spectacles and pageants. Sometimes the menagerie of wild beasts (including Leo X's favourite white elephant, Hanno) would be paraded on the lowest level.

The Mannerist garden

The Sacred Grove, also known as Parco dei Mostri (Park of the Monsters) of the gardens of Bomarzo, Viterbo, is an extreme example of Mannerist allegory, fantasy and storytelling. Another Mannerist characteristic is a loosening up of the formal *bosco* into more natural parkland, with isolated sculptures and fountains placed informally through it.

Also in Viterbo is the Villa Lante, now beautifully restored. This was described by George Sitwell in *On the Making of Gardens* (1909) as 'as much a work of art as any poem, painting or piece of music', and is a celebration of water and water tricks. It was partly designed by Vignola (the architect who took over at St Peter's from Michelangelo), who has made the central axis a water channel that moves through all the terraces at varying speeds and in different guises, sometimes helped by automata.

The house was built on a steep volcanic ridge, the perfect situation for water to stream and drip, first from the Deluge Fountain at the top, through moss and ferns down from the grotto into a pool, making its next entrance in the Fountain of the Dolphins, then flowing into the famous water staircase, the *cordonata*, edged with a stone crayfish pattern each side in tribute to the owner, Cardinal Gambara (*gambero* being Italian for crayfish).

Ice-cold water is channelled to a marble table to chill the cardinal's wine – a concept undoubtedly taken from Pliny the Younger's floating dishes. Montaigne described the Pyramid Fountain as surrounded by 'four small lakes, clear and pure and brimming with water. In the middle of each is a little stone boat, with two men carrying arquebuses [firearms]

in each, who draw up water and shoot it at the pyramid; there is a trumpet in each boat which likewise draws up water.'

The most famous Mannerist garden is that at the Villa d'Este, created for Cardinal Ippolito d'Este in Tivoli, north of Rome. Villa and garden were designed by Pirro Ligorio, the excavator and recorder of the remains of Hadrian's Villa of AD 118–138.

Villa d'Este has a classic geometric layout with a central axis from the villa. The sloping and lopsided site, perched on the top of a hill, was evened out as much as possible by hefty earth-moving. The design plan for the four labyrinths was unusual. Each was to be planted with 'different types of wood' – 'orange trees with hedges of myrtle; arbutus with hedges of honeysuckle; pines with laurustinus and firs with hedges of privet'.

At the Villa Lante, near Viterbo, a central axis sweeps up into the hills, making the garden the ideal situation for fanciful waterworks, playful water tricks and other Mannerist flights of fancy. A fresco in the loggia of the villa.

The Mannerist garden of Villa d'Este, Tivoli, which is full of heroic symbolism and larger-than-life waterworks, is one of the great period pieces of the Italian Renaissance. Illustration from *View of Villa d'Este*, by Etienne Duperac, 1575.

Accounts of 1582 confirm that the divisions of the labyrinth were made of espaliered trees. A French visitor remarked that the hedges were head height.

Two hundred years later Goethe was to comment that 'the whole complex of its landscape, with its details, its views, its waterfalls, is one of the experiences which permanently enrich one's life.'

Cardinal Ippolito d'Este's illustrious ancestors are represented by Hercules, patron of the Este family and also of the historic town of Tivoli. The white eagle on the family crest holds the three golden apples that Hercules stole from the Hesperides. Hercules' labours are illustrated in the Fountain of Dragons and his temptations in the Grotto of Venus.

Villa d'Este has the ultimate musical fountain. Montaigne described in 1580 'true music, naturally created . . . made by water which falls with great violence into a cave, rounded and vaulted, and agitates the air, which is forced to exit through the pipes of an organ. Other water, passing through a wheel, strikes in a certain order the keyboard of the organ. The organ also imitates the sound of trumpets, the sound of cannon, and the sound of muskets, made by the sudden fall of water.'

The revival of topiary

Alberti shares Pliny the Younger's delight in figurative topiary, echoing his sentiment that there should be 'box shrubs clipped into innumerable shapes, some being letters which spell the gardener's name or his master's'. In the flower gardens of Villa Quaracchi there were 'spheres, porticoes, temples, vases, urns, apes, donkeys, oxen, a bear, giants, men, women, warriors, a harpy, philosophers, Popes, Cardinals'. Some were clipped out of the hedge and some were free-standing. It was noted that in Villa di Castello there were 'elephants, a wild boar, a ship with sails, a ram, a hare with its ears up, a wolf fleeing from dogs, an antlered deer'.

Hypnerotomachia Poliphili

One of the great influences on the early Renaissance garden was a flight of fancy, *Hypnerotomachia Poliphili* or *The Strife of Love in a Dream*, published in 1499. Written by a Dominican monk, Francesco Colonna, it was richly illustrated with Roman architectural detail, including topiary, knots and parterres.

Probably the first book ever written as a stream of consciousness, it is an erotic romance in a pagan setting (a surprisingly profane work for a monk, perhaps). It tells the story of Poliphilus, who, while searching for his beloved nymph, Polia, comes to the mystical garden island of Cythera, home of the goddess of love. There we are transported to the classical ruins of ancient Rome – amphitheatres, peristyle courtyards, 'pycnostyle' colonnades (with double columns) made of 'splendid shining jasper'.

The original book was a lavish folio publication printed in Venice with 174 woodcut illustrations by an unknown artist. The pictures showed statues, fountains, grottoes, labyrinths and groves of cypresses, and were to prove a most useful resource for Renaissance architects and garden designers. The *Hypnerotomachia*'s influence spread quickly, as it was translated into French and partially into English.

The imaginary island of Cythera is a circle of level ground, hedged by clipped myrtle and cypress. Concentric circles within the boundaries are divided up into vegetable and botanical gardens, orchards and 'gracious woods and delightful shrubs'. The woods comprise bay, laurel, oak, pine and nut trees. One wood is filled with cypress, juniper and rosemary for scent. An enclosure for animals is hedged with myrtle and citrus trees. Meadows are divided up with covered walks and shaded with trellis.

Colonna describes topiarized arbours covered in woven and clipped greenery 'dense with leaves and elegantly joined, showing a perfect shearing in which no branch exceeded another, unless for the sake of grace and beauty'.

Knot in pattern of acanthus leaves.

Knot gardens – the first to appear in print – came with detailed descriptions and elaborate planting plans and topiary. In one knot the first 'band' was densely planted with marjoram edged with alternate pennyroyal and rue to make a pattern of acanthus leaves 'pointing in different directions'. Interlaced thyme and marjoram flowed into a central pattern. The spaces were filled with germander, violets the colour of amethysts, as well as white and yellow ones, coriander, cyclamen and primulas. In the centre of the loops there rose 'stems of mallow, three cubits high, coloured pink, purple, mauve, many-leaved and five-petalled, with a large crop of flowers'.

A complicated geometric pattern was made up of squares, with 'intersecting bands . . . at their midpoints', surrounded by octagons, so forming more squares on the diagonal, thereby making lozenge shapes. These 'also met transversely at right angles; and this mutual interference neatly formed another octagon surrounding the first one, harmoniously enclosing nine squares. With all its bands interwoven, alternately above and below one another, the whole pattern made an attractive and elegant knot-work of multiple decorative shapes that filled this entire square.'

Knot made of squares and octagons.

Knot with heraldic eagle.

Knot with eagle and pheasant.

A creation of box trees.

The pattern was outlined in white marble bordered on either side by 'simples'. 'Within the boundaries of this stone enclosure there grew various little herbs, dense and level in a perfect representation of the pattern; and all of this was repeated in every such artfully constructed square.' 'By Jupiter,' Colonna writes, 'it was a wonderful exhibition, giving great delight to the senses!'

In another knot a heraldic eagle in the centre was surrounded by a border with letters described in marjoram and edged with rue. 'The band, loops and circle were planted densely with rue; the eagle with wild thyme . . . the surrounding letters were of marjoram outlined with ajuga. One of the loops was filled with purple flowers, another with yellow and the third with white, all very prolific in their blossoms, never dropping them but constantly in flower. In the centre of these rings were planted four spherical balls of dense and regular myrtle, on two foot stems and so in all the others.'

Yet another portrayed an eagle and a pheasant, beak-to-beak. The letters around them were spelt out in 'wild thyme' and the spaces were filled with 'golden-hair' (lichen). Periwinkle, aquilegia, foxgloves, wild nard (hazelwort), wormwood and lavender infilled spaces within the knot. There were standard lavender and a 'ball of savin and one of juniper, three feet high'. 'All the herbs had beautiful foliage, freshly green and lovely to behold. It was a wondrous work of accuracy, amenity and delight. Tiny pipes in orderly arrangement irrigated it with a spray of fine droplets.'

Even more extravagant were the figurative topiaries. One was a 'remarkable creation made of box trees'. On a chest of soap-coloured chalcedony (quartz) was a box tree in the form of an antique vase from which arose a giant supporting two turrets. On top of these were clipped balls, their trunks 'each issuing at the same angle and bending so as to meet and join like the arch of a building'. 'Another thin, straight stalk arose, supporting a conical finial smaller than the ball beneath . . . Another ball was attached below the middle of this arch, like the one on stalks.' Above the arch was a 'slightly hollowed shell, a little less across the mouth than the width of the arch'. To crown this was 'a shape like a lily with its petals curved back all round'. Finally, 'out of the lily's cup came box trees divided into eight pillars, bending gradually and tapering to the summit.' It was remarkable indeed, as 'in all this rare topiary there no sign whatever of wood except in the straight stalks; everything was thickly covered with leaves and smoothly cut with all the care and art of the topiarist.'

Savin in cypress shape.   Box in circular container.   Circle-shaped apple tree.   Convex hemisphere.

Out of one knot 'grew a savin [probably *Juniperus sabina*] in compact cypress-like shape . . .'

A 'clipped box tree' rose out of 'a circular container with the usual decorations, three foot high and two paces across its opening, with the decorative lineaments . . . the container was of fine lapis lazuli.'

An apple tree was 'shaped by topiary into a thick circle like a coronet with its opening facing the pavilion . . . the sides of this stepped container were of beautiful mirror-like jasper, seeded with golden specks, mingled with spots of yellow, with serpentine blue veins and red transverse veins mixed with undulation of chalcedony, and squared off with graceful wave-moldings.'

Another fruit tree was 'shaped in a convex hemisphere' – this was one of many that 'teemed with fruits, flowers and ever-falling leaves, offering the height of pleasure to the spectator. Their branches did not stick out untidily to the side or tangle each other but were neatly arranged in different patterns.'

It is interesting that, though Renaissance garden designers were greatly influenced by *Hypnerotomachia,* they did not follow Colonna's ideas for fancy patterns within the parterres. Unlike the French designers who were to follow them, the Italian school preferred simple geometric shapes, very often the four equilateral simple squares of the *quadrato*. For the top level of the Belvedere Court the Vatican gardener, Lucerta, was requested to make four compartments in 'a simple quartered design, divided by wide gravel paths'. The many parterres at Villa Lante are based on circles and squares, and are reminiscent of the tiled floors which were popular at the time. The parterre patterns at elaborate Villa d'Este were equally unpretentious.

Sebastiano Serlio on parterres and caprices

The seven volumes of *D'architettura*, written – in the vernacular rather than in Latin – by the artist and architect Sebastiano Serlio (1475– *c*.1554), offered practical advice on building and perspective drawing to architects and builders.

Serlio carried forward Alberti's law of repeating patterns between house and garden, drawing up plans based on triangles and semicircles that could be used for ceilings inside the house and *compartimenti* outside. *D'architettura*, first published in 1537, was translated into French, Flemish and German and later into English, and became well known throughout Europe, especially when Serlio was summoned to France by François I to join the Italian team at Fontainebleau. His work on theatrical sets, employing Vitruvius' perspective and idea of the vanishing point, proved an inspiration, not only for the theatre, for also for architecture and garden design.

The fashion for simple geometric shapes lasted throughout the Renaissance. Francesco Pona, author of *Il Paradiso de' fiori* (1622) wrote that – for practical reasons as much as for taste – a garden should be composed of four perfect squares divided by spacious avenues. He recommends circles, squares and ovals as being 'preferable to long strips, star shapes, curves, and other intricate designs, because plants are choked when constricted by acute angles'. 'The plots should be marked off by means of divisions and designs of various sorts, and these above all be striking and elegant, but not deeply cut.'

The banker Vincenzo Giustiniani, when returning from France to his great Palazzo Giustiniani in Rome, had been impressed by the French covered and shady *allées*, but much less so by their elaborate *broderies*. 'It was not a good idea', he wrote in a letter, 'to go for intricate designs of close-cut lawns and flowers which need meticulous care to protect them from the four extremes of weather.'

Giovanni Battista Ferrari

This view was echoed by Giovanni Battista Ferrari (1584–1655), a Sienese Jesuit, botanist and professor who wrote the influential *Flora, seu de Florum Cultura* (*The Culture of Flowers*), published in 1633. Beautifully illustrated with copper engravings, this lavish production was financed by the Barberini family, who had a magnificent palace in Rome and to whom the book was dedicated.

Li giardini sono ancor l'oro, parte de l'ornamento della fabrica, per il che queste quatro figure differente qui sotto, sono per compartimenti d'essi giardini, ancora che per altre cose potrebbono seruire, oltra li dua Labirinthi qui adietro che a tal proposito sono.

He advises against a tapestry of complicated shapes, as 'they break the foliate work of parterres into little divisions, unsuitable for planting.' His illustrations for parterres are quite complex but not free-flowing. Within an outer rectangle or square, he keeps almost entirely to the inner square, rectangle, hexagon, octagon, circle, with only the odd formalized star or daisy shape. The paths, he says, should, in the old style, be narrower between the beds but wider in the periphery and in the centre. The beds, also, should not be too wide for the gardener to tend them from the paths.

Si cui uolupe sit cælestis ciuitatis beatissimam sedem æternæ stabilitatis in quadro positam terrenæ amœnitatis hortensi ambitu designare, cæloq, quodammodo in terris assuescere: hoc illi proponitur, quod in quadratos hortos quadrat, exemplar.

Si mundi ornatissimam rotunditatem hortensis ornatus rotunda imagine lubet æmulari: uel ætati floreæ nouum orbem condere: orbiculatum habes rudimentum quadrata in area lineatum: cuius continenti muro circunseptæ superuacaneis quatuor in angulis tum hortensis supellectilis cellas, tum congruentia floribus a uiaria poteris excitare: ut florea in silua siluestres Orphei ne desint. Cauebis tamen, ne munimentum circa extructum uel altitudine nimia, uel minimo interuallo areolas incommode opacet. Quare caute excitandum, et latiore ambulacro distinendum erit.

At uero si enormis ambitus aream denormans pulcherrimæ, optatissimæq, formæ non permittit optionem: quantum spatij licebit ad normalem figuram reuocabis: reliquum areæ tum in obeliscu, tum in alias non incongruentes imagines conformabis. Quod proponitur exemplar, ab denormata mutilaq, capacitate felix est; simili, enim pyramidis miraculo Ægyptiacæ magnificentiæ celsa fastigia æmulatur.

C 2.

Si uelis deniq, floreæ curæ quàm facilem aditum, tam difficilem exitum hortensi repræsentare simulacro: tuos hortos in labyrinthum implica, cuius hic imago aliqua exhibetur. Possunt autem labyrinthi areolæ uel cæterarum instar humiles subsidere, ut oculi tantùm implicatis flexibus irreniantur: uel ad quatuor circiter palmos lateritia structura excitari, ut pedes quoq, inter flores errabundi iucundissimè impediantur.

C 3

Edgings for parterres

Ferrari does not like boxwood for edging. He comments on its 'foetid' smell (a common complaint) and the cost of constant 'tonsuring'. He prefers thorn bushes as being 'hardier and less expensive'. He also recommends edgings of the classic thin Italian terracotta *pianelle* bricks, and quotes, as an example of a geometric parterre with a particularly fine *pianelle* edging, that of the Duke of Sermoneta.

Citrus plants (*above*) and (*below*) the classic Renaissance Italianate garden of Villa Giusti, Verona, with a central axis, complex geometric parterres, an outline of slim cypresses, a labyrinth, and steps to the top of a hill opening up to a view. By Johann Christoph Volkamer, who, it is said, introduced a citrus collection into the garden in 1714.

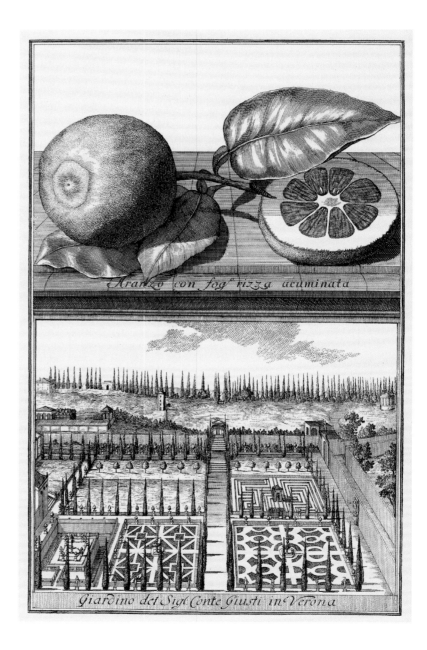

The Florentine agronomist Giovanvettorio Soderini, author of *Trattato della cultura degli orti e giardini* (1590's), reckoned that, among hedges of viburnum, roses, rosemary, myrtle and holly, 'it is the boxwood that will suffer most from sea air' – a view thought more likely to have been taken from one of Pliny the Younger's letters than from personal experience. He gives a list of more favourable plants for low hedging (*spallierette basse*), mostly consisting of herbs – thyme, hyssop, calamint, pennyroyal, marjoram, rosemary, lavender and cotton lavender, sage, santolina and – the odd one out – avocado. This accords with Colonna, who speaks of using contrasting green- and grey-leaved plants and recommends that any gaps in summer should be filled with flowers.

Other plants favoured by garden designers were hyssop, privet, daphne and butcher's broom (*Ruscus hypoglossum*). However, in general, it would seem that myrtle and laurustinus, or *Viburnum tinus*, were the most popular for edging and hedging, at least in Rome. A drawing for the replanting of Villa d'Este specifies myrtle hedges to enclose the compartments, between pedestals with vases, and carries instructions that the edging for the interior patterns should be kept no taller than a *palmo* (about seven inches). Giovanni Battista Sanga, secretary to Cardinal Bibbiena – friend and patron of Raphael – recommends planting myrtles, but if they fail to survive, due to the cold, they should be replaced with boxwood.

The walks

Criticism of mown grass walkways came mostly from English visitors. Gilbert Burnet, Bishop of Salisbury, noted in a letter of 1685 that the Italians 'have no Gravel to give them those firm and beautiful Walks that we have in England.' Almost a century later John Northall, in his *Travels through Italy* (1766), was to express much the same opinion, saying that there was 'one great defect in the Italian gardens – the want of gravel for the walks'. Another Englishman, a surgeon, Samuel Sharp, in his *Letters from Italy* remarked that 'as the Italians cannot have either green grass, or fine gravel, [there is] the want of some of the proper materials to render a garden perfectly beautiful.'

Ferrari's instruction for paths and walkways is to cover them with clay or clay mixed with *morchia* – the squeezed-out dregs of olives. This should be rolled or stamped in, then left to dry before being given a fresh topping. The alternative of lime or sand mixed with gravel, soil or brick, he warns, can be slippery in winter and is only too quick to become covered in moss.

Palissades and hortulan architecture

Edith Wharton, the American novelist and author of *Italian Villas and their Gardens* (1904) expressed the view that the 'Italian garden does not exist for its flowers, which are a late and infrequent adjunct to its beauties . . . the more permanent effects are obtained from three other factors in garden composition – marble, water and perennial verdure and the achievement, by their skillful blending, of a charm independent of the seasons.'

During the Renaissance, perennial verdure – the manipulation of trees, shrubs and climbers trained and clipped, with or without frames, to clothe walls or trellis or provide the structure of arches or *palissades* – was a fundamental element. The contrast of the vibrancy of living plants with stone or marble and water – plus the gift of the Italian countryside and sunlight – resulted in gardens that were superb sculptural artworks.

An undated document of the 1570s gives a list of shrubs and trees suitable for training in this way. Suggested evergreens are holly, box, pyramidal cypress, juniper, holm oak, laurel, cherry laurel, mastic tree

Green architecture: *berceaux* surmounted by pompoms, at the Villa Arconati-Visconti at Castellazzo, Lombardy. An engraving by Marcantonio Dal Re.

TOPIARY, KNOTS AND PARTERRES

(*Pistacia lentiscus*), privet, blackthorn and myrtle. Seville oranges and lemons are recommended for groves in warmer climates. Other favourites of the period include the strawberry tree, honeysuckle, pine and fir trees for the *spalliere* and pomegranates and oleanders for the groves. Topiary in its fullest sense was used with characteristic flair and imagination.

Fra Mariano Fetti, a patron of the arts (and said to have been the 'favourite buffoon' of Pope Leo X), lived next to the church of San Silvestro at Quirinal Hill. He described his garden as a 'labyrinth where you may see small groves and sylvan ornaments and a homely hodgepodge of one hundred varieties and a thousand caprices'. A visitor to his garden in 1544 told of 'topiary dining rooms, walkways, intercolumniations (spaces between columns), all swathed in ivy'.

A Renaissance classic is the green outdoor theatre. Edith Wharton was enchanted by the one at Villa Gori in Tuscany. 'Both pit and stage', she writes, '[are] enclosed in a double hedge of ilex, so that the actors may reach the wings without being seen by the audience; but the stage setting consists of rows of clipped cypresses, each advancing a few feet beyond the one before it, so that they form a perspective running up to the back of the stage, and terminated by the tall shaft of a single cypress which towers high into the blue in the exact centre of the background. No mere description of its plan can convey the charm of this exquisite little theatre approached through the mysterious dusk of the long pleached alley, and lying in sunshine and silence under its roof of blue sky, in its walls of unchanging verdure.'

The twentieth-century landscape architect Sylvia Crowe concludes in *Garden Design* (1956) that the quality that gives the Italian Renaissance gardens their unmatched appeal is the inherent harmony between garden and landscape. 'The piled-up hill towns and vertical accents of church towers', she writes, 'are reflected in the aspiring compositions of columns, statues and cypresses. The strong pattern and mosaic shadow of the vine leaves and the gnarled trunks of the olives are the parents of the carved and patterned stonework. These sublimated elements of nature give a unity between the garden and the landscape. Because of the harmony there is a peculiar serenity about Italian gardens. Although they are an expression of man's spirit in ascendency over nature, it is an ascendency which transmutes her, rather than conquers.'

Perhaps she is right in pinpointing this as the fundamental difference between the Italian Renaissance gardens and the 'ruthless mastery' of the sophisticated seventeenth-century French gardens they were to inspire.

The French Renaissance

15th–17th centuries

WHEN CHARLES VIII OF FRANCE and his army retreated from Naples in 1495 they were loaded down with tapestries, paintings and sculptures and generally what were described by one chronicler as 'countless marvels'. The French king had been greatly inspired by the splendour of the Italian gardens. Once home he wasted no time before addressing the cramped gardens of the Château d'Amboise on the Loire.

His first step towards transforming it from a decrepit medieval castle into something along the lines of an Italian Renaissance palazzo was to summon Italian artists and engineers. He had already brought the Neapolitan hydraulic engineer Pacello da Mercogliano with him to direct water from the Loire up to the gardens at Amboise. The sculptor Guido Mazzoni, who arrived next, was later given a knighthood and was commissioned to make the life-size figure of Charles VIII for his tomb when he died in 1498. Colonna's *Hypnerotomachia Poliphili* and the works of Alberti, Vitruvius and Serlio were translated into French.

Leonardo da Vinci, who brought the *Mona Lisa* with him (leading to much future controversy), and the architect Domenico da Cortona were both invited by the 'builder king', François I (r.1515–1547), to work on Château de Chambord, the royal hunting lodge. François was so much taken by the pope's collection of ancient Roman sculpture at the Belvedere Court that he commissioned a marble Ulysses from Michelangelo and a garden fountain from Tribolo (the Castello architect) and ordered some casts of Roman sculptures.

François was related by marriage to Cardinal Ippolito d'Este. The French king and the Italian cardinal, who were friends as well as relatives, must surely have discussed the exciting plans in hand at the time for the gardens at Villa d'Este.

The early French gardens

The French 'gardener kings' (who included Charles VIII, Louis XII, François I, not to mention Louis XIV) were trained soldiers who brought

The height of the French Renaissance. Louis XIV, the Sun King, enjoyed taking his guests on a tour around the gardens of Versailles. Painting by Étienne Allegrain, 1688.

TOPIARY, KNOTS AND PARTERRES

military precision and technology to ever more astounding feats of engineering. They took pleasure in moving mountains, flattening vast areas of terrain, wiping out villages, diverting rivers and syphoning them off to supply their hydraulic systems.

Royal gardens at the turn of the century were still in the medieval style, as can be seen in the beautiful illustrations by the court painter Jean Bourdichon for the books of hours composed for Louis XII and his wife, Anne of Brittany.

Jacques Androuet du Cerceau

A record of the next stage of the early French Renaissance gardens was provided by Jacques Androuet du Cerceau (1510–1584), architect to Charles IX (r.1560–1574). None of his work survives, but he is remembered for his fine engravings of architectural features, gardens and garden ornaments of the 1550s and 1560s. In his book *Les Plus Excellents Bâtiments de France* (1576–9) du Cerceau shows how the French nobility had adopted the idea of the Italian *compartimenti* of geometric beds but

OPPOSITE At the end of the fifteenth century the gardens of the French royal family were still in the enclosed medieval style. *Bathsheba Bathing*, a miniature by Jean Bourdichon for *Les Heures de Louis XII*, 1498–9.
BELOW The French nobility largely designed their gardens around their old castles. The Château de Verneuil, near Chantilly, was built to a revised plan of du Cerceau. It has a strong central axis in the Italian manner, and the geometric parterres, ornamental potagers and vineyards are lined up around it. An engraving from *Les Plus Excellent Bâtiments de France*, 1576–9.

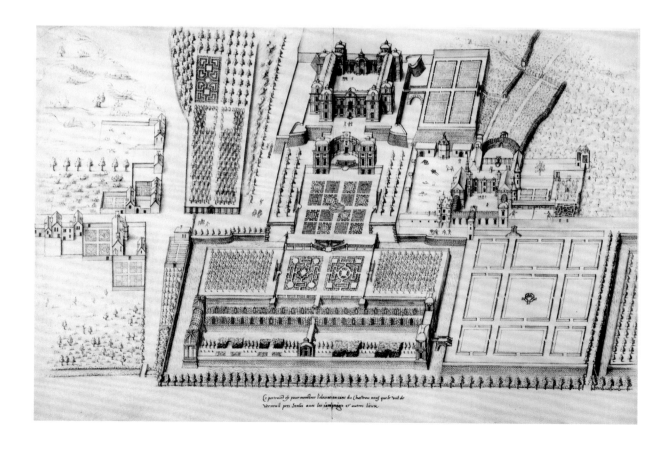

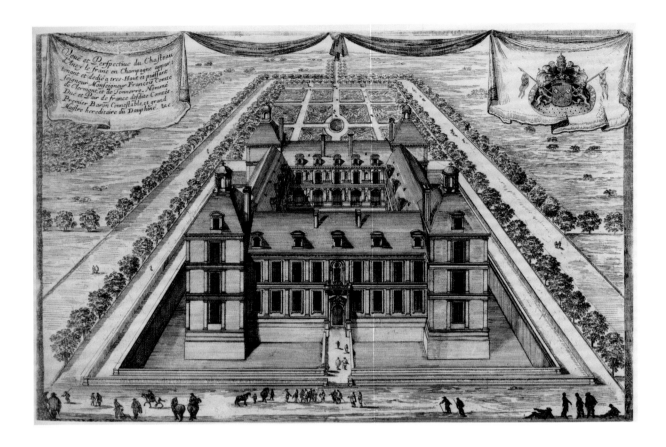

The gardens of Château d'Ancy-le-Franc, designed by Sebastiano Serlio in 1544–50, break new ground. The old château was replaced and the new house and garden were created as a unified whole in the Italian Renaissance style.

had yet to conceive house and garden as a single architectural entity. Rather than build anew, the French nobility generally adapted their fortified castles. The old ramparts and towers were turned into belvederes looking over the Italian-style *compartimenti* and the countryside beyond.

Sometimes the architect got round the problem of the relationship between house and garden by divorcing them, as at the Château de Vallery in Burgundy, which belonged to the Maréchal de Saint-André, a favourite of Henri II. The garden was otherwise laid out on Alberti's principles, with arcaded galleries and a raised walk from which to view the still-geometric parterres. A long canal divided it in half. Twin pavilions were set square in the corners of a piece of perfect symmetry with a viewing gallery in between.

Philibert de l'Orme

Two notable gardens created by Philibert de l'Orme (*c.*1514–1570) also illustrate the early stage of the French Renaissance. Son of a master mason, de l'Orme had studied architecture in Italy and worked for the pope before he took charge of the royal buildings in France in 1545.

The gardens of Château d'Anet, in the north of France, and those of the Château de Chenonceau, on the Loire, were both commissioned by Henri II for his mistress, Diane de Poitiers. They remain fundamentally inward-looking, with no attempt at vistas or views. However, both have parterres designed to be seen from above – particularly at Chenonceau, where the garden is surrounded by a raised promenade.

When Henri died in 1559, his widow, the powerful Catherine de' Medici, acquired Chenonceau by forcing an exchange on Diane, and also built her own rather similar enclosed garden on the other bank of the river Cher.

The gardens of Saint-Germain-en-Laye were the first really Italianate gardens in France. A series of spectacular terraces descend to the river Seine on a strong central axis, with grottoes and fabulous waterworks in the mode of Villa Lante. The parterres, claimed to be the first *parterres de broderie*, were laid out by Claude Mollet for Henri IV in 1595. Engraving by Alexandre Francini, a member of the family of famous Italian fountain-makers, 1614.

However, as a Florentine brought up with the Boboli Gardens as her personal playground, she also did much to establish the Italian garden in France. The daughter of Lorenzo the Magnificent, she entertained in a manner so extravagant that her *magnificences* were to be surpassed only by those at Versailles in the seventeenth century. At Chenonceau she erected a triumphal arch and made hedged rooms, topiarized green tunnels and green theatres. Limitless money was also poured into Fontainebleau, where she installed a moat, a painted gallery, statues and parterres.

Philibert de l'Orme was also involved in the design of Saint-Germain-en-Laye near Paris – the most Italianate garden of the period. One of the problems in making Italian-style gardens in France was the difference of terrain. Unlike Italy, France is largely flat. However, Saint-Germain-en-Laye was designed as a series of terraces down to the Seine on a long central axis and it had wide views of the city. It is here that the *parterre de broderie* was introduced in 1595. The spectacular fountains, grottoes, waterworks and water-driven automata were installed by two Florentine hydraulic engineers, the brothers Tommaso and Alessandro Francini. Their descendants, under the name 'Francine', became the leading fountain-makers in France for generations to come.

The sixteenth-century parterre

A book that was to have considerable influence on knots and parterres was *Praedium Rusticum*, by a physician, Charles Estienne (1504–1564). It was updated by his son-in-law, Jean Liébault, translated into French as *L'Agriculture et maison rustique* (1572) and into English as the *Countrie Farme* in 1600 by Richard Surflet and in 1616 by Gervase Markham. Though mostly on matters agricultural, there is a useful chapter on the practicalities of knots and parterres.

Proportion, the author says, depends partly on the gardener and partly on the pleasure of the master, 'the one whereof is lead by hops and skips, turnings and windings of his braine; the other by pleasing the eye according to his best fantasie'. In the 'inwards' are 'knots, mazes, armes, braunches or any other curious figures whatever', which are divided by 'slender rowes, or lines of hearbs, flowers, turfes, or such like'. The outside borders are 'what figure, knot or deuife you fancie', and are divided into 'alleyes, hedges, deepe borders, and such like'.

It is recommended to make the knots from 'sweet smelling herbs', the best being 'pennyroyal, lavender, hyssop, daisies, basil and other such' and for the outer borders, one-year-old lavender and rosemary. As 'for boxe, in as much as it has a naughtie smell, it is to be left off and not dealt with.'

Laying out the plan on the ground is best done from a basic grid, multiplied up and marked on the ground with lines and pegs. The plants need to be kept short so as 'not to hinder the view of the garden, though in the corners you could have taller specimens to give grace unto the little quarters'. It is allowed that 'you may worke some small birds, men, or other such portraits in Rose-marie.'

The inward quarters where you 'place the knots' may be 'circumferenced or bound in with fine curious Hedges, made Battlement-wise, in sundry forms – Pyllasters, Flowers, shapes of Beasts, Birds, Creeping things, Shippes . . . and such like . . . especially if your ground be little, or flattened, because these Hedges take not halfe so much roome as the Borders.' A quickset hedge is recommended 'so you will have fruits, flowers and sweet smelling herbs which will also keep your knots more safely as they are less likely to get pulled down by man or beast.'

Latticework

The book also threw light on the traditional method of latticework still in use in France in the sixteenth century. A low lattice support about two feet high is erected, then it is a matter of 'fashioning the battlements in such manner as you intend your Hedge shall grow'. Hedge plants are planted into the lattice and wound in as they grow to keep them within the framework, or, 'as need shall require, either with your sheeres or hook, you cut them to shape.'

A seventeenth-century French design for latticework screens.

Blacksmith's shears (possibly invented as far back as ancient Egypt), working on a simple spring system, were the tools medieval and Renaissance gardeners used to trim topiary. It was not until 1815 that secateurs were invented by an aristocratic émigré from the French Revolution, Antoine Bertrand de Molleville.

Olivier de Serres and the elaborate parterre

Olivier de Serres (1539–1619) was an agriculturist whose main interest was estate management. To help the French nobility maximize the profit from their estates, Serres came up with some original ideas – specifically, silk production and a line in exotic plants to be placed in the patterns of parterres.

His guide, a hefty 1,000-page work, *Le Théâtre d'agriculture et mésnage des champs* of 1600, proposed growing mulberry trees for silkworms, and introducing from tropical countries exotic vegetables and novel varieties of flowering plants which could be grown in the new glasshouses or under cloches.

Serres expanded the idea of the parterre compartments to cover the whole estate, with sections for different types of agriculture. These would include grazing and arable land, the *potager* or kitchen garden, poultry rearing (with an explanation of how to set out the coops) and the mulberry orchards.

In the parterres nearest the house would be valuable medicinal plants. The flower borders nearby would be used to display to the world the exquisite taste and refinement of the owner. Instructions were given for creating a parterre with 'letters, patterns, animals, birds, buildings and boats made and edged with sweet-scented herbs – lavender, rosemary, sage and thyme, among others – or with short bushes of myrtle and box'. The author noted that a parterre of box would last longer as, 'the beauty of box foliage stays the same in any weather, even in ice and snow. Its hardiness gives it long life and easy maintenance.'

The compartments would be laid out each side of the *grande allée* that would start from the building and stretch out into the landscape. Any swamps or rivers in the way of the plan would be dredged or diverted, the source of water channelled into irrigation or water routes to market. The rows of trees would be spaced more widely in the distance (a trick of perspective to be developed further in years to come). The aim was for an immaculate and ordered landscape in sharp contrast to the surrounding countryside. This was *aménagement*, a strict layout of land where nature was dominated and subdued. The flat terrain would prove trumps in the end as it provided the perfect terrain for the immaculate carpets of the *parterres de broderie.*

Dressing the land in floral embroidery

Aménagement and particularly the *parterre de broderie* were to become tools to market French commodities. The parterres, designed to be admired from the state rooms on the first floor, the *piano nobile,* were reflected in the decor and artefacts within. Flower patterns arranged like parterres appeared on china, the faience plates, ceilings, mantelpieces, and notably in the floral embroidery on the clothes of the nobility. Patterns with crowns of laurel and flower garlands represented military glory. On

Gobelins tapestry of a hunting scene, made to a design by Charles Le Brun, *c.*1679–1720. Many of the motifs displayed in this tapestry – tassels, urns, flowers, swags, architraves, acanthus leaves, *guilloches* (interlaced ribbons), birds, wings and letters – also appear in the *parterres de broderie.*

This needle lace (*point de France*) flounce is thought to have come from the court of Louis XIV – a clue being that the figure under a laurel wreath held by flying putti and crowned by a sun must surely be the Sun King himself. Motifs of crowns and heraldry, flowers and scrolls provided inspiration for the *parterres de broderie*.

the Île de la Cité in Paris, near Notre Dame, there was an instructional garden for plant identification where ladies would go to get inspiration for their embroidery patterns.

As the richer members of the Third Estate (the commoners) began to ignore social conventions and take to luxurious silks and satins, so the aristocracy sought out ever more extravagant dress to show their continuing superiority. For ideas, they looked to the royal courts of other countries. However, this inclination was quickly stamped on by Jean Baptiste Colbert (Louis XIV's powerful Controller of Finance – also in charge of trade and industry, the Navy, the development of Paris and the advance of science). He advised Louis to require his courtiers to wear clothes of French manufacture, so that, like the garden parterres, they were living advertisements for French fashion and fabrics.

Silk was at the heart of the trade in luxury goods. In 1662, Colbert, whose family were in textiles, bought out the famous Parisian factory Gobelins, to provide the finest tapestries and furniture exclusively for the Crown. He permitted manufacturers to invite skilled lacemakers from Flanders and Venice to teach their trade to the French artisans.

Jacques Boyceau

A former military officer, Jacques Boyceau (1560–1633), was in charge of Louis XIII's gardens. He designed the gardens for the Luxembourg Palace and laid out the original plan for the gardens of Versailles.

Boyceau's *Traité de Jardinage selon les raisons de la nature et de l'art: Ensemble divers desseins de parterres, pelouzes, bosquets et autres ornements* (posthumously published in 1638) is the first French gardening book to emphasize the aesthetics rather than the practicalities of gardening. The principal reason', he writes, 'for the existence of a garden is the aesthetic pleasure which it gives to the spectator.'

L'Habit du jardinier – a gardener ready for work, with a parterre behind. Grotesque from *Travestissements*, after Nicolas de Larmessin II, *c.*1695–1720.

Jacques Boyceau's refined, lace-like design for the parterre for the Luxembourg Palace. The boxwood parterres are filled with a pattern traced with a *rinceau*, or foliage motif – a winding stem-like pattern with leaves at equal intervals. Monograms of Marie de' Medici were incorporated around the central fountain. Engraving from Boyceau's *Traité de jardinage*, 1638.

Despite this, he does mention his basic, practical requirements for an apprentice. He should be like a young tree 'of straight trunk, well-grown, well-supported by roots on all sides, and of good descent'. He should work alongside the labourers 'learning well to cultivate the earth . . . to trace upon the ground his design . . . to plant and clip the parterres, and trim the *palissades* with a long handled sickle'. Mathematics is key. The garden designer 'must ascend to geometry, fundamental for all plans, departments, measures and alignments' to achieve the 'beauty of proportions' and 'the decorum of all the parts'.

In Boyceau's book are sixty engravings of his designs. Some are of *bosquets* and *salles de verdure*, but most are of the delicate lace-like parterres which he describes as 'the low embellishments of gardens, which have great grace, especially when seen from an elevated position: they are made of borders of several shrubs and sub-shrubs of various colours, fashioned in different manners, as compartments, foliage, embroideries, moresques (Moorish patterns), arabesques, grotesques, guilloches, rosettes, sunbursts, escutcheons (shield shapes), coats-of-arms, monograms and emblems.'

His 1615 design for the grand parterre for the gardens of the Palace of Luxembourg consisted of one large square with a semicircular end. It was divided into compartments filled with intricate embroidery, including the crowned monogram of his client, Marie de' Medici, widow of Henri IV.

The Mollets and the first *parterres de broderie*

The Mollets were a dynasty of distinguished royal gardeners who have gone down in history for their *broderie* parterres and also for bringing back boxwood as the key parterre plant. Jacques Mollet was gardener at the Château d'Anet and designed the parterres at Fontainebleau and had special responsibility for those at the Tuileries Palace, where there were the *allées* of white mulberries for silk and *palissades* of Judas trees clipped into arcades or *berceaux* in the Jardin Neuf.

His son Claude (*c.*1564–*c.*1649), apprenticed to his father, rose to be principal gardener to the king, working mainly for Henri IV and Louis XIII. He was the author of *Théâtre des plans et jardinage*, which was published posthumously by his three sons in 1652. For the parterre, Claude recommends low-growing flowers – violets, marguerites, anemones, cowslips and pansies – saying that, when planted together, they give the impression of a Turkish carpet. Later, flowers were generally kept away from the main parterres in the gardens of the royal establishments. For height to set off the flat parterres, Claude recommended planting *allées*, *bosquets* and *palissades* in yew, beech or hornbeam.

He claims to have invented the *broderie* parterres and introduced them at Saint-Germain-en-Laye, where he was encouraged by the garden designer Étienne du Perac to try one large unified design. 'They were', he writes, 'the first *compartiments en broderie* which have been made in France'. Having suffered a disaster in the Jardin Neuf at the Tuileries when the clipped cypress *palissade* died one winter, he resolved to use boxwood henceforth, with the taller variety, *Buxus sempervirens*, for waist-high hedging. He then persuaded the king to let him use the

Parterre design by Claude Mollet for the Jardin Neuf at the Tuileries, for which he persuaded Henri IV to allow him to use dwarf 'Dutch' boxwood (*Buxus sempervirens* 'Suffruticosa'). Published in Olivier de Serres's *Le Théâtre d'agriculture et mésnage des champs*, 1600.

low-growing *Buxus sempervirens* 'Suffruticosa' (known at the time as 'Dutch' box) for the sharply clipped lines of the newly refined flowing, intricate parterres.

He writes, 'Few people of rank had box in their gardens, so I planted my *compartiments en broderie* with several kinds of garden plant to give a variety of green. But such plants cannot last long in this French climate, because of the extremes of heat and cold that we have here. It was the great labour and expense of remaking and replanting the *compartiments* every three years that led me to experiment with box.' Claude Mollet's patterns for parterres for the royal gardens did not appear in his own book but he agreed to allow de Serres to use them in his *Théâtre d'agriculture et mésnage des champs* of 1600.

Le Jardin de plaisir

Little is known of André Mollet's life – not even his birth date, though it is thought that he died in the plague year of 1665. The most remarkable of Claude's three gardener sons, he was trained by his father and probably designed the plates for his work. He entered the service of the Dutch

A plate from *Le Jardin de plaisir*, 1651, showing the elegant scrollwork typical of the parterre designs of Claude and André Mollet. The Mollets stayed with the square and quartered design but would fill their *broderie* patterns with coloured earth, stones or low-growing flowers which were replaced each season.

Stadtholder, Frederik Hendrik of Orange, was in England during the Commonwealth, and designed St James's Park for Charles II, who had taken a great fancy to the French gardens during his exile.

In 1648, André was summoned to take the post of royal gardener to Queen Christina of Sweden. Though his garden plans for her, which included a maze and a 'compass' made up of box hedging and flowers, were never completed (as she abdicated in 1654), he left a folio of plans. *Le Jardin de plaisir,* illustrated with copper engravings, was published simultaneously in Swedish, French and German in 1651. The bulk of the book is a manual of gardening. Only in the last chapter does he tackle 'Embroyder'd Ground-Works, Knot-Works, Knot-Works of Grass, as likewise in Wildernesses, and others'.

The English version of 1670 consists of the last chapter alone, with a presentation of the plan for London's St James's Park. It was aimed at a wider readership, to include 'all the chief Gentry and Nobility of this Kingdom', who were invited to enjoy 'the pleasant Green, and inimitable Tapistry, composed of the Fruits and leaves of the Espaliers, the Counter Espaliers and of the Palisades'.

The boxwood parterre

Generally the Mollets divided the parterre plots into four, or at least multiples of two, in the old way. Sometimes the beds are on the diagonal to 'vary the ordinary custom'; occasionally they are lozenge-shaped or have oriental-style tops to them. But if the compartments were simple in shape, the interiors were complex and flowing, with extravagant swirls and arabesques, feathers and flowers, shells and trumpets, mythical beasts, urns and vases.

The 'ground works', André instructed the gentry and nobility, 'ought to be framed as near as possible to the house, that they may be perfectly seen from the windows, without the obstacle that could be caused by trees, palisades or other high work.'

Tricks of perspective, learnt from the Italians, were used to great effect. The French were to be the masters of *trompe l'œil*. André specified that the 'groundworks the most remote from the eye ought to be drawn of a Larger Proportion, than those that are nearer; for it is certain, that if they be very exactly proportion'd to the distance of the sight, they will thereby appear much more beautiful.'

Within the knots, which generally were infilled with coloured earth and stone, he placed square stones 'fit to bear Flower-pots', and small, 'choice, green trees, some clip't and crop't like Globes, and the others in Piramidal form' and 'all sorts of low flowers'. 'The main flower garden should be separate and it is not recommended for it to be part of the pleasure garden.' Flower beds were usually placed in the *plate-bande* – a border alongside the parterre, against a wall or hedge. He recommends that the plants should be chosen so that, as one set goes over, another replaces it. This way, they 'will greatly add to the ornament of the *compartiment*.' It took an army of trained gardeners to keep up the supply.

The turf parterre

André introduced the turf parterre to the fashionable French garden. 'Parterres', he writes, 'can be made two ways, viz. with box or with turff. Those of box are more fit for the neat and small Embroidery, because that the Box can be planted and clipped into what shape one will, and that there is less pains required in preserving and keeping it than that of Turff, which is often mow'd and roll'd.'

'Turff must be chosen on which sheep commonly feed which ought to be free of all other Herbs except Camomile, then you must have a slicer with a long and crooked handle, to cut the laid Turff in direct Lines, still remembering to slope your hand while you cut, that if the Turff chance to be raised it may be neatly rejoined and pit together again, so it will seem as if it was made long since.'

He recommends laying the turf at Michaelmas, as, if you wait until spring, it could dry out. Aftercare involves rolling it to get rid of the worm casts, then rolling it again to render it 'firmer and more tight'. This has to be done every day, or 'at least every other day', and it must be mowed twice a week.

Instructions are given precise measurements. Sometimes the boxwood parterre leads on to a parterre of turf. After the formal gardens come the wilderness, tree plantings, ponds, 'grass-plots', in the midst of which might be erected arbours and summer banqueting houses. Lime trees should not be used, nor elms, as they 'spread their roots too wide in the earth'; they should be 'banished absolutely from gardens'.

On boxwood

Of boxwood there are three sorts, 'viz. the Great box or Wood-box, which growth high enough if left alone, but that may be as well kept very low; for being cropt and clipt every year twice according to Art, it will not grow above three or four inches in ten years' space; and this is what is required in our Embroidery Ground-works. The second sort of box is called dwarf-Box, which never grows higher than one foot and a half, but is much tenderer than the other . . . The last kind of Box is between both the former, both in respect of its leaf and growth, but does not afford so pleasing a Green.'

'I know that in this Country most part have an aversion to all kind of Box, by reason of its strong scent, but that happens only when it is suffered to grow high; for being kept short and low, it scarce smells at all, especially the dwarf-Box.'

He warns against cypress trees, which 'must be kept always cropt in Pyramidal form and not suffered to grow above six or seven foot in height'. They should be left to 'their liberty', only clipped and cropped at the top and 'round about'. They should not be tied too tightly, as if left 'without air within they wither and become full of dead wood'. The 'wild thistle' (holly) is highly regarded as a green tree with its 'glittering foliage, sharp thorns' and resistance to cold.

Paths and *allées*

Mollet's comment on the paths and *allées* is that to have 'fair Walks, in which one may walk in all weathers with ease, there must be chosen a gravelly Sand, without the leaf mixture of any earth, except Clay, in case the gravel be too stony'. Small shells crushed on the surface should prevent worms from 'piercing through'. Paths should be raised in the middle for good drainage.

Transferring the designs on to the ground took skill. André did it by dividing both the plan and the bed (scaled up) into squares.

The Golden Age of the Sun King

Louis XIV was King of France for seventy-three years (1643–1715), and ruled as an absolute monarch from 1661. His famous dictum 'L'Etat, c'est moi' ('I am the State') describes his unwavering conviction of his divine right as appointed by God. France was the richest country in Europe and Louis's ambition was to outdo Rome in military glory and to rule a European empire. As a result, much of his reign was spent in warfare. Between times, however, he was a great patron of the arts and – perhaps surprisingly for a warrior king – he was passionate about his garden at Versailles.

André Le Nôtre

It was in this hothouse atmosphere that André Le Nôtre (1613–1700), France's greatest garden designer, was to take up the challenge of making the finest gardens that the world had ever seen.

Born in 1613 in a cottage on the edge of the king's gardens at the Tuileries, where his father was head gardener, André came from a long dynasty of royal gardeners. Originally from Blois, the family had arrived in Paris with Catherine de' Medici. André's grandfather, Pierre, was one of the head gardeners at the Tuileries, in charge of the great parterres. His father, Jean, worked under Claude Mollet, head gardener to three kings, before becoming head gardener himself. The two families were close. Claude Mollet's wife was André Le Nôtre's godmother.

André set out at first to be an artist. At the age of fifteen, he was apprenticed to Simon Vouet, a fashionable society portraitist who had spent time in Rome and is credited with introducing the Italian baroque style of painting to France. Le Nôtre spent six years at the Louvre Arts Academy studying painting, architecture, mathematics, perspective and construction – all of which would prove to be vital for his future career. A fellow apprentice was the artist Charles Le Brun, who was to be his lifelong friend and who would work alongside him at Vaux le Vicomte and Versailles.

After his apprenticeship, Le Nôtre was drawn back into his family's profession. Early influences in garden design included his superintendent,

Louis XIV, dressed as Apollo for the ballet *La Nuit*. An anonymous drawing of 1653.

Boyceau, and the Mollets. He was soon appointed principal gardener to the king's brother, Gaston, duc d'Orléans. Later, he succeeded his father as head gardener at the Tuileries and was made 'Draftsman of Plants and Terraces' for Anne of Austria, the queen mother. In 1645–6 he was put in charge of the restoration of Fontainebleau. Other major long-term projects included the royal residences at Saint-Cloud and Saint-Germain-en-Laye.

Vaux le Vicomte

The first garden of regal proportions that Le Nôtre designed from scratch was Vaux le Vicomte, near Paris, for Nicolas Fouquet, the ambitious superintendent of France's finances. Le Nôtre was tipped off about the post by his friend from the academy days, Charles Le Brun, who was back from studying with Poussin in Rome, and had taken on responsibility for the paintings and sculptures at Vaux. In designing the 189 acres of garden Le Nôtre was to break every rule in the book.

A major departure was to break away from the Humanist ideal of the *divina proportione* and the Vitruvian Man of Renaissance Italy. Instead, he treated the garden as a single dynamic whole on a central axis that stretched out to where the horizon meets the sky. He extended and divided the existing main parterre into matching halves (rather than the usual four) to strengthen the forward thrust of the garden's half-mile length.

Le Nôtre's quantum leap, though, was the advance in *trompe l'œil* and tricks of illusion. He had studied Descartes, Euclid's *Optics*, and the

La Maison de Vaux le Vicomte.
Etching from *Vues des belles maisons de France*, 1680.

LA MAISON DE VAUX LE VICOMTE *appartenoit à Monsieur Fouquet du temps de sa surintendance, le sieur le Véau, en fut l'Architecte, elle fut commencée en 1659. et a esté mise dans la perfection ou elle est avec une promptitude et une despence extraordinaires. Elle appartient presentement à Madame Fouquet. fait par Perelle.*
A PARIS Chez N. Langlois rue s.t Iacque a la Victoire. Avec Privilege du Roy.

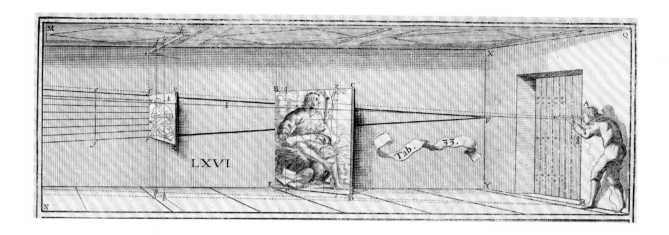

techniques of *anamorphosis abscondita* or hidden distortion. André Mollet had introduced the idea of foreshortening in *Le Jardin de plaisir* and Serres had also touched on it for the reverse effect when spacing trees further apart as they went into the distance, but Le Nôtre now took the idea much further. To prevent the garden from fading into insignificance at the distant focal point and to bring it back larger than life, he employed a trick of 'reversed' or 'braked' perspective, *perspective ralentie*.

To foreshorten the land he sloped it towards the viewer. In the gardens at Vaux the lawn parterre in the mid-distance is three times larger than the embroidery parterre immediately outside the château. In the same way, the figures in the grotto (which turn out on closer appraisal to be humanoid abstracts of limestone and concrete flanked by two river gods) are much larger than the figures on the nearby terrace.

They appear to be at eye level, yet on closer approach you realize that they are actually placed in a hollow. This uses a theory of Euclidean geometry that states that when a surface is below eye level, the more distant parts will appear higher. The giant Farnese *Hercules* at the furthest point of the garden is twice the size of the figures in the grotto and the same goes for the pools, which also increase in size the further away they are. The central path, La Grande Allée, widens subtly as it stretches into the distance.

On a windless day, a further matter of utter wonderment is that when you look into the square pool, the Carré d'Eau, from the far side you will see the château reflected in it, although it is a great distance away. This is achieved by getting 'the angle of incidence' to correspond with the 'angle of the reflection'. Le Nôtre is believed to be the inventor of *le miroir d'eau*, using still water like a mirror. It adds another dimension to this cleverly

Studies in *anamorphosis abscondita* – a trick of hidden distortion used by Le Nôtre. From *La Perspective curieuse ou magie artificielle des effets merveilleux* (*The Curious Perspective or Artificial Magic of Marvellous Effects*) by Jean François Niçeron, 1646.

The grandeur of Versailles. *L'Orangerie et la Pièce d'Eau des Suisses*, by Jean Cotelle, 1693.

manipulated garden – even the sky seems to be captured within the pool by its reflection.

Another illusion is that the grotto appears to sit right on the water's edge, when it is a considerable distance away. Experts say that the engineering for the grotto was taken directly from the latest advances in military fortress architecture. Standing by *Hercules* (who was in the plan but not put in place until the nineteenth century) and looking back at the château, the view has changed character completely. Instead of the single axis sweeping away into the distance, the many horizontals and differences of planes are revealed to provide a completely different aspect, with the interplay of levels now in full view.

But Fouquet's magnificent garden was to provide the setting for his downfall. The story is legendary. In 1661 his grand party set in the garden to display his great success in life and his service to the king ended in tragedy for him. The party was too extravagant. There was music by Lully, a poem by La Fontaine, both composed in honour of the host, and the play, *Les Facheux*, was a newly commissioned comedy ballet by Molière, who made a personal appearance. The grotto became an 'amphitheatre of fire' and fireworks flew off the cupola the length of the garden to the Grand Canal. The fountain-makers put on a breathtaking display. This show of wealth – exceeding that of the twenty-two-year-old king – was a disastrous faux pas. A jealous young monarch had Fouquet arrested and locked up for life.

Versailles

By this time Louis had decided to move the court away from Paris and build a palace outside the city at Versailles. His plan was to control the powerful nobles by keeping them trapped in a gilded cage under his watchful eye. Here he would hold lavish entertainments, with plays by Molière and Racine, ballets, firework displays, masked balls and *grandes fêtes*.

With Fouquet safely under arrest, Louis XIV's first step was to have the trees and the statuary (along with treasure from the interior of the house) removed from Vaux le Vicomte. He then engaged Fouquet's team of the architect Louis Le Vau, Le Nôtre and his friend the artist Charles Le Brun, along with legions of stonemasons, sculptors, hydraulic engineers, armies of artisans, fireworkers, fountain-makers and specialist gardeners. These included Jean-Baptiste de la Quintinie, lawyer turned gardener, who would be in charge of the king's magnificent *potager* at Versailles.

The task ahead was to expand the gardens of Louis's father's hunting lodge from a modest 250 acres of swamp into 4,000 acres (not counting 15,000 acres of forest) of immaculate gardens and the seat of a mighty empire.

The parterre of the Grand Trianon was full of flowers, possibly because it was created for the pleasure of the King's mistress. *Le Grand Trianon vu des parterres*, by Jean Cotelle, *c.*1693.

When back from his wars, the king turned his attention to the gardens. Sometimes he could be seen with clippers in hand. He liked to do a daily tour with Le Nôtre, whom he ennobled. Le Nôtre wisely charmed everyone when he humbly requested three snails and a cabbage heart for his coat of arms. When André was too old to walk any more, the king ordered that he should be carried in a sedan chair. The Sun King rode alongside.

Le Nôtre and Versailles

It is assumed that Le Nôtre started his plan at Versailles on the existing plan put down by Boyceau, enlarging it and working on it piece by piece, incorporating the lawns known as *boulingrins* (cf. 'bowling greens'), the water features, the steps, the *salles de verdure* and all the other glories. As at Vaux, Le Nôtre played with illusions and levels and *perspective ralentie*. In the Grand Canal there appear to be three pools of the same size, but this is a trick, as the furthest pool is three times bigger than the nearest. He lengthened the existing parterres in front of the Palace of Versailles so that they would appear square in perspective.

For Louis XIV's entertainments, Le Nôtre designed many *bosquets* – delightful outdoor rooms, each a small masterpiece, hidden within woodland. It is said that Versailles is a book that tells a story, and the message it unmistakably carries is that of the king's total power. His emblem was the sun. For the *Roi Soleil* the gardens faced east to west, directly illuminating the king's bedchamber at midday. A statue of Apollo, the sun god, was placed in the central fountain. Louis would sometimes himself perform in the guise of Apollo, just to drive home the message.

Le Nôtre and the parterre

Le Nôtre always put extensive parterres in front of the palaces. He followed the gradations by which the eye passed from the highly ornate *broderie* parterre to the simple grass ones, finally giving way to open countryside beyond the parameters. In the 1660s he introduced to Chantilly, Fontainebleau, the Tuileries and Versailles itself a simplified parterre of wide sweeping curves and broader *plates-bandes,* sometimes ending in scrolls. His parterres might be punctuated with clipped yew, box or orange trees, myrtle or bay. He also used a wider variety of plants than the Mollets (who kept to low-growers).

Yet he appeared in later life to lose interest in them. He was quoted in the memoirs of the duc de Saint-Simon as saying that parterres were 'only for nursemaids who, unable to leave their charges, could wander about them with their eyes and admire them from the second floor'.

Possibly Le Nôtre found the parterres too feminine. His most floriferous parterres certainly had women in mind – the Parterre du Midi could be viewed from the queen's apartments, and those of the Trianon were where the king would withdraw from court life for some peace with his mistress.

Immaculate yew topiary in the form of abstract, architectural shapes was everywhere at Versailles – so much so that when, in the next reign, Louis XV held a Yew Ball to celebrate the marriage of the dauphin, the king disguised himself as a yew topiary. (He had good reason to keep a low profile, as he had his eye on a pretty lady dressed as Diana, goddess of the hunt – the future Madame de Pompadour.)

On pruning

The standard of clipped topiary was rigorous. Jean-Baptiste de La Quintinie, in charge of the king's *potager*, scorned the amateur pruner, saying that 'everybody cuts but few prune', and that he was 'persuaded that pruning is not only a very useful but also a curious thing, and capable of affording pleasure to those who understand it. But at the same time, it must be acknowledged that it is likewise pernicious or dangerous when performed by unskilful hands.'

Patterns for topiary in yew, early eighteenth century. From *La Théorie et la pratique du jardinage* (*The Theory and Practice of Gardening*), by Antoine-Joseph Dezallier d'Argenville, 1709.

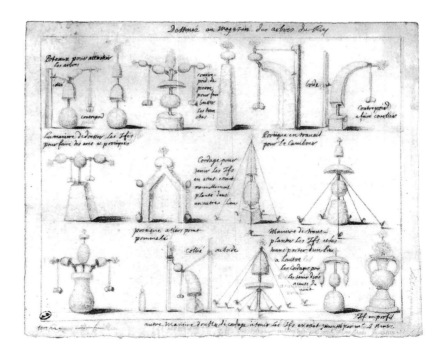

TOPIARY, KNOTS AND PARTERRES

Palissades

At Versailles much use was made of green architecture – the *palissades*, tall green walls made either of clipped shrubs or of shrubs trained on lathes. They were entirely smooth and even, furnished right to the ground, clipped on both sides as tall perpendicular perfection, often with decorative tops. They were designed to screen or be combined with latticework. Sometimes they would be used to enclose entire *cabinets de verdure.*

In the 1660s the Sun King had the gardens remodelled. Extra *parterres de broderie* appeared on top and by the side of the Orangerie, in new northern terraces and below the Latona fountain. All were embellished with new sculptures representing the continents, the times of day, the five Aristotelian elements – earth, air, water, fire and ether – the seasons, the poets and the passions. Great vases marked the borders and thousands of flowers were raised for the flower gardens both at Versailles and at local nurseries.

As Le Nôtre had left little record of his great work other than the gardens themselves, it is fortunate for posterity that the king's secretary, Antoine-Joseph Dezallier d'Argenville (1680–1765), who had an amateur interest in gardening, wrote down what he had learnt from him in *La Théorie et la pratique du jardinage*. The book went into several editions, was translated into German and finally, in 1712, into English by the architect John James as *The Theory and Practice of Gardening.*

On *palissades* Dezallier d' Argenville writes that either yew or box can be used, as both have the advantage of being evergreen. They should be of a 'good and lively green . . . inclining to dark'. The 'proper' box for *palissades* is the 'woodland' box. Yew, however, is the favoured plant, as it can be clipped to an immaculate finish for sheer walls up to thirty feet high.

Palissades are 'often cut into Arches . . . and Balls or Vases may be made on the Head of each Peer; the Vases are formed by shoots of Horn-beam rising out of the Palisade . . . this Decoration composes a kind of Rural Architecture . . . Natural Arbors are formed only by the Branches of Trees artfully interwoven, and sustained by strong latticework, Hoops, Poles, etc., which make Galleries, Porticoes, Halls and Green Vistas, naturally cover'd. These Arbors are planted with Female-Elms or Dutch Lime-Trees, with Horn-beam to fill up the lower part.' The *berceaux*, arched arbours, enclosing the *bosquets*, were usually made from oak, beech, ash, wild cherry, lime, elm or chestnut.

According to Dezallier d'Argenville, parterres fall into four categories.

'Parterres of Embroidery' are the most magnificent and 'sometimes are accompanied by knots and scrolls of Grass-work.' These should be in the principal place next to the building and extend to full width.

ABOVE, LEFT TO RIGHT A parterre of *compartiments*; a parterre in the English manner; a parterre of cut-work for flowers.

OPPOSITE, LEFT ABOVE Plan for a parterre.

OPPOSITE, LEFT BELOW A *parterre des compartiments*, from *La Théorie et la pratique du jardinage*, by Dezallier d'Argenville, 1709.

OPPOSITE, RIGHT Surveyor's tools. *From top to bottom*: a 'semicircle'; a level; a protractor; a 'whole circle' or 'square'.

'Parterres de *compartiments*' have the same symmetry of design at the ends and sides and are usually made of scrolls and other grass-works and borders for flowers. These may accompany the parterres of embroidery.

Parterres 'after the English manner' are 'plainest and meanest of all'. They consist of 'large grass plots all of a piece or cut but little', with a path around, and borders of flowers. These are used to 'fill up the greater spaces and in the Orangeries'.

'Parterres of Cut-work' should be 'cut with symmetry', with no grass or embroidery. Only the borders for flowers should be edged with box. These are 'proper for small places where you would raise flowers'. Where there are flowers it is a 'Parterre Fleuriste'.

'The dwarf box for the parterres should be young, small and fibrous and not too dry.' The one with the most delicate leaf is the 'most esteemed'.

Practicalities of the parterre

In the second half of his book, Dezallier d'Argenville concentrates on the theoretical principles and practice of the art of fine gardening. Instructing on the laying out of the parterre, he demonstrates the use of the semicircle, the protractor with a swivelling arm, the sea compass for use on a tripod and the 'square' to find the 'line of aim' or the 'visual ray'.

Levelling to a perfectly flat surface for parterres is ideally achieved by cut-and-fill of the existing terrain with use of a mason's line. Where the gradient is too steep, it would be necessary to terrace.

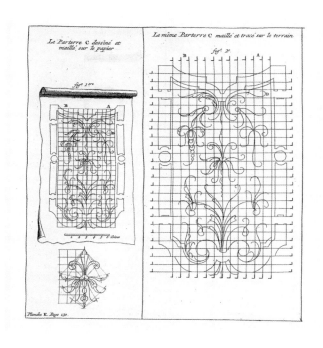

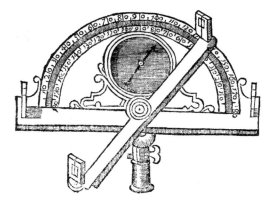

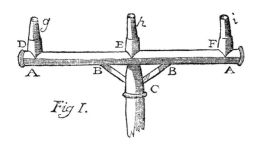

Fig I.

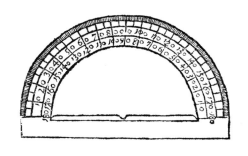

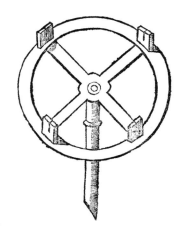

The labyrinth

Labyrinths and mazes, *Maisons de Dédalus*, followed naturally on from the floor mosaics in the medieval cathedrals. Horace Walpole was to remark in *On Modern Gardening* (*c*.1780) that 'a square and a round labyrinth were so capital ingredients of a garden formerly, that in du Cerceau's architecture, who lived in the time of Charles IX and Henry III, there is scarce a ground plot without one of each.'

The low-hedged labyrinths came in the seventeenth century (around the same time as the parterres), when floral and 'block' type mazes were popular in France, England and Holland. These were made from shrubs planted in blocks, 'plashed', or woven together, to make a leafy wall quickly.

High *palissades* in the most artistic labyrinth ever made – the labyrinth of Versailles.
BELOW LEFT The entrance, flanked by statues of *Love* and *Aesop*.
BELOW RIGHT *Le Milan et les oiseaux* – one of the thirty-nine fountains illustrating *Aesop's Fables*. From *Le Labyrinthe de Versailles*, with engravings by Sébastien Leclerc.

Louis Liger of Auxerre, writing in *Le Jardinier solitaire* (1706), described the labyrinth as 'a Place cut into several Windings . . . the most valuable Labyrinths are always those that wind most, as that of Versailles, the contrivance of which had been most wonderfully lik'd by all that have seen it. The *Palissades*, of which Labyrinths ought to be compos'd, should be ten, or twelve, or fifteen foot high; some there are that are no higher than one can lean on, but those are not the finest. The Walls of the labyrinth ought to be kept roll'd, and the Horn-beams in them shear'd, in the shape of Half-moons.'

Needless to say, the labyrinth at Versailles was the ultimate in both luxury and entertainment. It was designed by Charles Perrault, the celebrated compiler of folk and fairy tales, for the education of the dauphin. It had thirty-nine fountains, each depicting a scene from *Aesop's Fables*. These were populated by 333 painted lead animals, designed so that water poured from their mouths in such as way as to give the impression that they were having a conversation.

The fountains were constructed by Swalm Renkin (or 'Rannequin') – the ordinary carpenter and unschooled genius who invented the wondrous Machine de Marli, which pumped water up from the Seine some five hundred feet above the water level to feed the fountains at Versailles.

The king took such pride in the gardens of Versailles that he even wrote a garden guide, the *Manière de montrer les jardins de Versailles,* which ran to six updated editions. The labyrinth was clearly prized, as he put it on the second stop after the Orangerie. Guests were expected, even obliged, to walk in the gardens and be massively impressed. In his memoirs, Louis wrote that when foreign visitors saw how 'well-ordered and flourishing the gardens were and how much money had been spent, that it would make a very favourable impression on them of magnificence, power, wealth and grandeur'.

The king and Le Nôtre had set a garden style that would be copied and developed in different ways in every royal court. When Le Nôtre died in 1700, his epitaph was justified in saying that France was not the only one to have profited from his 'rare talent'. Indeed, 'All the princes of Europe wanted to have his designs.'

Britain
The Tudors and Stuarts

1509–1613

Britain lagged behind France when it came to princely gardens. The Wars of the Roses of 1455–1487, and the period of austerity that followed, meant that it was not until the succession of Henry VIII in 1509 that royal thoughts could begin to turn to anything so frivolous. A new flamboyant era was set in 1520 with the meeting between the French and the English kings at the Field of the Cloth of Gold (so called for the extravagant use of gold thread on the pavilions and other furnishings) in the then-English Pale of Calais. Henry's aim was to outshine his rival, François I, with an ostentatious show of tournaments, revelry, feasting and jousting.

The Tudor knot

Whereas the French king had already invited Leonardo da Vinci to work on the Château de Chambord, had commissioned work from Michelangelo and was planning the rebuilding of Fontainebleau, it was still to be some years before Henry would embark on his first garden.

He purloined Hampton Court from Cardinal Wolsey in 1528 (following Wolsey's failure to get a dispensation from the pope to dissolve the king's marriage to Katherine of Aragon). Little is known of what the garden was like in Wolsey's time, other than that it was enclosed by galleries, and that it had, in the words of George Cavendish, Wolsey's loyal courtier servant and biographer, 'knots so enknotted, it cannot be exprest'.

My galleries ware fayer; both large and long
To walke in them whan that it lyked me beste;
My gardens sweet, enclosed with walles strong,
Embanked with benches to sytt and take my rest:
The knots so enknotted, it cannot be exprest . . .

The Tudors loved complicated, symmetrical patterns. They were to be seen in the architecture, in plaster ceilings, carved on to furniture and

Isaac Oliver, *A Young Man Seated under a Tree*, c.1590–95, against the background of an early parterre.

RIGHT Floral motifs from Part Four of Trevelyon's *Miscellany* of 1608, a book of patterns taken from historical sources for use in architecture, crafts and design, including garden knots and mazes. OPPOSITE *Lettice Newdigate aged Two*, 1606. In this portrait, by an unknown artist, there are three Tudor knots in the garden behind the little girl.

woven into cloth or embroidered into clothes. Thomas Trevelyon, a Protestant writing master who lived near Blackfriars in London, produced a 'commonplace book' of patterns taken from diverse sources – almanacs, historical chronicles, husbandry manuals and other commonplace and pattern books from different countries. It was primarily intended for embroidery and other such crafts, but one chapter is devoted entirely to joiners and gardeners 'as Knots and Buildings . . . with many other thinges to serve their use very well'.

A further record of the use of knots among the fashionable includes a receipt for payment of a gardener in 1502 for 'diligence in making knottes' to be viewed from open galleries at Thornberry Castle, in Gloucestershire. At Alnwick Castle, Northumberland, in the same year, a payment is recorded to 'attend hourly in the garden for setting of erbis, and clypping of knottes'. A poem by Stephen Hawes of 1509, *Passetime of Pleasure or the Historie of Grande Amoure*, also speaks of knots and topiary.

> With flora paynted and wrought curiously
> In dyveres knottes, of mervaylous gretenes
> Rampande lyons stoode up wonderfly
> Made all of Herbes with dulcet swetnes . . .
> Of dyvers floures made full crafetly
> By flora coloured with colours sundry.

Lettice Daughter of Sᵒ Inᵒ Newdigate Kᵗ Wife to Bolton

The knot represents eternity. The knot, being without beginning or end, is the symbol of an everlasting bond associated with marriage. Intertwined snakes in a figure of eight go back to the caduceus, the winged wand or 'herald's staff' of Greek mythology, associated with Hermes (the Roman Mercury), messenger of the gods. The figure of eight is the Greek symbol for infinity. The snake itself also represents eternity and rebirth as it sloughs off its skin and emerges renewed.

A popular conceit was to have the lovers' initials interlaced in the middle of the knot. It is recorded that when Henry arrived with his new bride, Anne Boleyn, at Hampton Court in 1533, there were many knots of their intertwined initials of 'H' and 'A'.

Heraldry was a major theme in Tudor gardens. Heraldic displays had became commonplace in England during the Wars of the Roses, to show allegiance. Receipts from London joiners for the House of Tudor for heraldic animals, displayed on poles painted in the Tudor stripes of white and green and bearing the Tudor rose or the royal arms, included greyhounds, lions, horses, antelopes, dragons, harts and hinds painted in bright colours, with the glitter of touches of gold. Such animals would also appear in topiary.

Topiary

Thomas Platter, a burgher from Basle who visited Hampton Court in 1599, gives an eyewitness account of the gardens, which he found to be 'the finest and most magnificent royal edifice to be found in England, or for that matter in other countries' and in which there was, he noted, most elaborate topiary. In an area which was like a chess board, with squares filled with red brick dust, white sand or green lawn, 'there were all manner of shapes, men and women, half-men and half-horses, sirens, serving maids with baskets. French lilies and delicate crenellations all round made from dry twigs bound together and the aforesaid quick-set shrubs, or entirely of rosemary, all true to life, and so cleverly and amusingly interwoven, mingled and grown together, trimmed and arranged picture-wise that their equal would be difficult to find.'

Even in Tudor times, Britain remained slow to take up the Italian Renaissance school. Henry's break from Rome in the 1530s caused a distance between the two countries. Also, unlike other European royal courts, British royalty did not customarily bring in architects, artists and skilled artisans from abroad. Royal architecture and gardens came under jurisdiction of the Office of Works and teams of master craftsmen would operate under the supervision of the Surveyor of the King's Works.

NON SINE SOLE
IRIS.

Nonetheless, it is known that Henry had a copy of Pietro de' Crescenzi's *Liber Ruralium Commodorum*, the *Book of Rural Benefits* (see page 37), in the library at Whitehall, and Pietro's influence was unmistakable in Henry's gardens. Crescenzi describes a garden fit for royalty as an outdoor palace with rooms and pavilions, walks and bowers made from trained trees, with much use of grafting and intertwining – a signature feature of Tudor gardens, with their outdoor galleries and fine 'carpenter's work'. A visitor in the Elizabethan era noticed that 'plants are trained, intertwined and trimmed in so wonderful a manner and in such extraordinary shapes, that the like could not easily be found.' He also remarked on the fact that rosemary was trained as a wall shrub so 'as to cover them entirely, which is a manner exceeding common in England'.

Work on the gardens at Henry's Hampton Court started with the Privy Orchard, followed by the Privy Garden, the Cloister Green, the Pond Garden and the Mount Garden (or 'Little Garden'). These were joined by covered walks in the Crescenzi style, and filled with heraldry and many sundials. The most outstanding feature of the Mount Garden was the Great Round Arbour, three storeys high, nearly all in glass with a lead cupola surmounted with the king's arms, from which to survey the king's Privy Garden, a view of the Thames, and the Pond Garden.

Henry's next great garden, also confiscated from Wolsey, was York Place in Whitehall. Later renamed the Palace of Whitehall, it was refurbished for the new queen, Anne Boleyn. Here we read of the Great Garden, where there were 'different animals carved in wood, with their horns gilt . . . set on top of columns, together with the flags bearing the Queen's arms'. In the centre was a quadrangular stone, described by

BELOW AND OPPOSITE *The Family of Henry VIII*, English School, *c.*1545. The view through the arches is of the Great Garden of Whitehall Palace, where the brick-edged beds are planted with low-growing herbs. The heraldic King's Beasts, here carved in wood and set on columns amidst the flower beds, were also often depicted in topiary.

a viewer as 'a beautiful work of art'. It was 'hollow in the middle and round like a baptismal fount'. On the stone there were 117 sun circles on which to see the hours. Tudor gardens were seen as places of science and learning.

Henry's greatest garden, however, was Nonsuch in Surrey (destroyed in 1682). As in France, fine English gardens were generally adapted to already existing castles and fortified manor houses, but Nonsuch was built from scratch. In the manner of Fontainebleau, the courtyards were richly furnished with antique sculptures and reliefs. Anthony Watson, Rector of Cheam, describing the view from the inner gatehouse through the arch, speaks of 'huge figures of gods and goddesses gleaming white . . . so moulded that they seemed to be leaping off the wall'. They were on 'golden frames, that shone so brightly, it looked as though the palace was on fire'.

In this garden there was a puzzle maze of 'hazardous wiles' and 'a tortuous path'. There was also topiary in the form of deer, horses, rabbits and dogs giving chase 'with unhindered feet' and which 'effortlessly passed over the green' – in much the same way as they did at Hampton Court.

Nonsuch Palace, a detail taken from a map of Surrey by John Speed, 1610. Each of the four gardens shown in front is divided into four or three sections and planted with clipped trees.

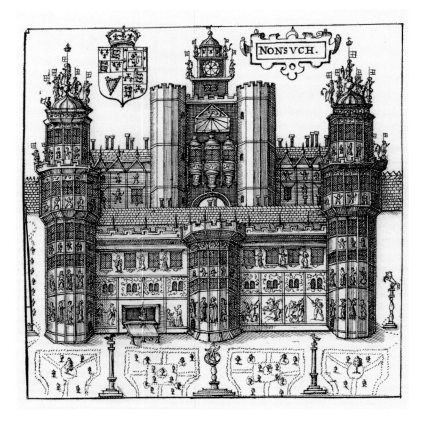

According to a 1650 Parliamentary Survey, the gardens were filled 'with quarters and rounds set about with thorn hedges, walks, arbours, covered alleys and seats painted green, blue and russet'.

William Cecil, Lord Burghley, for many years Elizabeth's prime minister, kept a magnificent establishment, Theobalds in Hertfordshire, which was frequented by the queen. The gardens were so large and the avenues so long that it was said that one could walk for as much as two miles without coming to the end. Paul Hentzner, a German lawyer (1558–1623), describes the garden in his *Travels in England, during the Reign of Queen Elizabeth*.

The property, he tells us, is surrounded by a large moat, which is used for a boating canal. There is a grotto with water 'streaming out of a rock into a basin supported by the figures of two slaves; on the ceiling is painted the Zodiac with sun and moon in their courses, and on each side six trees, with bark, leaves and birds'-nests, all complete and natural.' There is a labyrinth called the Hill of Venus (as it has a mound in the middle) and this is 'one of the fairest places in the world'. At the end of the garden is a summer house with marble sculptures of the twelve emperors of Rome. On the porch are portraits of all the kings of England.

The parterre is laid out in nine beds. In the Privy Garden there is a 'handsome quicksett hedge cut into formes'. There are several square knots, each surrounded by a whitethorn or privet hedge, 'cut into a handsome fashion' and with a cherry tree at the 'angles'. There is a white fountain in the central knot, while another has the royal arms 'exquisitely made'. A third is planted with 'choice flowers'. Two have 'figures of wainscot [finest quality oak imported for woodwork], well carved', while the others are 'handsomely turfed'.

When the queen was entertained there in 1591, a speech was given in her honour by the poet and playwright George Peele. In it, he assumes the character of a gardener and describes the making of the 'maze' (probably a knot or a parterre) at a nearby garden, Pymms.

The moles destroyed and the plot levelled, I cast it into four quarters. In the first I framed a maze, not of hyssop or thyme, but that which maketh time itself wither with wondering: all the Virtues, all the Graces, all the Muses winding and wreathing about your majesty . . . all this not of potherbs, but flowers, and flowers fairest and sweetest; for in so heavenly a maze, which astonished all earthly thought's promise, the Virtues were done in roses, flowers fit for the twelve Virtues, who have in themselves, as we gardeners have observed, above an hundred; the Grace of pansies partly-coloured, but in one stalk, never asunder, yet diversely beautified; the muses of nine several flowers, being of sundry natures, yet all sweet, all sovereign.

On the writing of knots

In the sixteenth century, the advent of printing, the interest in new and exciting scientific discoveries, the introduction of plants arriving from recently discovered territories and the burgeoning national passion for gardening among the now-literate middle classes all came together to bring on a rush of herbals.

The first printed herbal, of 1525, was by Richard Bankes, while Peter Traveris's *Grete Herbal* was published the following year. John Fitzherbert's *Boke of Husbandry* was written in English rather than the customary Latin, as was William Turner's *Herball*. A practical book on pruning was Leonard Mascall's *Booke of the arte and manner how to plant and graffe all sorts of trees*. It included an illustration of the pruning tools, which, incidentally, were little changed since the Romans. The more readable *Herbal or General History of Plants* by John Gerard was published in 1597.

Contemporary with Gerard was Francis Bacon (1561–1626), Lord Chancellor, statesman, politician, philosopher, author and an influential scientist. In his famous *Essay of Gardens*, he was ahead of his time in expressing a distaste for topiary and parterres. For his part, he declares, he does not like images 'cut out in juniper or other garden stuff; they be

Illustrations from Leonard Mascall's *A Booke of the arte and manner how to plant and graffe all sorts of trees*, 1589.
RIGHT Three stages of cleft grafting.
OPPOSITE Pruning and grafting tools.

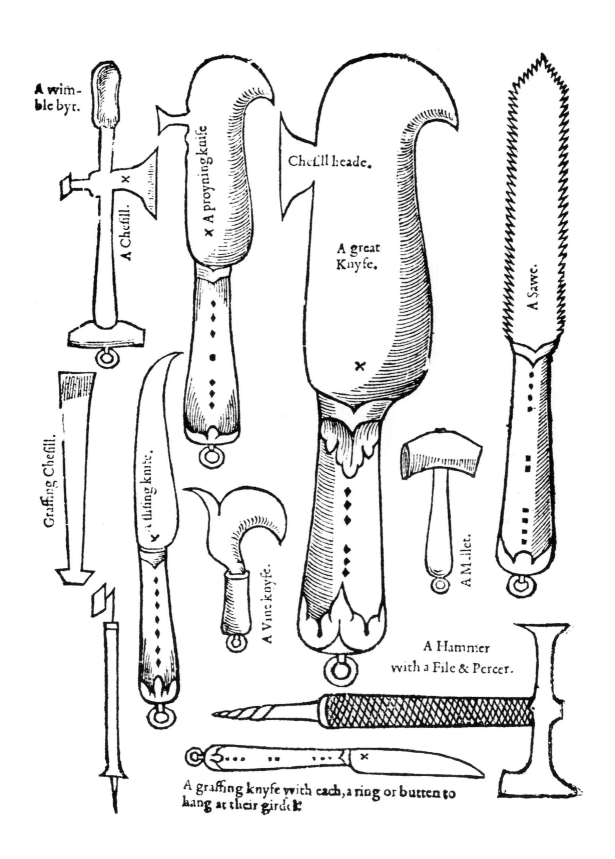

A wimble byt.

A Chesill.

A proyning knaife

Chesill heade.

A great Knyfe.

A Sawe.

Graffing Chesill.

A thing knife

A Vine knyfe.

A Mallet.

A Hammer with a File & Percer.

A graffing knyfe with each, a ring or butten to hang at their girdel.

for children.' 'As for the making of knots, or figures, with divers coloured earths, that they may lie under the windows of the house on that side which the Garden stands, they be but toys; you may see as good sights many times in tarts.'

However, he did not object to little low hedges around 'welts' and 'pretty pyramids'. In his ideal kingly garden he would have none of those knots or figures of coloured earth. It would be set round with trellis screen and arches, varied with turrets and plates of coloured glass for the sun to 'play upon'. In the centre would be a large mount crowned with a banqueting house. There would be plenty of fountains but no standing water, as pools 'mar all, and make the garden unwholesome, and full of flies and frogs.' This had been experienced at Versailles, where the croaking of bullfrogs kept the French court awake at night.

Thomas Hill

In 1563, there appeared the first gardening book to concern itself with knots and the pleasure garden written in English for the ordinary householder: *A Most Briefe and Pleasaunte Treatyse, Teaching how to Dresse, Sowe, and Set a Garden*, by Thomas Hill (or 'Hyll'). Hill was an astronomer but wrote on a wide range of subjects, including mathematics, dreams and physiognomy, as well as gardening. The publishers described the book as 'collected from

Woodcut of Thomas Hill's suggested design for a simple enclosed garden in *The Proffitable Arte of Gardening*, 1586.

TOPIARY, KNOTS AND PARTERRES

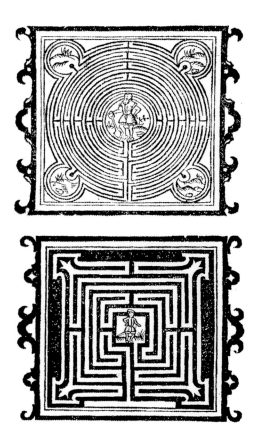

the best approved Authors besides forty years experience in the Art of Gardening'. It was later reprinted as *The Proffitable Arte of Gardening*.

Thomas Hill gave two designs for mazes, recommended for larger gardens. These could be used for recreation and to provide decoration. He suggests planting fruit trees in the corners, with a 'herber decked with roses . . . or els a fair tree of rosemary' in the centre, and recommends that 'in wet places the beds should be raised two foot high.'

Another of Hill's books was *The Gardener's Labyrinth*, which appeared in 1577, under the pseudonym Didymus Mountain, and was so popular that it continued to be reprinted into the mid-seventeenth century. *The Gardener's Labyrinth* of 1577 includes twelve knot designs, similar to those used in embroidery and marquetry and on carpets.

The 'herber' or 'circular arbour', Hill writes, 'may be framed with Juniper poles, or the willow, either to stretch, or to be bound together with Osiers, after a square forme, or in arch maner winder, that the branches of the Vine, Melone, or Cucumber, running and spreading all ouer might so shadow and keepe both the heat and sun . . . there under.'

Patterns for mazes (left) and for knots (right) by Thomas Hill, from *A Most Briefe and Pleasaunte Treatyse*, 1563.

A design for a quartered garden with knots and heraldry, from Gervase Markham's *The English Husbandman*, 1613.

Gervase Markham

Gervase Markham (1568–1637), author of *The English Husbandman* of 1613, had been a soldier in the Low Countries and in Ireland, and a horse-breeder (reputed to have imported the first Arab horse), before embarking on his career in horticulture. He makes the first mention of the parterre in English. He reports that it is being taken up among the fashionable classes. He writes that while knots were, with mazes, 'the first that were received into admiration' and are 'most ancient and at this day of most use amongst the vulgar', they are in modern times 'the least respected with the great ones, who for the most part are given over to novelties'. Clearly, the 'novelties' are the French parterres. He notes that these are filled with costly 'powder of marble', but 'our own grauell is in euery respect as beautiful, as dry, as strong, and as long lasting.'

In 1616 he made a fresh translation of Charles Estienne's *L'Agriculture et maison rustique*, a work that had been influential on his *English Husbandman*. 'You shall understand Beds filled with flowers they were generally simpler than those without any and these were now known as "open knots".' In these the patterns were set out with low-growing shrubs and herbs or would be filled with chalk for white, clay for yellow or chamomile for green, whereas the 'closed' knots would be filled with flowers of a single colour.

In Markham's plan for *The English Husbandman*, the orchard is planted in a quincunx pattern so that 'which waysoever, a man shall cast his eyes, yet he shall see the trees every way stand on rowes, making squares, alleys and devisions, according to a man's imagination.' The garden of pleasure would be laid out in knots and dwarf shrub mazes, some as coats of arms 'to be seen in the gardens of Noblemen and Gentlemen which may beare coate armour'. Straightforward knots of lavender and other herbs were for the housewife to spread out her 'linen cloths' to dry.

These knots and other devices may be 'circumferenced or bound in with fine curious Hedges made Battlement-wise, in sundry forms – Pyllasters, Flowers, shapes of Beasts, Birds, Creeping things, Shippes . . . and such like . . . especially if your ground be little, or flattened, because these Hedges take not halfe so much roome as the Borders.' Plants – eglantine, privet, hawthorn and sweet briar – can be woven into the latticework and will protect the quarters and knots.

William Lawson

William Lawson's *Countrie Housewifes Garden* and *A New Orchard and Garden* were published together in 1618 and went into several editions. *A New Orchard and Garden* has the first plan of the garden for an ordinary country house rather than for a grand manor or palace.

In this plan, the six squares, over three terraces, are defined by trees with 'ornaments' in between. There is a mount, 'M', in each of the four corners, from which to enjoy the garden and countryside beyond. 'N' marks the still houses. The horse and the man signify topiary figures. 'C' is a knot with a Tudor Rose at its centre. The orchard ('B') is in a quincunx pattern. There is a bridge and a kitchen garden, beehives and walks. The outside fence would have been 'set' with stone fruit.

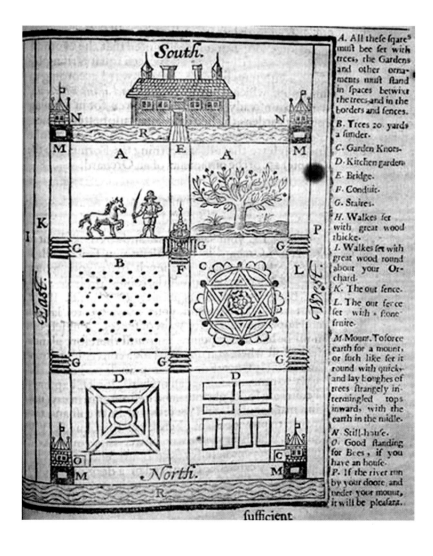

An early design for a productive and ornamental country house garden (generally considered to be an Elizabethan garden), published in William Lawson's *A New Orchard and Garden*, 1618.

TOPIARY, KNOTS AND PARTERRES

Where there is a maze, Lawson recommends that it should be made of fruiting shrubs and trees 'well framed a man's height so as to make your friend wander in gathering of berries till he cannot recover himself without your help'. A pleasant river 'with silver streams' would be a good addition to the orchard: here you could sit on your mount and 'angle a peckled Trout, sleighty Eel or some other daintie Fish'. He suggests relaxing when tired on banks and seats of chamomile, pennyroyal daisies and violets.

Lawson's *Countrie Housewifes Garden* is said to be the first published book expressly written for women. He goes into some detail on the design and layout of the garden and orchard, 'together with divers new knots for gardens'. However, keeping in mind the endless possibilities, he says he will leave 'every Housewife to herself – let her view these few, choice, new forms, and note this generally, that all plots are square'.

Lawson's books spring from his own experience of gardening – as a Protestant Yorkshire vicar – in the north of England over forty-eight years. Refreshingly, the product was entirely his 'sole experience, without respect to any former-written Treatise'.

John Parkinson

In 1629 John Parkinson's *Paradisi in Sole Paradisus Terrestris – Park-in-Sun's* (pun on 'Parkinson') *Park on Earth*, generally known as *Paradisus*, was published. It was dedicated to Henrietta Maria, wife of Charles I. Little is known about Parkinson's life, other than that he was born in 1567, probably in Nottinghamshire, and became apothecary to James I and Botanicus Regius Primarius to Charles I.

Considered by many to be the most beautiful gardening book in the English language, *Paradisus* also marked a departure from the herbals of the day, being as much about the aesthetics of plants for the 'Garden of pleasant and delightfull Flowers' as about plants for their practical uses. The book is aimed at the middle classes as well as the aristocracy: he points out that 'many Gentlemen and others are much delighted to bestow their paines on grafting themselves.'

He recommends a four-square quartered design for knots and gives six examples of geometric patterns for 'true knots'. He suggests – as Lawson had before him – that 'every man . . . take what may please his mind'. These six patterns are included because 'many are desirous to see the forms of trayles [possibly 'trellis'], knots and other compartiments'. Like Gervase Markham, he specifies that 'open knots' are 'are more proper for . . . outlandish flowers; I have here caused some to be drawne to satisfie

OPPOSITE ABOVE An illustration by William Lawson from *A New Orchard and Garden*, 1618.
OPPOSITE BELOW Guidance offered by William Lawson in *The Countrie Housewifes Garden*, 1618, showing how to set out a knot on the ground with pegs and lines, together with some suggested knot patterns.

their desires.' ('Outlandish' flowers being imported plants or exotics, generally bulbs such as the tulip, as opposed to native plants.)

Knots fall into two categories – the one is of 'living herbes and the other are dead materials, as leade, boords, bones, tyles etc.' Lead, though costly, as well as too hot in summer and too cold in winter, 'delights some' and is 'sometimes cut out like unto the battlements of a church'. Boards should be made of hefty oak four or fives inches broad. Sheep's shank bones – which should be placed thin end down – fade to white in time and 'prettily grace out the ground', whereas edging beds with jawbones, as 'used by some Low Countries and other places beyond the seas', is 'too grosse and base'. Tiles are good but easily broken. There is a new fashion for 'whitish or bluish pebble stones'.

Parkinson notes that boxwood is still not widely used: it is only growing in the gardens of those who are 'curious'. Nonetheless, it 'serveth very well to set out a knot or border or any beds, for besides that it is ever-greene, it be reasonable thick set, will easily be cut and formed into any fashion . . .'

For the knots of living herbs, Parkinson recommends cotton lavender (*Santolina chamaecyparissus*), 'being of the highest respect for late daies, accepted both for the beauty and forme of the herbe' but generally only found in the gardens of 'great persons'. Thrift, he says, is the 'most anciently received for making knots . . . and will give much delight' as it will grow 'thicke and bushie . . . etc. and may be kept, being cut with a pair of Garden sheeres'. However, it may die in the frost and has the disadvantage of 'sheltering snails and other small noisome worms so plentifully that gillyflowers and other fine plants are much spoiled by them'. He also suggests hyssop, germander, marjoram, savory, thyme, juniper and yew – though the last two 'soon grow too big'.

With the English love of a good path, Parkinson recommends 'the fairer and larger your allies and walks be, the more grace your garden shall have.' They should be open, turfed or sanded or planted with 'sweet smelling herbs that release their scent when trodden on' – such as burnet, wild thyme and water mint – or 'shady alleys with under arched trees' or the 'thick pleached allée' – privet, sweetbriar or hawthorn – 'enlaced together' with a few roses and covered walkways with carpenter's work.

The Jacobeans

In 1603, James VI of Scotland took the throne as James I of England. There followed, remarkably, nearly four decades of peace, before the outbreak of the Civil War in 1642. The Jacobean era was one of extravagance in England on a scale not seen since the reign of Henry VIII.

Two characters shone out in bringing French and Italian influences to British gardens: the great architect Inigo Jones and the French hydraulic engineer and designer – and grandson of Jacques Androuet du Cerceau – Salomon de Caus.

Inigo Jones

Inigo Jones (1573–1652), one of England's most remarkable architects, was the son of a Smithfield clothmaker. He rose to be Surveyor General to James I. His redoubtable talents were seen and promoted by benefactors, particularly the great patron of the arts Lord Arundel, who introduced him to Italy in 1613–14. There Inigo Jones attended the theatrical events of the Medici court in Florence, and he later designed sets and costumes for some five hundred performances of masques for the Jacobean court, most notably with the playwright Ben Jonson. In his stage sets, he quite often included images of the Italian Renaissance gardens of the day.

Inspired by Palladio's *Quattro libri dell' architettura* (*Four Books of Architecture*) – which he read in Italian – and by the teachings of Vitruvius, Inigo Jones went on to introduce Italian Renaissance architecture to

Of His Britannick Majesty's Palace of White Hall the Park Side. A view from the St James's Park side of the planned new palace of Whitehall, designed by Inigo Jones in 1638 but never built. The garden is like a parade ground marked by topiary cones alternated with classical statues. Engraving by D.M. Muller, 1749.

Britain's elite. He designed the Queen's House, Greenwich – the first classical building in England. Other works included the Banqueting House for the Palace of Whitehall (with a ceiling painted by Rubens), the Queen's Chapel at St James's Palace, the Piazza at Covent Garden and the remodelling of St Paul's Cathedral. He was to be influential on a number of eighteenth-century architects and garden-makers – not least Lord Burlington and William Kent, the duo who would be key in bringing to Britain the Palladian villa, classical references and a more 'natural' garden, as inspired by the Italian *campagna*.

De Caus: Salomon and Isaac

At the same time, the French hydraulic engineer Salomon de Caus was bringing word of the French Renaissance to English garden designers.

Born in 1576 in Dieppe, Salomon de Caus had visited Italy at the age of nineteen and spent three years there, and had then studied architecture in France. He came to England to work from 1607 to 1613 for Anne of Denmark, wife of James I. His principal job was to tutor Henry, the Prince of Wales, in mathematics, and he was also drawing master to the other royal children.

During this time he made many designs for entertaining fountains and waterworks for Richmond Palace, which were published as *Des Grots et fontaines pour l'ornement des maisons de plaisance et jardins*. He later produced *Les Raisons des forces mouvantes*, describing how to make hydraulic toys and effects – singing birds, hooting owls and musicians playing the flute. It is assumed that he was the 'Frenche Gardiner' referred to both at Somerset House and Greenwich.

De Caus's major garden design work in England was for Robert Cecil, Lord Salisbury, first minister to King James. Like his father, Lord Burghley, Cecil was a great garden enthusiast and had added to the already magnificent garden at Theobalds, which he had inherited on his father's death. However, when the king took a fancy to Theobalds, an exchange was suggested (or perhaps rather imposed). Lord Salisbury was to give Theobalds to the king: in return, he was offered the run-down Tudor palace of Hatfield House.

Undaunted, Cecil set to work to supervise a large building programme at Hatfield, calling on the services of Inigo Jones as architectural consultant. De Caus was commissioned to create the great water parterre and fountains in the East Garden.

Salomon's nephew, brother or son (the dispute continues) Isaac de Caus, also a hydraulic engineer, designed at Wilton House, Salisbury,

for the Earl of Pembroke, an inspired interpretation of the Renaissance garden which is also a landmark in English garden history.

His daring departure was to make a wilderness in the centre so as to conceal the river Nadder, which runs diagonally through the garden, thus preserving the symmetry of the view. On the house side of the wilderness are the 'Platts embroidered' (as *parterres de broderie* were known in England) in the latest chic Mollet style, and on the other side of a broad bridge, a circus, another garden of *allées*, cherry-lined walks and arbours. There are central statues and additional parterres with fountains and marble statues bordering the main garden.

At the far end stands the focal point – the Borghese Gladiator in front of the grotto, a de Caus masterpiece. The grotto was a mechanical theatre full of monsters, gods and singing birds worked from a water system held in reservoirs on the roof and powered by gravity. John Woolridge in his *Systema Horti-Cultura* (*The Art of Gardening*) of 1667 wrote that it was the 'most famous that this Kingdom affords . . . wherein you may view . . . the best of waterworks'.

In 1623 the labyrinth of Wilton House was described by the 'Water Poet', John Taylor, as being circular with wider paths on the outside, 'as the Rinds of an Onion are greatest without, and less towards the Centre'. He described the hedges as 'so thickly set' that it was impossible to see through them and therefore 'the Work seems endless'.

During the Civil War Puritanism put paid to lavish living, and many of the gardens were deliberately destroyed. However, when, in 1660, Charles II was restored to the throne, there was another dramatic change. Charles, in his years of exile, had acquired a taste for the *jardin à la française*. He would employ André Mollet to design the parterres in St James's Park and the ornamental 'Dutch' canals at Hampton Court. This would cause John Evelyn to comment that Hampton Court, formerly 'a flat, naked piece of Ground', was 'now planted with sweete rows of lime-trees and the Canale for water now neere-perfected'.

Meanwhile, Elizabeth Stuart (1596–1662), sister of Henry, Prince of Wales and of the future Charles I, had in 1613 summoned her former drawing master, Salomon de Caus, to Heidelberg in south-west Germany. She was now married to the Elector Palatine, Frederick V, who instructed him to lay out the gardens of the palace of Heidelberg, no expense spared and with 'toutes les raretés qu'on l'on pourroit faire'.

The garden at Wilton House, designed by Isaac de Caus, with French parterres. From *Hortus Pembrochianus*, 1645–50.

War in Europe
and the Dutch Golden Age

1613–1702

N 1613, when Salomon de Caus arrived at Heidelberg Castle to design what would become known as Germany's finest Renaissance garden, Europe was on the brink of the Thirty Years War. Three decades of religious persecution, witch-hunting and power-mongering, between 1618 and 1648, would see the fragmentation of the Holy Roman Empire and leave Europe – especially Germany – considerably the poorer.

The war grew from the conflict between Catholic and Protestant princes within the Holy Roman Empire. On 23 May 1618 a group of Protestant noblemen stormed Prague Castle and threw three imperial counsellors out of a window. This, the Defenestration of Prague, marked the beginning of the Bohemian revolt, and with it the Thirty Years War. Bohemia's largely Protestant electorate went on to reject the dynastic Catholic heir, Ferdinand of Styria, offering the crown instead to the Protestant Elector Palatine. Frederick was crowned king on 4 November 1619.

His reign was brief. Defeated in 1620 in the Battle of the White Mountain, Frederick escaped with his family to a life of exile in the Netherlands. The uncompleted garden at Heidelberg Castle was abandoned to its fate. Fortunately, Salomon had produced a book, *Hortus Palatinus*, which was dedicated to Frederick with the hope that the garden would be finished in more peaceful times. Undoubtedly, de Caus also had it in mind to take it as his calling card as he hastened back to France to work for Louis XIII.

Heidelberg

The gardens at Heidelberg had been built on an intractable site high above the town and the river of Neckar. Swathes were sawn out of the mountainside and a series of five terraces was put in place. Because of the difficulties of the site de Caus left out the classic central axis, but he included many other Renaissance features: a labyrinth, gazebos, pools, grottoes and his speciality – the musical waterworks that never failed to astonish and delight.

OPPOSITE The gardens of Castle Heidelberg, considered to be Germany's finest Renaissance garden, were designed by Salomon de Caus for Prince Frederick. The elaborate *broderie* pattern of this parterre incorporates a crown topped by the Greek cross – a part of Frederick's heraldry. His name is spelt out around the centerpiece statue of Urania, the Muse of Astronomy. From *Hortus Palatinus*, 1620.
OVERLEAF Jacques Fouquières, *The Gardens at Castle Heidelberg*, 1620.

133

One contemporary commentator remarked that, while the garden was designed in the grand manner, the superb detail made it also 'curious'.

The message of the garden was one of political power and domination over both man and nature. On the top terrace stood a statue of Frederick. Beneath him were Neptune, Hercules, Apollo and the river gods. In the opening to the grotto there was a lion, symbol of the Palatinate. De Caus did not look for unity in the design but variety within unified themes. An *entrelac* parterre would be alternated with a *broderie* one. Narcissus, who loved only himself, contrasted with Ceres and Pomona, the goddesses of fertility.

In *Hortus Palatinus* de Caus described the garden design in some detail. The Parterre of the Column, which had a central Ionic column, was surmounted by a Greek cross, part of Frederick's heraldry. It was surrounded by four quarters with elaborate *entrelac* parterres. Orange trees were arranged in order, one large, one small, around each quarter, with a taller one in the centre.

The Parterre of the Column. The central feature is a column surmounted by Frederick's Greek cross. Each pattern in the parterre is designed to be a little different, as de Caus liked variety within his themes.

TOPIARY, KNOTS AND PARTERRES

The neighbouring garden was on the same lines but with a statue of Urania in the centre and a pair of muses at each of the four entrances. Each of the quarters had a crown within the parterre design and an inscription to Frederick. On the far side of this was the Parterre of the Orangerie, heavy with the scent of orange blossom in May. It was laid out as an eight-pointed star within a circle (said to be a cosmic diagram expressing a harmonic order). Some parterres were laid out in the striking French way of clipped boxwood set against white sand, a style adopted by Jacques Boyceau in the Luxembourg Palace and by the Mollets in the 1630s.

Beyond there was a water parterre, a labyrinth (never completed) and a circular 'Bed of Seasons'. This was constantly replanted so as to be in flower all year round. It let on to a panoramic view across the countryside. Further from the palace, raised up on terraces on the side of the hillside, the parterres were in the simpler Italian style of geometric shapes.

BELOW LEFT The Parterre of the Orangerie was laid out in as eight-pointed star within a circle.
BELOW RIGHT Another of de Caus's parterre designs, this one marked by orange trees in pots.

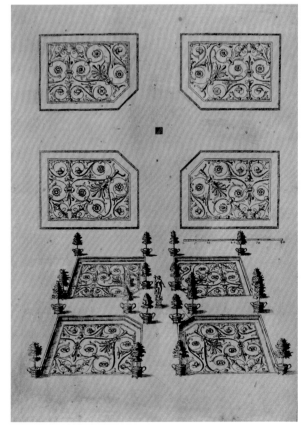

Herrenhausen

Many years after the 1658 Treaty of Westphalia ended the Thirty Years War, Sophie, the youngest daughter of Frederick and Elizabeth, set out to make a garden. Just as her parents had created the greatest Renaissance garden in Germany, Sophie would now make what was to be considered Germany's finest baroque garden. Sophie was married to Ernest Augustus, Elector of Brunswick-Lüneburg, and their son would be George I of Britain. Her garden masterpiece was at their summer house, Herrenhausen, near Hanover.

Although well aware of the Le Nôtre school – she corresponded regularly with her niece Liselotte, the second wife of Louis XIV's brother, Philippe, duc d'Orléans – Sophie also favoured the symmetrical Dutch style, familiar to her from her childhood. She sent her head gardener, Martin Charbonnier, who had been trained at Versailles, to the Netherlands for further instruction.

The Grosser Garten (Great Garden) was almost completely flat and an exact rectangle, bounded on three sides by a canal, with the palace on the fourth side. On either side of the strictly central axis were twin garden rooms, mirror images of each other. The central parterre with its *bassin* was surrounded on three sides by high hedges, salons, cabinets and trees arranged in quincunxes. To one side lay the maze and to the other a hedge theatre – the only part of the garden on more than one level. It had an orchestra pit, wings of clipped hornbeam and an array of Dutch gilt figures.

RIGHT The celebrated garden theatre at Herrenhausen, set with wings of clipped hornbeam and flanked by Dutch gilt figures. Engraving by J. van Sasse after J.J. Müller, *c*.1720. OPPOSITE Bird's-eye view of the Great Garden of Herrenhausen, designed in the Dutch style. Artist unknown, 1708.

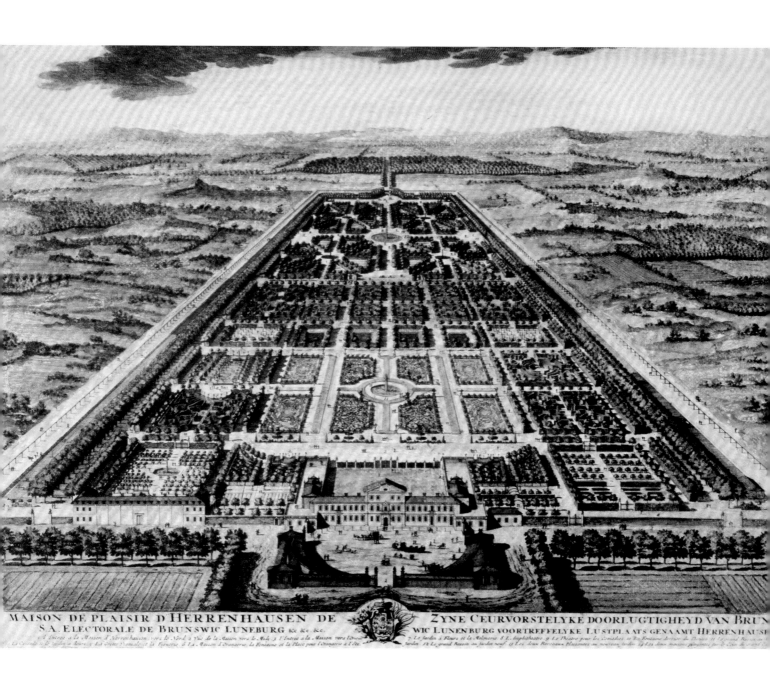

MAISON DE PLAISIR D'HERRENHAUSEN DE   ZYNE CEURVORSTELYKE DOORLUGTIGHEYD VAN BRUN
S.A. ELECTORALE DE BRUNSWIC LUNEBURG &c &c &c.   WIC LUNENBURG VOORTREFFELYKE LUSTPLAATS GENAAMT HERRENHAUSE

The Dutch Golden Age

The seventeenth century saw the flowering of the Dutch Golden Age. With the Dutch East and West India Companies, founded in 1602 and 1621, the Netherlands came to surpass even Venice in trade and in banking. Science and the arts flourished in this era of Rubens, Rembrandt, Vermeer and van Dyck. The ruling House of Orange produced distinguished generals, men of culture – and influential garden-makers, most notable among them Maurits, Frederik Hendrik and, not least, the British king, William III.

Exotic flowers

Exotic florists' flowers were always centre stage in the Dutch garden. The seafaring Netherlands had been renowned for their horticulture since the Crusades, when their ships brought in subtropical plants from the Levant and the Indies. In the seventeenth century, Haarlem was the European centre for flower and bulb nurseries, as Boskoop was for trees. It was normal practice for large landowners in England at the time to get their indigenous trees from home and the fruit and forest trees from Holland or Flanders.

Erasmus

A significant early influence on the Dutch Renaissance garden was Erasmus (Desiderius Erasmus Roterodamus, 1466–1536), a Catholic priest and classical scholar, who describes in his *Colloquies* (1518) gardens that are both Christian and Humanist.

Erasmus writes of square walled enclosures, 'neatly kept and in perfect order . . . designed for the entertainment of the Sight, the Smell and the Refreshment of the very Mind'. The garden walls should be covered in frescoes depicting animals, trees and flowers. He notes that 'one piece of ground will not hold all sorts of plants . . . the kitchen garden and that's my Wife's; the other is a physic garden.' One enclosure is nothing but sweet herbs and those 'only choice ones too'. A meadow with a quickset hedge is where he 'diverts himself with good company. There is a nursery of foreign plants and the aviary and bees.' A fountain would 'refresh and cleanse the soul'.

An 'Erasmian' style emerged in the Netherlands, with galleries, statues, a cruciform shape or square, *trompe l'œil* backdrops and parterres filled with prized flowers.

Hans Vredeman de Vries

Hans (or Jan) Vredeman de Vries (1527–*c*.1607) was another influence on Dutch garden design. De Vries was born and raised in Friesland. He trained in the Netherlands and later worked in Antwerp, Frankfurt, Danzig, Prague and Amsterdam. Having made a particular study of Vitruvius and Serlio, he carried the logic further to extend the single-point perspective to the multi-point perspective. In *Perspective* (1605), dedicated to Prince Maurits and subtitled 'The most famous art of eyesight', he establishes the basic principle of vanishing points, from which he diverges and elaborates. All parallel lines converge on a horizon line. However, the 'eye point' might not be on the centre. His beautifully executed engravings include exciting views down vaults and up into domes, where different rules may apply. Though his theories were not entirely original – nor entirely correct – he took a leap forward, and his book was the bible of his architect contemporaries. Even the great painter Johannes Vermeer had a copy in his library.

De Vries was an architect, a fortifications engineer and a painter. He was untiringly prolific, producing pattern books of designs, sometimes

A multi-perspective by Hans Vredeman de Vries. From *Perspective*, 1605.

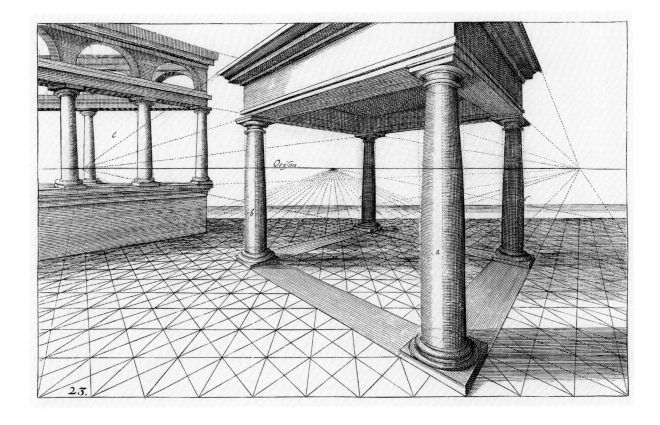

every few months – some five hundred images over his lifetime. They were of dreamt-up palaces, architectural details, decorative effects and much else – not least garden plans, designed for his students and everyman.

The *Hortorum viridariorumque elegantes et multiplicis formae ad architectonicae artis normam affabre delineatae* of 1583 was devoted to model, rather than actual, garden plans and mazes. The book cast a contemporary interpretation on the classical masters and was a source of stylistic ideas for many garden details, including fountains, cartouches, grotesques, railings, garden buildings, mazes and walks. Among the parterre patterns it included the *parterre de pièces coupées*, a novel idea then but ideal for the Dutch garden designers with their penchant for exhibiting rare and exotic plants to best effect.

De Vries often used designs inspired by 'strapwork', which has the appearance of flattened strips of leather or parchment interwoven to make geometric patterns. Very popular in northern Europe, it was a style much

A design inspired by strapwork, shown in an engraving by Hans Vredeman de Vries, *c.*1555–60.

used in architectural designs, stucco, furniture, stained glass, ceramics, embroidery, tombstone decoration, frescoes, book bindings – and parterres.

He divided the gardens into the classical orders, perhaps somewhat fancifully. The square geometric patterns were captioned 'Doric', the spiralling and circular ones were captioned 'Ionic' and the labyrinthine patterns were 'Corinthian'.

Though only one of his garden plans is known to have been put into practice,[1] details from his pattern books with their Flemish Mannerist intricacy were much adopted by garden practitioners and designers. Notable among those he influenced were his student Hans Puechfeldner, who worked for the Holy Roman Emperor Rudolf II (and produced fifty-six pen and ink drawings of designs), and Jan van der Groen, head gardener to the House of Orange.

Palace Garden with Poor Lazarus in the Foreground. This painting by Hans Vredeman de Vries shows a Dutch palace garden in the typical Dutch sixteenth-century style, with neatly fenced topiary parterres, a central fountain, a domed garden building and green tunnel walks.

[1] The garden of Duke Julius at Wolfenbüttel for whom Hans Puechfeldner served as architect and engineer in 1589.

Jan van der Groen

Jan van der Groen (1626–1671) produced *Der Nederlandtsen Hovenier* (The Dutch Gardener), a book that was so popular it was reprinted nine times, and translated into both German and French. It contains much practical advice on the running of an estate but also delves into the artistic design elements of the garden, throwing some light on seventeenth-century Dutch gardens.

'Nature', van der Groen writes, 'can be disobliging but be made pleasurable by art . . . In the same way that marble has to be worked to achieve shape and become a garden statue, so the making of a garden can only be achieved by subduing natural phenomena to the laws and rules of mathematics and art.'

Van der Groen was especially interested in parterres. The use of the orangerie and the gradual introduction of the hothouse in the late seventeenth century broadened the choice of plants available to decorate parterres. In 1638 the *Hortus Botanicus* of Amsterdam was founded. This brought in a fresh raft of introductions from afar and whipped up even more enthusiasm for newly introduced plants.

For containers on the parterre, van der Groen recommended tender plants including the climbing 'flame lily' (*Gloriosa superba*) from Ceylon, the 'lady-of-the-night' orchid (*Brassavola nodosa*) from the West Indies, the 'blood flower' (*Haemanthus coccineus*) from Africa, the belladonna lily (*Amaryllis bella-donna*) from the West Cape and the balsam apple (*Momordica balsamina*) from tropical Africa, along with peppers, tomatoes and the Asian tea plant, *Camellia sinensis*.

Agaves, *Aloe vera* and *Yucca gloriosa* were recommended for structure. For height, van der Groen suggested training morning glory up poles. A cypress tree was often used to mark the central point of the parterre. Clipped orange, lemon and lime trees, as well as myrtle, bay and jasmine, were standard for the *parterre de l'orangerie*. They were usually grown in barrels or tubs for ease of moving them under cover in winter. The *plates-bandes* of parterres would be filled with coloured earth, stone chippings or grass, and the tubs placed on top. An exedra, a semicircular shape like the stage of a theatre, was a popular design for the display.

Van der Groen further commended fig, prickly pear, pomegranate, olive, oleander, myrtle, laurel and strawberry, carob and Judas trees. For edging the parterres, various primulas, lavender, autumn crocus and thymes are considered suitable, and tall black and white mulleins (*Legusia speculum veneris*) and toadflax are among the many plants suggested

OPPOSITE
Den Nederlandtsen Hovenier (The Dutch Gardener) by Jan van der Groen.
ABOVE LEFT The cover of the book, showing the gardener inviting you in to see the garden and to read the book.
ABOVE RIGHT The Orangerie.
BELOW LEFT Design for a garden.
BELOW RIGHT Knot pattern.

TOPIARY, KNOTS AND PARTERRES

The Orange Grove, an engraving by
S. Kleiner, 1724, showing orange
trees in pots being put out for the
summer months.

for the corners. Along the walks and paths, chamomile may be grown
for its scent.

He noted that the gardens of Holland were 'filled with all kinds of
delights'. They were, he said, like small personal museums displaying
collections of *objets d'art* and natural curiosities brought in from foreign
shores – unusual shells, coral, insects, birds and other exotica.

Another particularity of the Netherlands was the stork's nest on a
pole high above the ground (it was considered to be an unlucky omen if
the nest remained unoccupied). In a watery country, ponds on different
levels, with dams, waterwheels and sluices, were frequently seen. The
Netherlands were also noted for their avenues of fine trees, often bordering
canals. In the 1640s, John Evelyn remarked that the Dutch towns were
'frequently planted and shaded with beautiful lime trees, which are set in
rows before every man's house'.

Maurits

The garden of Buitenhof in The Hague, designed for William the Silent's
second son, Maurits (1567–1625, Prince of Orange from 1618), is
considered to be the first example of a classic Dutch garden. Appropriately

for the soldier Stadtholder, the garden was made on the strictly symmetrical and mathematical lines characteristic of military architecture.

A canal running down one side of the garden was to become a classic feature in a country overflowing with water. The castellated walled garden was divided into two identical squares containing identical circular arbours and with pavilions placed in each corner. These would be another common feature of the Dutch garden, bringing a rare element of height in a flat country.

Within twin circular tunnel walks was a concession to the French style – the *parterres de broderie,* on this occasion arranged around the letter 'M' for Maurits. A fountain marked the centre of each circle and was in turn encircled by bronze containers for flowering plants. According to Constantijn Huygens, Secretary to the House of Orange, the two circles represented Alexander the Great's regret that there was only one world to conquer. A more unusual feature was that one side of the house, fronted by a gallery, formed part of the fourth wall of the enclosed garden and was constructed with the same brickwork.

The garden of Prince Maurits at Buitenhof, The Hague. Engraving by Hendrik Hondius, 1622.

Frederik Hendrik

The reign of William the Silent's third son, Frederik Hendrik, from 1625 to 1647, coincided with the height of the Dutch Golden Age. He is credited with introducing the glamour of Versailles into Dutch gardens. He invited André Mollet to design the parterres for his various gardens. These included the Hague summer palace of Huis ten Bosch, the classical French palace of Rijswijk in southern Holland and Honselaarsdijk, the Princess Dowager's house. For this last Mollet designed a *parterre à l'anglaise* to one side of a heraldic lion and a *parterre de broderie* on the other. Mollet had been rather taken with fine grass 'plats' favoured by the English and now combined the two.

Mollet's technique at this time was to use white stone or white marble chippings on near-black earth or slag to describe the twists and turns

of the finer lines of the flower and leaf designs. The low-clipped box was reserved for the bolder designs. Some of the *plates-bandes* would be planted with low-growing flowers including anemones, ranunculus and tulips, while others would be left as blanks, edged with box but filled with sand or, sometimes, with red earth.

The Dutch designers were aware of the concepts of the Italian Renaissance and also the doctrines of Versailles, which they adopted to a degree. While generally there is little trace of the Albertian concept of unity between house and garden, nor scope for the grand vistas, the Dutch took up the geometry, elegant ironwork, fountains, parterres and topiary, while retaining a certain Calvinistic restraint. In the gardens of wealthy burghers or the gentry, the visitor was more likely to be greeted by a statue of St Peter than by a Hercules or a Colossus.

Two views of the summer palace, Huis ten Bosch, and its gardens, designed for Frederik Hendrik and his wife, Amalia, in southern Holland. Paintings by Jan van der Heyden, 1665–75.

William and Mary

In 1672 William III (1650–1702) stopped the invading French army, achieving a first in defeating Louis XIV. Hailing him as 'Redeemer of the Fatherland', a grateful populace elected him as both Stadtholder and Captain-General of the Dutch Republic. He went on to marry his cousin Mary Stuart, the daughter of James II of England, in 1677. In the Glorious Revolution of 1688, he accepted an invitation from a group of high-powered Tories and Whigs to depose James, his unpopular Catholic father-in-law, and was crowned joint monarch with Mary.

William, who was to confess in a letter to a friend that his two passions in life were hunting and gardening,[2] inherited from his father the fine gardens made by his grandfather, Frederik Hendrik. He had made a start on garden design himself with his hunting lodges – Soestdijk (where he put in a game reserve, woodland and gardens) and Dieren (where his garden included a water labyrinth inspired by Versailles).

By 1684 he had felt in need of a larger hunting lodge and bought an old castle, Het Loo, in fine country near Apeldoorn, central Netherlands. Jacob Roman (1640–1716), sculptor turned architect, designed a new building in the Palladian style.

In the male-only Prince's Garden to one side of the castle, there was a *cabinet de verdure* with pleached *allées*, serpentine walks, a 'bolingrin' (a lawn which was kept immaculate by an English gardener called Ralf) surrounded by low box hedges, gilded lead fountains and box trees clipped into many shapes. In the Queen's Garden, on the other side, there were tunnel walks and the parterres were filled with flowers, along with Mary's treasured collection of exotics in pots or barrels.

The Lower Garden, which was a more public space, was viewed from a terrace with fan-shaped steps leading down to statues of the gods of the local rivers, the Rhine and the IJssel. Eight square *parterres de broderie* were filled with flowers and four simpler *parterres à l'anglaise* contained statues. Beyond was a handsome park with *bosquets*, ponds, aviaries and yet more statues. Fountains, cascades and rills were major features.

The second stage for the garden came when William, by now King of England, found that the newly built Het Loo needed to be bigger and grander still. In 1698 the caricaturist Romeyn de Hooghe noted that William now 'gave thought to change this princely model into a kingly garden of pleasure'. The building was transformed into a palace and a new raised Upper Garden was added to the Lower Garden with a 'green colonnade' of oaks running between the two.

[2] 'Chasse et . . .jardinages vous savez estre deus de mes passions'. Letter to Hans Willem Bentinck.
[3] Journal of Edward Southwell (1696).

A central feature of the gardens was a statue of Hercules strangling a pair of writhing serpents with his bare hands (presumably there was a message there to any intending invaders). The focal point was an obelisk, in front of which was a octagonal water basin and the King's Fountain which shot water up forty-six feet – higher than anywhere else in Europe at the time. A visitor noted that 'one of the greatest beauties of the garden' was a reservoir 'planted with limes . . . [and] Ewe trees in pyramids'.[3] It was fed by natural springs day and night. Another water parterre spelt out the monogram of William and Mary.

Though there were no 'perspectives', as in Nôtrian gardens, at Het Loo, there was a strong single central axis and French influence in the parterres.

The gentlemen's domain of the 'boulegrin' with a parterre behind, in the Prince's Garden at Het Loo. Engraving by Romeyn de Hooghe, *c.*1700.

ABOVE The fountain with the water parterre framing the monogram of William and Mary at Het Loo. An etching made by P. Schenk, in the seventeenth century.

OPPOSITE Daniel Marot designs taken from *Das Ornamentwerk des Daniel Marot*, Berlin, 1892. The vibrant patterns and motifs were used in furniture, decor, fabrics, tapestries and other artefacts – and also for parterres.

[4] After the 1685 revocation of the Edict of Nantes, which had extended some tolerance to the Huguenots.

William's closest friend, Hans Willem Bentinck, a keen gardener who took charge of the garden while William was away, had caught enthusiasm for the *jardin à la française* while posted as ambassador in Paris.

To design the gardens for William III at Het Loo, Bentinck recommended Claude Desgotz (*c.*1655–1752), Le Nôtre's nephew, and Daniel Marot (1661–1752), a highly talented Huguenot refugee fleeing persecution in France.[4] Marot was only twenty-four when he was first engaged by William to design at Het Loo, and later he followed William to Hampton Court. He had a prodigious gift for designing any and every form of architectural ornament for both interiors and exteriors. For the gardens, he would turn his hand to railings, statues, cascades, fountains, and – not least – the *parterres de broderie*.

Unlike André Mollet, who preferred low plants in single colours in the *jardin de plaisir*, Marot splashed out in flamboyant baroque style, combining plants of different colours, shapes and heights, with climbers wound round sticks planted between clipped topiary balls and cones.

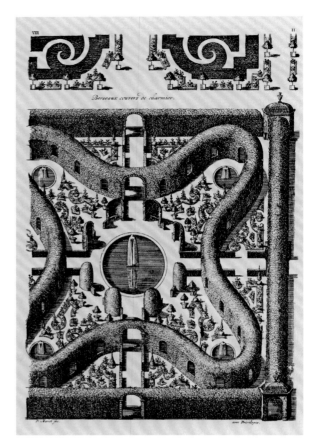

Taken from a book of
garden designs for Het
Loo and Hampton Court,
Gartenwerk: *The New Book
of Parterres with Twenty-
four Different Engravings
by D. Marot, Architect to
William III,* 1892.
ABOVE LEFT A fashionable
design for an orangerie
with an exedra at the top.
ABOVE RIGHT A *berceau* or
covered walkway, possibly
of yew, with windows
clipped out to view the
garden from every side.
RIGHT An 'Arc de
Triomphe'.

In the spirit of Sebastiano Serlio, who designed the same patterns for both ceilings and parterres, Marot brought motifs from within the house out into the garden and used them in simplified form.

Drawing inspiration from antiquity and the great designers of Louis XIV's court, he played with patterns such as 'C' scrolls (often back to back with a short bar joining them), acanthus scrolls and volutes (the spiral shapes on the capital of the Ionic column) and the cartouche (an oval-topped shape with a flat base, a design often seen in windows). He would incorporate these patterns into the parterres and echo them in the benches, the hedge designs, the *bosquets* and *berceaux*. Added to this mix was the 'grotesque' – a word coined from 'grotto', implying the dark shades of the gargoyle, the licentious, the comic and the absurd. The 'arabesques' were mostly the flowing lines of intertwined plants and foliage.

Hampton Court

William was asthmatic and did not enjoy the polluted air of London any more than he did the frivolities or the intrigues of court life. Rather than settling in the Palace of Westminster like his predecessors, he decided instead to enlarge and embellish Hampton Court. Daniel Defoe, in his *Tour through the Whole Island of Great Britain,* noted that 'King William fix'd upon *Hampton-Court*; and it was in his reign that Hampton-Court put on new cloathes and being dress'd gay and glorious, made the Figure we now see it in.'

Hans Willem Bentinck, now Lord Portland and Superintendent of Royal Gardens, was in charge of the gardens at Hampton Court. In addition to bringing over a large Dutch team, Bentinck hired the Englishman George London as his deputy. Christopher Wren, the Surveyor of Works, and his assistant, William Talman, drew up plans for a new east front of Hampton Court. The Great Parterre (later known as the Fountain Garden, as it contained so many) was designed within a semicircle of limes with wide lime walks radiating off it. Marot designed the *parterres de broderie*, which were punctuated with some three hundred yews clipped into obelisks and silver holly globes in 1689. The Privy Garden was also remodelled. England's earliest surviving hedge maze, planted in hornbeam in Tudor times, was replanted in the 'Wilderness' between 1690 and 1695 by George London.

William and Mary bought Kensington Palace (then Nottingham House) in 1689 as their London base. With only 30 acres to play with, they took great pleasure in making around the house a very Dutch garden, divided into small rooms, with flower and cut-work parterres, dwarf trees, a canal and fountain and two labyrinths.

OVERLEAF Leonard Knyff, *View of Hampton Court*, *c.*1703 (detail). The Fountain Garden at Hampton Court with the *broderie* parterre and the *patte d'oie*.

The plants were supplied by the nearby Brompton Park Nursery, and George London drew up the plans for the 12-acre southern garden.

After Mary died of smallpox, aged only thirty-two, in 1694, William lost interest in his gardens. A contemporary wrote that 'Upon the death of that illustrious Princess, gardening and all other pleasures were under an eclipse with that Prince; and the beloved Hampton Court lay for some time unregarded.'

The great Dutch gardens that they had developed were characterized by their mathematical neatness and regularity, clever hydraulics, canals and waterworks, ornamental pavilions, orangeries, rare exotics displayed in pots, small garden rooms, ornamental grilles, garden theatres, lead statues and vases, immaculate hedging and topiary.

Daniel Defoe in *A Tour through the Whole Island of Great Britain* observed in *From Richmond to London* that William had revived a love of gardening in England:

> His Majesty was particularly delighted with the decoration of the ever-greens, as the greatest addition to the beauty of a garden preserving the figure in the place even in the roughest part of an inclement and tempestuous weather. With the particular judgment of the king, all the gentlemen of England began to fall in; and in a few years, fine gardens, and fine houses began to grow up in every corner; the king began with the gardens of Hampton Court and Kensington, and the gentlemen followed everywhere, with such a gust that the alteration is indeed wonderful throughout the kingdom.

The Nôtrian garden abroad

So desirable was the Nôtrian style among Europe's rulers that a certain competitiveness had grown among them. Charles II, having spent years in exile in France absorbing the culture, wrote to Louis XIV in 1662 asking him to release Le Nôtre to help with the gardens at Greenwich and Hampton Court. The French king's reply was gracious. It was that, although he needed Le Nôtre 'continually' and the gardener was very 'occupied at Fontainebleau', Louis would consent as Charles 'so desires'.

A Dutch garden of the seventeenth century, possibly in Noordholland, north of Amsterdam. The elegant *broderie* parterre is kept simple, filled with plain earth and embedded in gravel. Immaculate high hedges lead the eye to farmland on the one hand and a seascape on the other. Painting by Johannes Janson, 1766.

There is no record of Le Nôtre travelling to England, but it would seem that he did send a plan. Charles wrote to his sister Minette (Liselotte's predecessor as duchesse d'Orléans), at Saint-Cloud, saying, 'Pray let Le Nostre go on with the modell, and only tell him this addition, that I can bring water up to the top of the hill, so he may add much to the beauty of the descent by a cascade of water.'

Peterhof

Peter the Great, who ruled from 1682 to 1725, missed Le Nôtre but persuaded Jean-Baptiste Alexandre Le Blond, Louis XIV's chief architect at Versailles, to come to St Petersburg as 'architect general' with an offer of five thousand roubles (great wealth) and a private mansion. Le Blond drew up a plan for the city and designed Peterhof Palace and the garden.

Peterhof, from *A Panorama of St Petersburg*, an engraving by Alexei Ivanovich Rostovtsev, 1717.

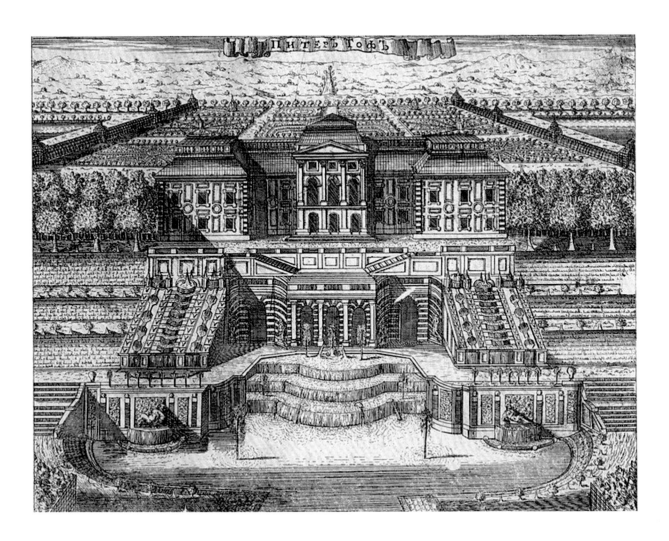

An immense and luxuriant royal palace, it was the tsar's playground on the Baltic Sea, known as the 'Russian Versailles'.

La Granja

Felipe V (r.1700–1746), the first of the Bourbon kings of Spain, grandson of Louis XIV and brought up at Versailles, converted the monastery grounds of La Granja into a royal palace with palatial gardens.

It took gunpowder, pickaxes and the toil of five thousand men to make a magnificent garden out of solid rock. All the soil had to be imported, but the rock paid off when it came to the fountain. La Granja's water jet (entirely powered by gravity) was the highest of any royal palace in the 1720s. Water shot up to a staggering 160 feet, far outdoing its closest rival at the palace of Nymphenburg (designed by another pupil of Le Nôtre, Dominique Girard), which reached a (still remarkable) 85 feet.

It must have provided much satisfaction to La Granja's French hydraulic engineer after the legendary frustrations at Versailles, where – if the waters were to be kept playing at all – a gardener had to hare from fountain to fountain turning water on as the king approached, and then off again.

Nymphenburg Palace

The Italianate garden of Nymphenburg Palace, summer residence of the Elector of Bavaria, Max Emanuel (r.1679–1726), was enlarged in the French style. Like Charles II, Max Emmanuel had acquired a taste for French gardens, having spent some years exiled in Paris after the Austrian occupation of Bavaria in 1704.

Around a central *bassin* with gilded statues were four *broderie* parterres. A certain Herr Gottfried Edler von Rothenstein, visiting in 1781, noted that there were 'vases and many beds between with many flowers, which each month present a different picture . . . Right in the front stand six gilt urns . . . next there are dragon fountains . . . In the parterre there stand twenty-eight gilt statues, groups, vases and urns, and near the espaliers seventeen statues made of white marble.'

A Dutch influence could be seen with the canals that surrounded the *schloss* so that it appears to be situated on an island within the park. The central canal ended in a great Italianate cascade. From a *patte d'oie* three vistas pointed towards three separate church spires.

OVERLEAF Joseph Stephan, *Nymphenberg Castle with its Fountains and Water Games*, 1761.

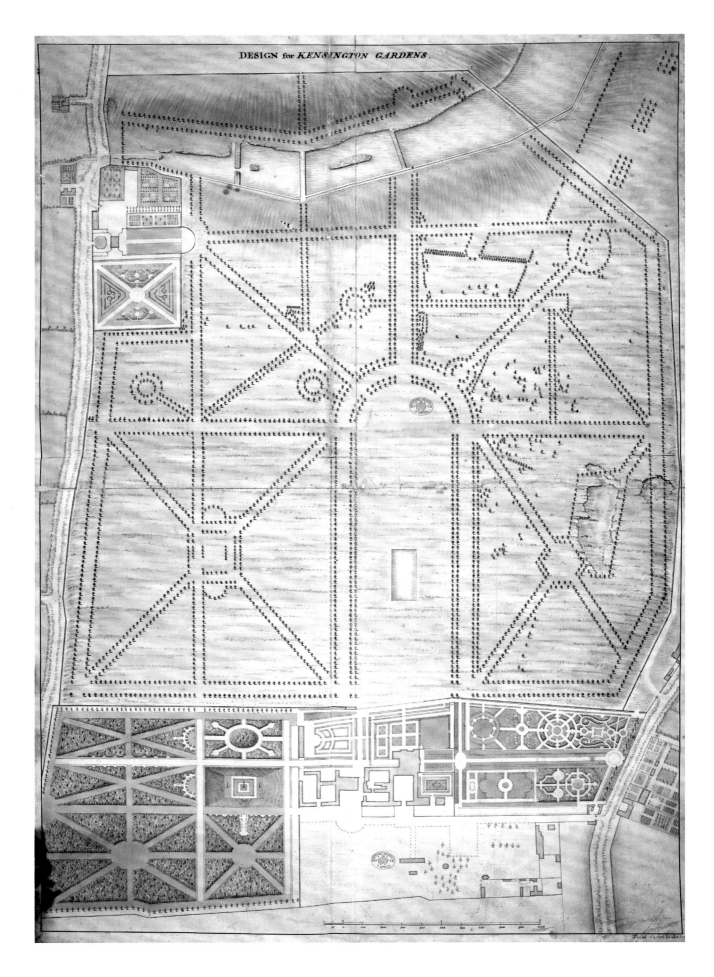

DESIGN for KENSINGTON GARDENS.

The Swan Song
of the Formal Garden

England at the turn of the 18th century

T HE LAST GRAND FLING of the formal garden in England came about largely thanks to two clever and hardworking entrepreneurs, George London and Henry Wise. As partners in the Brompton Park Nursery, in Kensington, they held a near monopoly in garden design for the great estates.

Their clients included the aristocratic owners of Blenheim Palace, Castle Howard, Longleat, Stowe and Chatsworth. They worked alongside the most eminent architects of the day, Christopher Wren (Surveyor of the King's Works), William Talman, Nicholas Hawksmoor and John Vanbrugh. And their booming nursery business was even more profitable than the design side. From Brompton Park, they provided enough trees and shrubs for the woodlands, forests and miles of sweeping lime and horse chestnut avenues required by large estates the length and breadth of the country.

Brompton Park Nursery

Undoubtedly their connections in high society were key to their singular success. George London (c.1640–1714) was royal gardener under Bentinck for William and Mary, and Henry Wise (c.1653–1738) would be royal gardener for both Queen Anne and George I. Stephen Switzer, one-time foreman to the nursery, remarked that 'Mr. London and Mr. Wise being join'd partners, and thus, as it were, both possest of the Royal Favour, and the Purses of the King, Queen, and Nobility, left no Stone unturn'd to carry on their Designs.'

The Brompton Park Nursery was founded by London and three others in 1681. Henry Wise came into the firm as an apprentice and by 1689 he and London were sole partners. It was a substantial enterprise, standing on a 100-acre site in Kensington that is today partly occupied by the Albert Hall and the Victoria and Albert, Science and Natural History museums. A contemporary hazarded a guess that that if each of the plants

Paul Sandby (1731–1809), lithograph showing *Design for Kensington Gardens as laid out by Henry Wise.*

in their stock were priced at a penny the total value would be around £40,000. The nursery was also a horticultural showcase, specializing in rare specimens from America.

John Evelyn, now Secretary to the Royal Society, deployed his considerable influence in their support. In an enthusiastic foreword to *The Compleat Gard'ner* (his translation of Jean-Baptiste de La Quintinie's book about the potager at Versailles) he praised their knowledge of soils, aspects, situations and of every type of plant, their expertise in 'Lines and Figures' and levelling of ground, and their judgment regarding the 'Proportions of Walks and Avenues, Starrs, Centers etc. suitable to the Lengths, etc.' He went on to applaud their 'numerous Collection of the best Designs, and I perceive are able themselves to Draw, and contrive other . . . Works and Parterrs of Imbroidery . . . and Flower Gardens . . . And where Fountains, Statues, Vases, Dials and other decorations of Magnificence are to be plac'd with most advantage.'[1]

Little is known of George London's background, but it is assumed that he was of humble origin. He is first recorded as apprenticed to John Rose, André Mollet's successor as head gardener to Charles II, who was a specialist in exotics. London relates in a letter of 1710 an extraordinary tale of how a 'duble-flor'd Indian Almond' was taken with other botanical specimens from a 'Dutch East Indie-Man' by an English plant enthusiast aboard a man-of-war during the Third Anglo-Dutch War. The plant was sent to the royal gardens where London 'wase then Apprentice' and where he had the good fortune to restore it to full health.

It is known that Rose sent him to France to learn about the French style; he may possibly have worked in Le Nôtre's team of over three hundred gardeners.

By 1675 he was working for Henry Compton, the Bishop of London, an avid plant collector who was said to have had over one thousand rare exotics in his 'stoves' and greenhouses at Fulham Palace. (Switzer described Compton as a 'Father of the Church but also of Gardening' and 'a great encourager of Mr. London, and probably very much assisted him in his designs'.) After William and Mary's arrival, he was appointed as deputy superintendent of the royal gardens, under Bentinck. He made a further trip to see French gardens – including Marly – with Bentinck in about 1700.

Even less is known of the early days of London's partner, Henry Wise. However, as his career progressed he had much to do with the creation of the garden at Blenheim and supervised the works at Longleat and Chatsworth. Later he concentrated on dealing with the business side of the nursery and being on call for his duties to the Crown.

George London, meanwhile, travelled tirelessly cross-country, riding 'fifty or sixty miles a day' on horseback. Switzer was to write: 'It will hardly be believed, in Time to come, that this one Person actually saw and gave Directions, once or twice a Year, in most of the Gentlemens and Noblemens Gardens in England . . . visiting all the Country-Seats, conversing with Gentlemen, and forwarding the Business of Gard'ning in such a degree as is almost impossible to describe.'[2]

John Wootton, *Bowater Vernon with Hanbury Hall and its Formal Garden designed by George London*, 1701. One of the many aristocratic gardens designed by the George London. Pictured here is Bowater Vernon, the dissipated legatee of Hanbury Hall, Worcestershire. The garden (now restored by the National Trust) had a viewing platform over a sunken formal parterre and fruit garden, with rides radiating through the park.

[1] Jean-Baptiste de La Quintinie, *Instruction pour les jardins fruitiers et potagers*, published posthumously in 1690. Translated as *The Compleat Gard'ner: or, Directions for cultivating and right ordering of fruit-gardens, and kitchen-gardens; By Mounsieur De La Quintinye. Now compendiously abridg'd* (1699).
[2] Stephen Switzer, *The Nobleman, Gentleman and Gard'ner's Recreation* (1715)

The Retir'd Gard'ner

In 1706 – a few years ahead of John James's 1712 English translation of the *La Théorie et la pratique du jardinage* (*The Theory and Practice of Gardening*), which was believed to contain the thoughts and ideas of Le Nôtre – London and Wise published *The Retir'd Gard'ner, in Two Volumes: the Whole Revis'd, with Several Alterations and Additions, Which Render It Proper for Our English Culture*. It was a translation (with some additions of their own) of a popular gardener's guide, *Le Jardinier Solitaire* by the French agronomist Louis Liger.[3] It was encyclopaedic in scope but was very clear on their specialism – the English interpretation of the baroque – not least with their definitions of the different types of parterre.

The book takes the form of a dialogue between a gentleman who is intending to repair to his seat in the country and a retired gardener who offers guidance on the cultivation and propagation of every type of plant. The chapter devoted to the parterre offers an insight into the many subtle complexities, the pros and cons of the different types of parterres for varying situations, the possible combinations of styles and a multitude of other considerations – both practical and aesthetic – that the skilled parterre planner must weigh up before proceeding.

In the opinion of the gardener,

> . . . there is nothing more ingenious belonging to a garden, than the different Ways of marking out different figures in a Parterre, especially where the Design happens to be well contriv'd, and the Execution of it perform'd by a skillful Hand . . . In former Times the Use of Box was not known; but now it is more used, and found much better and more delightful than any other Plant, for Edging of Borders and all sorts of Imbroidery.
>
> . . . some Parterres are said to be imbroider'd; others partly imbroider'd, and partly Cut-work with Borders; a third sort compos'd of Grass-work only; a fourth made up of Imbroidery and Grass-work; a fifth only Cut-work; a sixth nothing but Cut-work and Turfs of Grass; a seventh of Cutwork of Grass and Imbroidery; an eighth whose middle is all Cut-work, and the Borders Imbroidery; a ninth on the contrary, whose borders are all Cutwork; and the Middle Imbroidery and lastly, another sort, whole middle is partly Imbroidery, partly Cut-work and green Turf, with Borders of Turf and Cut-work.

On practical matters, the retired gardener advises that box parterres should be planted out not with rooted cuttings but with unrooted slips.

[3] *Le Jardinier Solitaire: The Solitary or Carthusian Gardener, being dialogues between a gentleman and a gard'ner containing the method to make and cultivate all sorts of gardens . . . Also the compleat Florist . . . by the Sieur Louis Liger d'Auxerre . . . newly done into English.*

THE
RETIR'D GARD'NER.

The SECOND VOLUME.

Containing the Manner of
Planting and Cultivating
All Sorts of
Flowers, Plants, Shrubs, and
Under-Shrubs,
Neceſſary for the
Adorning of GARDENS:

In which is Explain'd,
The Art of Making and Diſpoſing of Parterres,
Arbours of Greens, Wood-Works, Arches, Columns, and other Pieces and Compartments uſually
found in the moſt Beautiful GARDENS of Country-Seats. The whole enrich'd with Variety of Figures, being a Tranſlation from the Sieur *Louis Liger*.
To this Volume is added, A Deſcription and Plan of
Count TALLARD's Garden at *Nottingham*.

The whole Revis'd, with ſeveral Alterations and Additions,
Which render it proper for our *Engliſh* Culture.

By *George London*, and *Henry Wiſe*.

LONDON: Printed for *Jacob Tonſon*, within
Grays-Inn Gate next *Grays-Inn* Lane. 1706.

Regum æquabat opes animis:———.
Vir: Geor: Lib. 4: ver: 132.

These should be taken from a healthy specimen plant that you judge best for your planting; and, having several of them in your Hand, and holding them as even as possible, cut their tops off horizontally, then taking a Dibble made for the purpose, you make Holes with it, and put them in the Ground, always observing to plant them in a straight Line, and upon the Level, as well in respect to the Surface of the Earth as the two sides of the Border, and lastly, that the Box may grow in the same manner you would have it, when you put it into the Ground, you always take care to press down the Earth of the Hole, holding your Hands side-ways against the Sides of the Plant.

Frontispiece of *The Retir'd Gard'ner*, the London and Wise bestseller, first published in 1706.

I
The Form of a Parterre only Imbroider'd

In this sort of Parterre there is commonly nothing planted; the Flourishes and the Branch-work which compose it being fill'd with greater Neatness with Earth, different from that of the Paths, which are always gravell'd. This sort of compartment is oftener made in small Gardens than in great.

Imbroidery is those Draughts which represent in Effect those we have on our Cloaths, and that look like Foliage, and these Sorts of Figures in Gard'ners language are call'd *Branch-work*. Below this foliage certain flowers seem to be drawn which is part of that of Imbroidery, which we call *Flourishings*.

II
The Form of a Parterre Imbroider'd, and whose Borders are Cut-work

The Imbrodiery of this Parterre may be fill'd with what Earth we please, provided it be distinguish'd from that of the Cut-work which gives these sorts of Compartment the finest *Relieve* that can be. The Paths of this Parterre must likewise be set off with yellow or white Gravel, and the Borders with Earth like that of the Cut-work.

III
The Form of a Parterre only of Green Turf

These Parterres look well in spacious Gardens, where there is something else to please the Eye, and are placed there only to create different Objects: For whoever in a small Garden should see nothing but a Grass-Plot without any other Ornament, his eyes would receive but little Pleasure; for which Reason this Way is very little practis'd unless of Men of undiscerning Judgment at Palates. A Grass-Plot looks also well in a small Court before a House, or upon a Terrass made on purpose to render the House more agreeable.

IV
The Form of a Parterre, compos'd of Imbroidery and Grass-Plots, with Borders of Cut-work

A Parterre compos'd of Imbroidery and Grass-Plots looks very well in little Gardens as well as in great, and since in these sorts of Works nothing pleases more than Variety, we take care in tracing out these Parterres to leave regular Spaces at equal Distances for the *Dutch* jars, in which we plant some Flowers or Shrubs; these Plots by a Surplusage of Ornament producing a wonderful Effect.

V
The Form of a Parterre all Cut-work, with Borders

This kind of Parterre will only look well in Gardens of a middling Size, and to say Truth is the most plain, and consequently the least agreeable of all; especially where the Compartments happen not to be artfully dispos'd, for then such Garden Plots will rather offend than please the Eye.

VI
The Form of a Parterre partly Cut-work and partly Green Turf, with Borders

These Parterres are esteem'd according to their Design, and their Symmetry. They look very well in great Gardens as well as in small, the Verdure of the Grass, and the Enamel of the Flowers with which the Compartments ought to be fill'd according to the different Seasons of the Year, present a charming Object to the Sight. These parterres may likewise be set off with such Pots as I mentioned before or surrounded with Boxes fill'd with Orange Trees, or with other Shrubs of like Nature.

A sample of the myriad parterre designs described in *The Retir'd Gard'ner* by London and Wise, 1706.

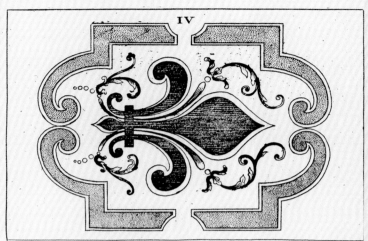

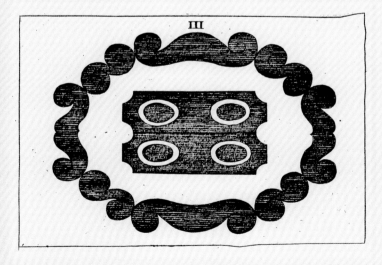

When it comes to planting out the flowers, it is recommended to make a hump 'so that it may lie in the Shape of a Carp's Back . . . so it will set off the Plants it contains, and make the Flowers appear much better than if they were flat.' The soil for the flowers should be refreshed every three years by taking away 'half a Foot' and replacing it with fresh soil.

In conclusion, the gardener points out that 'Altho' I have given the Designs of some Parterres, that does not hinder but everyone may use those he thinks fit; my intention being only to show what a Parterre was, and how many sorts of them are commonly used.'

The advice on the planting of parterres reflects the London and Wise style of a profusion of flowers, or, in the gardener's words, 'a cloth of Tissue of divers Colours, wherein, the chief Beauty of a Garden consists'. This was entirely different from the Dutch way, where each plant was kept separate.

However, the planting is not to be done haphazardly but in a methodical grid system, with the tallest plants in the back and repeated patterns of 'such plants that are of a middle Stature, as Snapdragons, Chrysanthemum, Indian Rose, Poets Pink, Amaranthus &c.'. Cautionary advice is that 'In planting Flowers you are, above all Things, to avoid Confusion, and by no mean to set one Sort where another ought to be.' The gardener adds that 'The great vacancy in the middle of the Borders are to be fill'd with clipt Yews and Flowering shrubs cut into Balls.'

The team at Brompton Park

Not surprisingly, London and Wise attracted an impressive team. Leonard Meager (c.1624–1704), their first foreman, was the author of several books, including a guide to growing fruit and flowers, *The New Art of Gardening; With the Gardner's Almanack* (1697). Stephen Switzer (c.1682–1745), Meager's successor as foreman, worked with Vanburgh and London on Castle Howard and Blenheim and designed the garden at Grimsthorpe Castle in Lincolnshire. He edited a magazine, *The Practical Husbandman and Planter*. In 1715 he published *The Nobleman, Gentleman, and Gardener's Recreation*, based on the work and ethics of London and Wise. In 1718 an expanded version was published as *Ichnographia*. He would become a nurseryman in his own right, an influential garden designer and a persuasive voice in favour of the 'natural' garden.

Charles Bridgeman (1690–1738), a gardener's son, was a skilled draftsman. It seems likely that London and Wise first employed him in that capacity and as a surveyor. After London died in 1714 Bridgeman worked in partnership with Wise and when Wise retired, ten years later, Bridgeman

took over his post as royal gardener. He designed many great gardens with professionalism and skill, spanning the gap between the formality of London and Wise and the inception of the more naturalistic school.

Knyff and Kip

Practically all the London and Wise gardens were later landscaped over. However, fortunately for posterity, many of their gardens are recorded in the topographical bird's-eye records of large estates made by the Dutch partners Leonard Knyff (1650–1722), surveyor and draughtsman, and Johannes Kip (c.1652–1722), engraver. Their engravings were published in 1707 as *Britannia Illustrata* and in 1724 as *Nouveau Théâtre de la Grande Bretagne*.

Longleat House

Longleat House in Wiltshire, the Elizabethan family estate inherited in 1682 by Sir Thomas Thynne, 1st Viscount Weymouth (1640–1714), had an impressive London and Wise garden.

Leonard Knyff, *A View of Wilton House*, c.1700. A fine example of Knyff's topographical work showing (top) Wilton House in its landscape, (bottom left and centre) Salomon de Caus's formal gardens, and (bottom right) the stables designed by Inigo Jones.

Two views of Longleat from
*Britannia Illustrata, or Views of
the Queens Palaces and also of the
Principal Seats of the Nobility and
Gentry of Great Britain* by Knyff and
Kip, 1707.

In characteristic London and Wise style, it was a beguiling fusion of the Dutch, the Italian and the French. The Dutch influence was manifested in immaculate canals, a bowling green, a labyrinth, an orangery and knot gardens filled with flowers or statues. The kitchen gardens were very Dutch indeed, being just as tidy as the formal ones, causing Canon Jackson, George London's former employer, to remark that 'the very gooseberry and currant bushes are drilled to grow in square and parallelogram, trimmed up as still and stately as the lords and ladies at the Court of Hague.'

Spectacular fountains and cascades bore the mark of the Italian school, while the long and elegant parterres, designed by Henry Wise, were entirely French. The garden was mapped out so that each enclosure led to the next – another surprise, another delight in store. In this era variety was key. There were orchards, a fir plantation, a hazel copse, woodland of beech and chestnut with formal rides cutting through from a *patte d'oie* and a designed 'wilderness'.

The mount, crowned with an arbour, and the plentiful topiary in the form of box or yew hedges clipped into dragons, unicorns and other mythical creatures might in England have appeared to be throwbacks to the Tudors, but they were still highly fashionable in the Netherlands. Pride in the English specialities, a luxuriant and perfectly tended green lawn and raked gravel paths, was expressed by an unknown poet.

> Versailles of statues, and Jet Eau's may boast.
> Where wealthy monarchs never spare the cost;
> But we all other Countries far surpass,
> In shining Gravel and the Carpet Grass.[4]

Chatsworth House

In the closing years of the seventeenth century London and Wise were called in by William Cavendish, 1st Duke of Devonshire (1640–1707), to create the massive parterres at Chatsworth in Derbyshire, where William Talman (*c*.1640–1714), who also worked with Christopher Wren at Hampton Court, was laying a new house over the old Tudor bones.

Daniel Defoe recorded that there were:

> greenhouses, summerhouse, walks, wildernesses, orangeries, and all the proper Furniture of Statues, Urns, Greens, etc. with Canals, Basons, and Water-works of various Forms and Contrivance; as Sea-horses, Drakes, Dolphins, and other Fountains that throw up the Water. An artificial Willow-tree of Copper spouts dropping

[4] *Paradise Regain'd or the Art of Gardening* (1728)

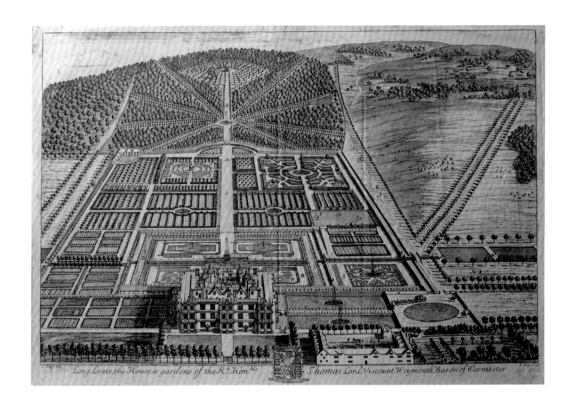

Long Leate, the House & gardens of the R^t Honble Thomas Lord Viscount Weymouth, Baron of Warminster

Long Leate, the Seate of the R^t Honble Thomas Lord Weymouth Baron of Warminster.

Long Leate, Maison du Seig^r Thomas Viscomte de Weymouth Baron de Warminster.

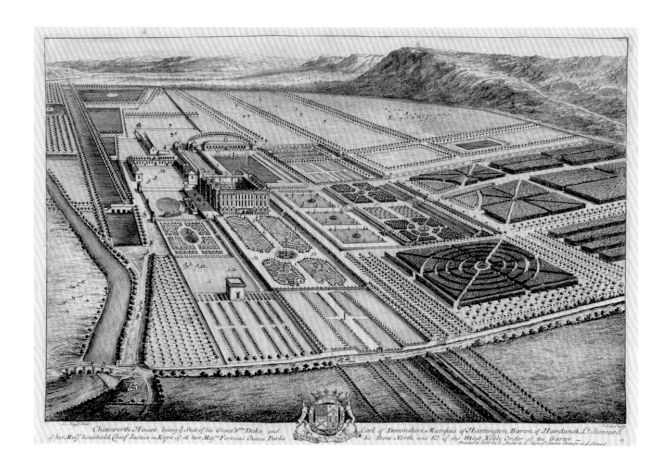

Chatsworth House from Knyff and Kip's *Britannia Illustrata*, 1707.

water from every Leaf. A wonderful Cascade, where from a neat House of Stone, like a Temple, out of the mouths of Beasts, Pipes, Urns etc. a whole River descends the Slope of a Hill a Quarter of a Mile in Length, over Steps, with a terrible noise and broken Appearance.

Castle Howard

At Castle Howard, in Yorkshire, Charles Howard, 3rd Earl of Carlisle (1669–1738), in 1699 commissioned John Vanbrugh (1664–1726) to design his mansion. A former soldier and the author of two Restoration comedies, Vanbrugh was described by Joshua Reynolds as 'an architect who composed like a painter'.[5] He was renowned for his theatrical and flamboyant buildings and gardens and Castle Howard has often been described as the first baroque private house in Britain.

London and Wise's gardens at Castle Howard, though still formal, gave hints of the naturalism that was to come. The entrance was through

[5] It was also said of Vanbrugh (by the 2nd Earl of Chesterfield, a relative by marriage) that he 'united conversational pleasantry with perfect good humour.'

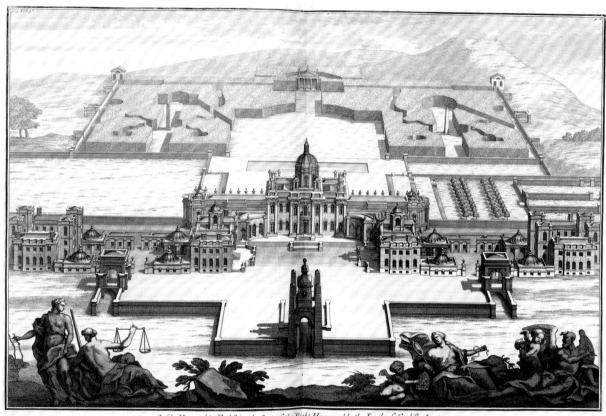

Castle Howard in Yorkshire the Seat of the Right Honourable the Earl of Carlisle &c :

a pyramid gate down a drive flanked by the 'Temple of Four Winds' and the 'Roman Bridge'. Variety was much in evidence. Horace Walpole remarked that nobody had told him that he should 'at one view see a palace, a town, a fortified city, temples on high places, woods worthy of being each a metropolis of the Druids, the noblest lawn on earth fenced by half the horizon and a mausoleum that would tempt one to be buried alive'.

Castle Howard, Yorkshire, from *Vitruvius Britannicus, or The British Architect, containing the Plans, Elevations, and Sections of the regular buildings both publick and private, in Great Britain* by Colen Campbell, 1715–25.

Blenheim Palace

When it came to Blenheim Palace in Oxfordshire, Vanbrugh sent off for a copy of Palladio. The palace was a gift from Queen Anne to the Duke of Marlborough in gratitude for his victory in the 1704 Battle of Blenheim. It was to be built in the grounds of Woodstock, the royal residence where, according to legend, Fair Rosamund – Henry II's mistress – had been locked within the labyrinth. Vanbrugh (who had served as a captain under Marlborough and spent time as a prisoner of the French) was chosen to

Detail of a plan for the gardens of Blenheim Palace, 1719. The scrollwork parterres south of the house lead to the formal woodland in the hexagon. To the east and west there are straight rides through the wilderness. On the west side, there is a *patte d'oie* designed by Henry Wise.

[6] From Addison's libretto for Thomas Clayton's opera *Rosamund.*

build the new palace and turn the 2,000 acres of rough parkland into a princely estate.

Ahead of his time, he wanted to keep the old Woodstock Palace as a romantic ruin and build Blenheim Palace on the far side of a chasm. The two would be linked by the 'Grand Bridge', once the sides of the valley had been hewn into shape by Wise.

The river Glyme, which meandered haphazardly through the landscape, was to be civilized into regular canals in the Dutch fashion. Perhaps Vanbrugh's bridge was a little too big in relation to them, as Alexander Pope was to remark that 'the minnows, as under this vast arch they pass, murmur, "how like whales we look, thanks to your Grace".'

A parterre the width of the south front, and half a mile long, stretched from the palace. An early ha-ha protected the parterre from rabbits and deer, an idea that would be much employed in future garden design to take down the barriers and open the garden to the countryside.

Immediately south of the house, the scrollwork parterres are flanked by compartments of pyramidal clipped yews and junipers planted in rows. The four divisions carry down through the 'Woodwork', a hexagonal area of formal wilderness which was planted by Switzer and stocked by the Brompton Nursery with '9,357 hedge yews of various heights', '5,900 hornbeam, privatt and sweet bryar' and 831 large and 1,478 small flowering shrubs. Henry Wise laid out the surrounding gardens of the hexagon leading to rides in a star shape to the east and in a *patte d'oie* to the west.

The patterns within the parterre were limited to cutwork and the flourishes were few. This was in accordance with the taste of the duchess. She did not approve of Vanbrugh's extravagance (which had caused Joseph Addison to rhapsodize, 'Behold the glorious Pile ascending, Columns swelling, Arches bending').[6] Nor did she allow the old Woodstock Palace to be kept as a picturesque ruin.

However, when the duke died, in 1722, a massive Column of Victory was erected and a collection of elms was planted in the strategic positions of Marlborough's troops at the Battle of Blenheim.

The garden of the Maréchal de Tallard

It is rare to see a design for a small garden at this time but fortunately one has been provided by the arrival of the Maréchal de Tallard among the defeated French generals brought back from the Battle of Blenheim in Marlborough's triumphal procession. Camille d'Hostun de la Baume, duc de Tallard (1652–1728), was a personal friend of Louis XIV and had been French ambassador to Britain at the Court of St James. He was to enjoy

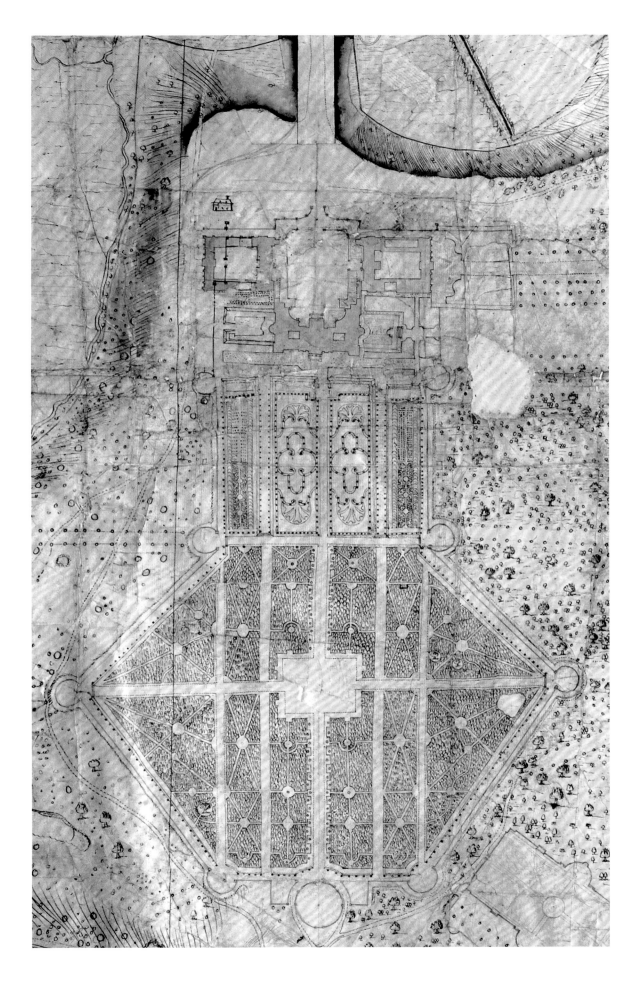

a not disagreeable stay as a prisoner of war entertained by the English gentry. According to Daniel Defoe, the garden of the house assigned to him, which was designed by London and Wise, was small but beautiful, 'after the French fashion and one of the beauties of Nottingham'.

The maréchal's parterres were described in *The Retir'd Gard'ner* as one oblong 'Quarter of Grass-work, which we call a Fund of Grass, upon which many Varieties of Works are cut out, as Angles of several Forms, Squares, Circles, Semi-circles, Ovals and Branch-works; all of which compos'd together the French call Gazon coupé, and we Cut-works in Grass. These Cut-works are cover'd with Varieties of Colours.' These might have been red sand, brick dust, coal dust mixed with yellow sand or with spar (crystals and minerals) from the lead mines, or crushed shells. The verges and corners were grassed. The finest gravel walks were in different colours, 'some of a yellowish brown some greyish, as the Country affords. At the several Centers are Pots and Plants.'[7]

The wilderness and the 'wiggle'

A first historic step into the more flowing lines of a landscape garden was taken with the wilderness and the 'wiggle'. In the Nôtrian *Theory and Practice of Gardening*, the rule for the arrangement of the paths in the *bosquet* or the grove had been 'the star, the direct cross, the Saint Andrew's Cross and the goose foot' (*patte d'oie*). The walks were to be of a specific measurement, the trees also, and the stems were to be kept bare for 10 feet. Gradually, however, designs for woodland paths were moving away from ramrod lines: they began to weave, twist and meander.

The breakthrough was made at Castle Howard, not by a professional but by its inspired owner, the Earl of Carlisle. Switzer describes how, for the gardens in Castle Howard's Wray Wood, 'Mr. London designed a star, which would have spoilt the wood, but that his Lordship's superlative genius prevented it, and to the great advancement of the design, has given it that labyrinth-diverting model we now see it.'

The design for Wray Wood was, Switzer claims, 'the highest Pitch that Natural and Polite gard'ning can arrive to'. It was a 'beautiful wood', made by a 'natural gardener', where the visitor was 'often surprised with little Gardens with Caves, little natural Cascades and Grotts of Water, with pieces of Grotesque Painting, Seats and Arbours of Honeysuckle and Jessamine . . . with all the varieties that Nature and Art can furnish him with . . . Tis there that Nature is truly imitated, if not excell'd, and from which the ingenious may draw the best of their Schemes in Natural and Rural gardening.'

[7] *The Retir'd Gard'ner*, vol. II (1706).

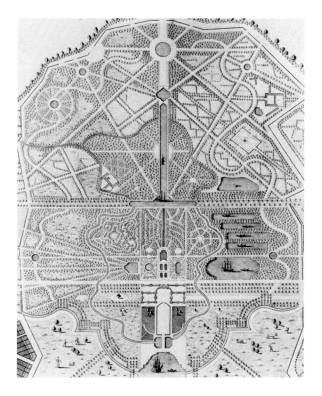

A slight loosening had also crept in at Marly, Louis XIV's relatively private retreat within the grounds of Versailles. Here the star-shaped linear rides were surrounded by undulating woodland and serpentine water features which London noted on his visit with Bentinck in 1700, and which caused him to comment in *The Retir'd Gard'ner* that 'The most valuable labyrinths are those that wind most, as that of Versailles . . .'

Though he was considered to be the last of the formalists, there is no doubt that George London was aware of the rumbles of revolution. His last garden was for Sir Richard Child at Wanstead, where he speaks (again in *The Retir'd Gard'ner*) of walks and *palissades* of hornbeams 'winding variously for the greater Ornament of Park, Labyrinths and Groves . . . Those that are irregular are not less esteem'd for the Variety of them, in great Parks, is what pleases most.'

The Enclosure Acts were changing the look of the countryside in England. Thousands of acres of the common land were being privatized, civilized and hedged off. Wolves no longer roamed. Nature was no longer seen as a threat that needed to be subdued and dominated.

Quite the reverse – a rugged, untamed 'natural' landscape was soon to become the romantic idyll.

ABOVE LEFT The Maréchal de Tallard's garden. A plate from *Les Délices de la Grande Bretagne et de l'Irlande* by James Beeverell, 1707. ABOVE RIGHT A plan by Stephen Switzer published in his *Forest, or Rural Gardening*, 1715, showing a daring move away from the rigid straight paths and the *patte d'oie* of the formal style towards the gentle curves and 'wiggles' of the serpentine.

The Landscape Movement

England in the 18th century

THE DISCOURSE ON THE 'NATURAL' GARDEN was opened by a small coterie of influential Whigs, largely members of the aristocratic Kit-Cat Club, probably so called from its early venue at the Cat and Fiddle in Gray's Inn, where the proprietor, Christopher Catt, took pride in his 'kit-cat' mutton pies.

The name may have been frivolous, but the club had a serious political purpose. Founded in the late seventeenth century, it supported the Whig objectives of a strong Parliament, a limited monarchy and the Protestant succession to the throne. Horace Walpole (1717–1797), son of Whig Prime Minister Robert Walpole (1676–1745), later remarked that while the members were 'generally mentioned as a set of wits, in reality [they were] the patriots that saved Britain'.

The Grand Tour

In the eighteenth century the Grand Tour provided inspiration for a revival of the Arcadian idyll in gardens. The young aristocrats who undertook the Tour had been schooled in the pastoral poetry of Virgil and Horace and were much moved by the ancient Roman ruins and the Renaissance buildings in Venice, Florence, Rome and Naples. Herculaneum, discovered in 1709, and Pompeii, in 1748, added to the fervour for classicism and the desire to transpose it to the English countryside.

Those interested in architecture took as their travel guide Andrea Palladio's *Le antichità di Roma* (*Antiquities of Rome*), of 1554, and the *Quattro libri dell'Architettura*. Palladio had worked with the classical scholar Daniele Barbaro on the illustrations and the text for the 1556 reissue of the ten volumes of *De Architectura*, written by Vitruvius in the first century AD as a building guide for Caesar Augustus.

The landscape

Palladio had, however, left no guide to garden design, as his architecture was sited in the open Italian countryside. The spirit of the eighteenth century was in accord with the romantic and naturalistic landscapes of the Italian

OPPOSITE Portrait of Francis Basset, future 1st Baron of Dunstanville and Basset, 1778 – a 'milord' on the Grand Tour – by Pompeo Batoni, 1778.
BELOW A plate showing the Villa Rotunda, from the edition of Vitruvius's *De Architectura* compiled by Andrea Palladio and Daniele Barbaro, 1556.

campagna as described by the Roman poets. The landscapes of Claude Lorrain, Nicolas Poussin, Gaspar Dughet (Poussin's protégé and son-in-law) and the theatrical Salvator Rosa, while differing from each other in style, all portrayed Italian landscapes filled with classical temples and ancient Roman ruins. Painterly designed landscapes became the mode. And the 'Claude glass', a convex mirror that reflected the garden as a picture in miniature form, became an essential tool for the garden-visiting cognoscenti.

Meanwhile, there was another thread running alongside the desire to create Arcadian gardens with ancient ruins that distilled the wild Italian *campagna*. Inspired by England's Augustan poets and wits, the Whig landed gentry would include literary references, moral messages, allegories and sometimes even barbed political references in the gardens of their great estates.

Johann Zoffany, *Mr and Mrs Garrick taking Tea and the Shakespeare Temple at Hampton, c.*1762. The garden of the famous actor David Garrick, in the very latest landscape movement style with a Palladian temple.

The literary promoters

Joseph Addison and Alexander Pope were the earliest literary publicists for the new style.

Addison (1672–1719), Fellow of Magdalen College, Oxford, a Whig politician and a founder member of the Kit-Cat Club, returned from his two-year Grand Tour brimming with ideas. He had long held the view that gardening was 'near akin to Philosophy' and from his Oxford days he had expressed his desire to 'to bring Philosophy out of Closets, Libraries,

Nicolas Poussin, *Un Temps calme et serein*, 1650–51. A reflective and peaceful landscape, with a shepherd and his flock in the foreground.

Schools and colleges to dwell in clubs and Assemblies, at Tea Tables and Coffee Houses'.

This he achieved when, in March 1711, he and Richard Steele (a schoolfriend from Charterhouse and the publisher of *Tatler*) launched the *Spectator* magazine, with the avowed intention to 'enliven morality with wit and temper wit with morality'. The *Spectator* maintained a conversational style, causing Dr Johnson to say that Addison's readers 'fancy that a wise and accomplished companion is talking to them'. During its short life of eighteen months, it appeared daily (apart from Sundays) and was a great success, particularly in the coffee houses, where it was passed from hand to hand.

As the fictional Mr Spectator, Addison kept up a lively conversation with an imaginary country squire, a faintly foolish hunting-shooting type, Sir Roger de Coverley. In his articles of 1712, Addison brings out a serious point regarding the crippling economics of maintaining a formal garden as opposed to a more 'natural' one.

'But why', Mr. Spectator asks, 'should not a whole estate be thrown into a kind of garden by frequent plantations, that may turn as much to the profit as the pleasure of the owner? A marsh overgrown with willows, or a mountain shaded with oaks, are not only more beautiful, but more beneficial, than when they lie bare and unadorned.

'Fields of corn make a pleasant prospect and if the walks were taken a little care of that lie between them, if the natural embroidery of the meadows were helped and improved by some small additions of Art and the several rows of hedges set off by trees and flowers that the soil was capable of receiving, a man might make a pretty landskip out of his own possessions.'

The earliest mention of the idea of the meander, the 'squiggle' or 'wiggle' demonstrated in the serpentine paths of Wray Wood as described by Switzer (see page180), had come from Sir William Temple (1628–1699), ambassador to The Hague and a negotiator of William III's marriage to Mary Stuart. A keen gardener at his own beloved (and formal) Moor Park, Hertfordshire, he was also an elegant essayist. His secretary, the satirist Jonathan Swift, collected and published his essays after his death.

Though he had never been to China, in *The Gardens of Epicurus* of 1685, Temple mused on the 'Chinese way of doing things' and whether forms that are irregular might yet 'have more beauty than the others'. He writes:

Among us, the beauty of building and planting is placed chiefly in some certain proportions, symmetries, or uniformities; our walks and our trees ranged so, as to answer one another, and at exact distances. The Chinese scorn this way of planting, and say a boy, that can tell an hundred, may plant walks of trees in straight lines . . . But their greatest reach of imagination is employed in contriving figures, where the beauty shall be great, and strike the eye, but without any order of disposition of parts, that shall be commonly or easily observed . . . And though we have hardly any Notion of this sort of Beauty, yet they have a particular Word . . . to express it; and where they find it hit their Eye at first sight, they say the *Sharawadgi* is fine or is admirable.

There is some debate about whether Temple was correct in his interpretation of the word *Sharawadgi*, but in any event he went on to warn Westerners against attempting it themselves, as it might prove too much of a challenge. There would, he warns, be 'More Dishonour if they fail and 'tis twenty to one they will; whereas in regular figures 'tis hard to make any great and remarkable faults.'

Considerably later, Addison published a response to Temple. In 1712, in the *Spectator*, he wrote that:

Writers who have given an account of China, tell us, the inhabitants of that country laugh at the plantations of our Europeans, which are laid out by the rule and the line, because, they say, anyone may place trees in equal rows and uniform figures . . .They have a word it seems in their language . . . (*Sharawadgi*) by which they express the particular beauty of a plantation that thus strikes the imagination at sight . . .

Our British gardens, on the contrary, instead of humouring Nature, love to deviate from it as much as possible. Our Trees rise in Cones, Globes and Pyramids. We see the marks of scissors on every plant and bush. I do not know whether I am singular in my opinion but, for my own part, I would rather look upon a tree in all its luxuriancy and diffusion of boughs and branches, than when it is thus cut and trimmed into a mathematical figure; and cannot but fancy that an orchard in flower looks infinitely more delightful, than all the little labyrinths of the most finished parterre.

Among the contributors to the *Spectator* was Alexander Pope (1688–1744), finest of the Augustan poets, translator of Homer, and wit. In 1713 Pope famously lampooned (in the *Guardian* newspaper, another Whig publication) some imaginary wilting topiary for sale in a fictitious nursery.

> Adam and Eve in yew: Adam a little shattered by the fall of the tree of Knowledge in the great storm; Eve and the serpent very flourishing . . .
> St. George in Box; his arm scarce long enough, but will be in a condition to stick the dragon by next April.
> A green dragon of the same, with a tail of ground ivy for the present. NB – these two are not to be sold separately . . .
> An old Maid of Honour in wormwood . . .
> A topping Ben Jonson in Laurel.
> Divers eminent modern poets in bays, somewhat blighted, to be disposed of a pennyworth.

He deplored 'people of the common Level of Understanding' (as opposed to 'Persons of Genius'), who were

> principally delighted with the Little Niceties and Fantastical Operation of Art, and constantly think that finest which is least Natural. A Citizen is no sooner Proprietor of a couple of Yews, but he entertains Thoughts of erecting them into Giants, like those of Guild-hall. I have known an eminent Cook, who beautified his Country Seat with a Coronation Dinner in Greens, where you see the Champion flourishing on Horseback at one end of the Table and the Queen in perpetual Youth at the other.

He wrote that 'the taste of the ancients in their gardens' was for 'the amiable simplicity of unadorned nature, that spreads over the mind a more noble sort of tranquility'.

The third member of the literary triumvirate was the Whig politician and philosopher Anthony Ashley-Cooper, 3rd Earl of Shaftesbury (1671–1713), who threw himself into the spirit in *The Moralists* (1709). Writing from his Philosopher's Tower on the Shaftesbury Estate in Dorset, he declared he would:

> no longer . . . resist the Passion growing in me for Things of a *natural* kind; where neither *Art* nor the *Conceit* or *Caprice* of man has spoil'd their *genuine Order*, by breaking in upon that primitive State. Even the rude *Rocks*, the mossy *Caverns*, the irregular

unwrought *Grotto's* and broken *Falls* of Waters, with all the horrid Graces of the *Wilderness* itself, as representing NATURE more, will be the more engaging, and appear with a Magnificence far beyond the formal Mockery of Princely Gardens.

The Dutch and their mournful family of yews

Among the English, the Dutch were beginning to get a reputation for fussiness, finickiness, fanciness, too many collections of shells and knick-knacks, ridiculous topiary and too much of it. The poet William Mason, in his epic poem *The English Garden* in 1731, spoke of the 'mournful family of Yews (that) came over with the house of Orange'. Batty Langley, the eccentric 'Gothick' garden designer, in *New Principles of Gardening* (1728), mused on 'how shocking is a stiff regular garden . . . first taken from the *Dutch* and introduced into *England* in the time of the late Mr. London and Mr. Wise.'

Plenty of 'wiggles' in Batty Langley's garden plan in his *New Principles of Gardening* (1728), in which he derides the 'stiff regular garden'.

Stephen Switzer

Stephen Switzer took the view that there were in England too many country estates where the 'crimping diminutive, and wretched Performances we everywhere meet with . . . the Top of these Designs being Clip't Plants, Flowers and other Trifling Decorations'. They were 'were only fit for little Town Gardens'. As to Hampton Court, the only fault of the Pleasure Gardens was that they were 'stuff'd too thick with Box, a Fashion brought over out of Holland by the Dutch Gardeners'. He derided the 'little Niceties and fantastical Operations' and the contortion of turning trees into 'monstrous shapes of Screws, Monkeys, Giants etc.' On the contrary, 'Rural life should be celebrated as by Virgil and Horace.'

Claude-Louis Châtelet, *Le Hameau, Petit Trianon*, 1786. Marie-Antoinette's enchanting *ferme ornée*.

Along with Bridgeman, Switzer had spanned the last of the formal gardens with London and Wise and was now promoting the 'natural' approach. He was greatly inspired by the idea of the *ferme ornée* – an Arcadian ornamental farm where the 'natural' landscape, with its framed views, careful planting and judicious placing of water and streams, would be enhanced by statues, follies, grottoes and attractive-looking livestock.[1]

He described himself as a 'promoter of this Farm-like way of Gardening, before it was used by anybody in any place in Great Britain, and must still think it not only the most profitable but the most pleasurable of any Kind of Gardening . . . It is really the truest and best Way of Gardening in the World, and such as the politics and best Genius of all Antiquity delighted in.'

He expanded his *Forest, or Rural Gardening – The Nobleman, Gentleman, and Gardener's Recreation*, which was based on the words of London and Wise, into the three-volume treatise *Ichnographia Rustica; or, Noblemen, Gentlemen and Gardener's Recreation*. Published in 1718, *Ichnographia Rustica* includes this 'kind of extensive gardening' with gardens 'open to all View to the unbounded Felicities of distant Prospect, and the expansive volumes of Nature herself'.

Two courts

1719 was the year Alexander Pope settled in Twickenham and started his famous garden, keeping the discussion alive. In that year too, Caroline, Princess of Wales (wife of the future George II) began to think about gardening at Richmond Lodge.

Caroline had met Addison previously when, on a diplomatic mission to Germany, he had visited Herrenhausen, the Hanover palace with its famous garden designed by the Electress Sophie, which had been the orphaned princess's childhood home. Now, in England, she adopted the 'Addison aesthetic', and claimed to be the 'patron of natural gardening'. This was a subject she discussed with her 'gardening lords', a privileged circle that included Addison and Pope. She also enjoyed holding *fêtes galantes*, as inspired by the paintings of Watteau, and generally helped the landscape aesthetic along by giving it the seal of royal approval.

Meanwhile Pope, at his villa in Twickenham, was holding his own court for his wide circle of influential friends. These included, of course, his patron Lord Burlington, the architect Charles Bridgeman and William Kent. Within the 5 acres of his much-publicized garden he created a grotto, an under-road tunnel, an arcade of trees, a shell temple and a mount overlooking the Thames. He was to write in a letter to Lord

[1] Very different from Marie-Antoinette's later make-believe farm, Le Hameau de la Reine, built in 1783 in the Petit Trianon, where the eggs were washed before the queen 'collected' them.

Atterbury in 1725, 'I am as busy in three inches of gardening as any man can be in three score acres. I fancy myself like the fellow that spent his life cutting ye twelve apostles in one cherry stone. I have a Theatre, an Arcade, a Bowling-green, a Grove, and a what not.'

The Architect earl and William Kent

Richard Boyle, Lord Burlington (1694–1753), a wealthy patron of the arts, is credited with making at Chiswick House the first private villa in the neo-Palladian style in Britain. His inspiration had come from his two Grand Tours, in 1714 and 1719. On returning from the first, he dismissed the baroque architect James Gibbs (1682–1754) from Burlington House in Piccadilly (now housing the Royal Academy) and replaced him with the Scottish architect Colen Campbell (1676–1729), who gave the building 'a true Palladian front'.

Burlington met William Kent (1685–1748) towards the end of the second tour, which he had undertaken to make a close study of Palladio's villas near Vicenza. At that time Kent was already an established artist. The son of a Yorkshire cabinet-maker, he had broken his apprenticeship as a coach painter in 1709 when Yorkshire benefactors 'raised a contribution and recommended me to proper persons in London'. From there he went on to Rome with William Talman (son of the architect for William and Mary at Hampton Court).

There, Kent prospered and notably painted a fresco on the ceiling of the baroque church San Giuliano dei Fiamminghi (St Julian of the Flemings). He was commissioned to paint some pictures for a cardinal and even won a Vatican medal for a religious painting organized by the Accademia di San Luca. On Thursdays he operated as a cultural guide for the young British bucks, the *milordi,* on their Grand Tour. He supported himself further by copying pictures for his sponsors, and seeking out paintings and *objets d'art* to send back to England.

Kent could turn his hand to anything in the decorative or artistic line. With equal ease and virtuosity he could paint ceilings or portraits, sculpt statues and design furniture or buildings or gardens. With fluent Italian and renowned charm, he had fallen into the very circle of the discriminating and artistic wealthy who would be his clients of the future.

Burlington and Kent came back to England together in 1719, and Burlington engaged Kent to decorate the interior of Burlington House. He would later decorate Kensington Palace for the queen and was much in demand by the beau monde in general. However, it is for his association with the gardens of Chiswick House, and later with those of Stowe and Rousham, that Kent is best remembered.

Chiswick House and garden

Before Kent's arrival on the scene, Burlington had already designed a rustic house with 'Vitruvian' doors for the garden of Chiswick House, as well as commissioning classical statues – to express his Whig sympathies – and various stone features or garden buildings or *fabriques*. These included the Pagan Temple, designed by James Gibbs, and the 'Bagnio', a neo-Palladian bathing house designed by Colen Campbell. Burlington had also put in a now old-fashioned, sharply geometric *patte d'oie* leading to focal points.

When Kent arrived at Chiswick in the 1720s, he softened the harsh lines of the paths and turned the Bollo brook that ran near the front of the house into a lake, using the excavated soil to make a viewing walkway

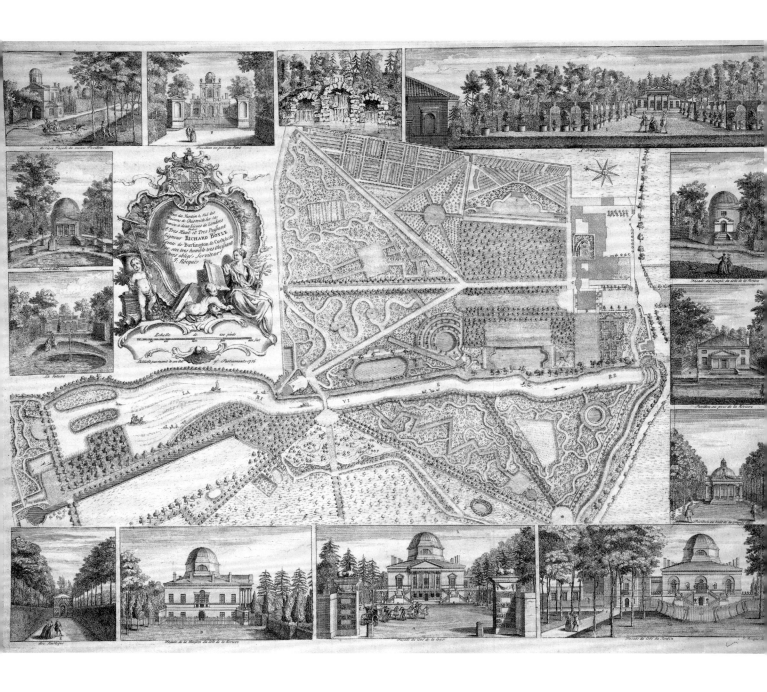

John Rocque, *Plan and Views of Chiswick House*, 1736.

over the garden and the more distant river Thames. He put in a ha-ha, created a cascade and the exedra – a green hedge theatre designed to display Roman statues.

Burlington's passion was primarily not for gardens, but for architecture. In his library he had every version of Vitruvius, Serlio, Bramante and Palladio. When Chiswick House burnt down in 1725, he replaced it

TOPIARY, KNOTS AND PARTERRES

with a neo-Palladian villa – a villa, not a palace, as this would have been offensive to Whiggish sensibilities. Ostentation (of which there was still plenty) was kept behind doors for reasons of 'taste'.

Burlington was a generous sponsor to Alexander Pope (who, as a Catholic, had not been allowed to attend university or even own property). Perhaps in gratitude, in 1731 Pope composed his *Epistle to the Right Honourable Richard Earl of Burlington Occasioned by his Publishing Palladio's Designs of the Bathes, Arches, and Theatres of Ancient Rome.* It is a poem about 'taste' – or the lack of it. He addresses Burlington:

> You show us, Rome was glorious, not profuse,
> And pompous buildings once were things of use . . .
>
> Who then shall grace, or who improve the soil?
> Who plants like Bathurst,[2] or who builds like Boyle? . . .
>
> Something there is more needful than expense
> And something previous ev'n to taste – 'tis sense . . .

He expresses his own view on how to make a garden:

> To build, to plant, whatever you intend,
> To rear the column, or the arch to bend,
> To swell the terrace, or to sink the grot,
> In all, let Nature never be forgot.
> But treat the Goddess like a modest fair,
> Nor overdress, nor leave her wholly bare . . .

and gives us his tenets:

> He gains all points, who pleasingly confounds,
> Surprises, varies, and conceals the bounds.

Above all else:

> Consult the genius of the place in all,
> That tells the waters or to rise, or fall;
> Or helps th' ambitious hill the heav'ns to scale,
> Or scoops in circling theatres the vale;
> Calls in the country, catches opening glades,
> Joins willing woods, and varies shades from shades,
> Now breaks, or now directs, th' intending lines;
> Paints as you plant, and, as you work, designs.

[2] The 1st Earl Bathurst, who created a famous landscape garden at his house, Cirencester Park in Gloucestershire.

Bridgeman at Stowe

Stowe, in Buckinghamshire, is the most celebrated, innovative and political of all England's eighteenth-century landscape gardens. Richard Temple, 1st Viscount Cobham (1675–1749), a distinguished soldier, Whig supporter (and member of the Kit-Cat Club), had the foresight to employ in succession the three most influential garden designers of the time – first Charles Bridgeman, then William Kent and finally Capability Brown. They created a masterpiece.

Between 1711 and 1733, Bridgeman took the first steps to a more 'natural' pastoral approach. He brought into view fields with crops and livestock. Contrary to general belief, he did not actually invent the ha-ha, but he deserves much credit for his imaginative use of it.[3] At Stowe, the 4-mile ha-ha sweeps across in front of the house and out to each side to

Jacques Rigaud, *View of the Queen's Theatre from the Rotunda*, 1733. While he was working at Stowe, Charles Bridgeman invited the draughtsman Rigaud to make a record of the garden with its many classical buildings, so bringing it overnight celebrity.

TOPIARY, KNOTS AND PARTERRES

open up the landscape. The garden appears to flow into the countryside to the Corinthian column on the distant skyline.

He replaced a parterre with a formal lake, causing Pope to remark in his *Epistle,*

> The vast parterres a thousand hands shall make,
> Lo! Cobham comes, and floats them with a lake . . .

He predicted the picturesque with the making of compositions along the network of walks that ties the garden together. These included the views of Temple of Venus on the raised Rotunda, which looks across to a statue of Queen Caroline mounted on a column. The architect Vanbrugh, who was a friend of Cobham, designed some follies and an Egyptian pyramid that was erected in 1724. Each walk was designed to end in a vista or focal point.

When Horace Walpole examined the evolving style in hindsight in his *Modern Gardening* of 1780, his view was that the tide had turned with Bridgeman's work at Stowe. Bridgeman had banished the topiary, knots and parterres – the 'verdant sculpture'. He abandoned 'the square precision of the foregoing age. He enlarged his plans, disdained to make every division tally to its opposite; and, though he still adhered much to straight walks with high clipped hedges, they were his only great lines, the rest he diversified by wildernesses, and loose groves of oak, though still within surrounding hedges.'

Kent at Stowe

In the 1730s, Kent pushed the ideas of the landscape movement further. In 1733, along with many other Whigs, Cobham had fallen out with Robert Walpole over the Excise Bill. This was when Kent created the celebrated Elysian Fields as a damning political comment. The Temple of the British Worthies looked across a stream named the river Styx to the Temple of Ancient and Modern Virtues. Here a beheaded Robert Walpole demonstrated Cobham's utter disillusionment with the government of the day.

Rousham

Rousham, in Oxfordshire, is widely considered to be Kent's masterpiece. There too he followed Bridgeman and worked from his plan of fountains and pools and the classical buildings which were placed on the 'swoops and swells' of the land. He put in what Horace Walpole described as

[3] It has been suggested that the ha-ha at Stowe may well have been Cobham's idea, as the concept was a military one.

'the sweetest little groves, streams, glades, porticoes, cascades, and river, imaginable; all the scenes are perfectly classic.' Unencumbered by the inhibitions of the trained architect or landscape designer, Kent approached the design boldly and with a fresh eye.

In Walpole's words, Kent was 'painter enough to taste the charms of landscape, bold and opinionative enough to strike out'.

> He leapt the fence and saw all nature was a garden . . . Adieu to canals, circular basins and cascades, tumbling down marble steps, that last absurd magnificence of Italian and French villas. The forced elevation of cataracts was no more. The gentle stream was taught to serpentize seemingly at its pleasure, and where discontinued by different levels, its course appeared to be concealed by thickets properly interspersed, and glittered again at a distance where it might be supposed naturally to arrive . . . A few trees scattered here and there on its edges . . .

Kent's 'great principles to which he worked were perspective and light and shade' and his 'ruling principle was that nature abhors a straight line . . . Thus dealing in none but the colours of nature, and catching its most favourable features, men saw a new creation opening before their eyes. The living landscape was chastened or polished, not transformed.'

The Arcadian landscape: Stourhead and Painshill

The concept of making a classical landscape, overflowing with poetic and artistic allusions, along a circuit of composed tableaux was carried forward by Henry Hoare (1705–1785) of Stourhead, in Wiltshire, and Charles Hamilton (1704–1786) at Painshill in Surrey. Both were creative gentlemen gardeners. Friends from their schooldays at Westminster, they had both been inspired by the Grand Tour and both designed their gardens from scratch.

Henry Hoare's father had built a Palladian mansion designed by Colen Campbell at Stourhead but, as at Rousham and Painshill, the garden design broke convention and was placed out of sight of the building. At Stourhead the gardens were arranged around the lake, approached from a bridge taken from Palladio's *Quattro libri*. As the path, backed by dark woodland, twists and turns, tantalizing glimpses of features appear in the distance – the Grotto, the Pantheon, the Temples of Apollo and Hercules, the River God, the Gothic Alfred's Tower, as well as other glimpses through to the landscape, half seen and tantalizingly eclipsed before being fully revealed further along the path.

The Garden at Stourhead. This painting of the eighteenth-century English
School shows a view of the pastoral idyll, with a temple beyond the bridge on
the far side of the lake.

The circuit at the 200 acres of Painshill took a route that led up hill and down dale from the man-made lake. Charles Hamilton did not have the great wealth of his banker friend Henry Hoare, but he put life and soul into his garden over three decades. It was a showcase for his important collection of evergreens and it also had many of the features of Stourhead. In addition to the classical garden buildings, which included the Temple of Bacchus (Hamilton kept vineyards), there is a Turkish tent, a hermitage (which briefly had a resident 'hermit') and what is possibly the largest and most glamorous grotto in Europe, with crystal stalactites that glitter like diamonds under candlelight.[4]

Hartwell House

The history of the garden at Hartwell House in Buckinghamshire – a beguiling mixture of the old and the new – is something of a mystery.

The house, which is largely Georgian, was partially designed for a Chief Justice, Lord William Lee, by James Gibbs (the baroque architect sacked by Richard Boyle from Burlington House in Piccadilly). It is considered likely that Bridgeman designed the garden, as it bears many of his hallmarks – the formal lake in place of a parterre and a network of cross-views ending in focal points of many different styles. Among them were a Hercules, a Jupiter and a Juno, a view through to the Grand Canal, a Tuscan-style pavilion, a Gothic tower, an Egyptian pyramid and a statue of William III. The grand plan also included a working farm with crops, and sheep or cattle grazing in the fields.

It seems likely that the new plan was imposed on the framework of an earlier garden which was mentioned in the nineteenth-century *Aedes Hartwellianae*.[5] It was reported that, around 1695, the grounds were 'squared out around the house, divided by walls and evergreen fences, with prim yews cut into architectural forms, and watered by canals as straight as a pikestaff' – all of which seems very Dutch or French but was set off to good effect by the freer Bridgeman landscape.

Lancelot 'Capability' Brown

The landscape movement reached its ultimate manifestation with the arrival of 'Capability' Brown (1716–1783). He had worked under Kent at Stowe (he was head gardener there at the age of twenty-four), and went on to explore the expressive possibilities of the 'natural' but 'improved' landscape. He had arrived on the scene with perfect timing to provide an innovative formula of his own that was exactly what was wanted.

[4] The cave-like grottoes so popular at this time gave the Rococo movement its name (derived from 'rock' and 'cockle shell').
[5] William Henry Smyth, *Aedes Hartwellianae*, 1851.

Working with 'natural elements', his gardens were twice blessed – they were both painterly and practical. Once installed – which could, indeed, involve the vast expense of moving villages and creating lakes – they were far less expensive to maintain than the old formal gardens. They consisted primarily of a lovely but totally contrived pastoral view of a serpentine lake, working farmland, informal groups of trees, and views across the rolling greenness of the English countryside.

Parterres were banished and lawns were brought right up to the house. Unsightly farm buildings were screened off with banks of trees, while any that were ornamental were made to double up as kennels, cottages or dairies.

After Balthasar Nebot, *The Topiary Exedra with a View of the Obelisk, Hartwell House, Buckinghamshire,* 1738. A superb example of theatrical green architecture, with the obelisk framed within the central arch.

Englishmen liked their sport, so plans would include a sporting estate with walks for the 'guns' and more ornamental rides for the ladies.

Brown thought out his garden designs in broad, sweeping terms. He likened his method to a form of punctuation. 'Now *there* I make a comma, and there, where a more decided turn is proper, I make a colon; at another part, where an interruption is desirable to break the view, a parenthesis; now a full stop, and then I begin another subject.'

He, personally, completed 150 commissions across the great estates of Britain. Examples included Chatsworth, which was flattened (bar the cascade and the sea horse), and Blenheim. A visitor to Longleat in 1760 recorded: 'The gardens are no more. They are succeeded by a fine lawn, a serpentine river, wooded hills, gravel paths meandering round a shrubbery, all modernised by the ingenious and much sought-after Mr Brown.' The superb green architecture at Hartwell was removed and the garden was 'laid out' as a landscape by one of Brown's followers. It is said that by the time he died 'Capability' Brown had set a fashion so sought after that there were four thousand landscape parks in England.

As the fashion spread to the Continent, the formal gardens of the Dutch palace of Rijswijk were demolished in favour of a *jardin anglais*, as was Honselaarsdijk, with its Mollet parterres. Louis Napoleon landscaped Het Loo and Catherine the Great wiped out Le Blond's Peterhof. In 1772, Catherine wrote to Voltaire, 'I passionately love gardens in the English style, the curved lines, the gentle slopes, the ponds pretending to be lakes, the archipelagos on solid ground, and I deeply disdain straight lines . . . I should say my anglomania gets the better of planimetry.'

However, there were those who regretted the loss of the old formal gardens. In 1909 Sir George Sitwell reflected in *On the Making of Gardens* that:

The new fashion spread like a plague over Europe, destroying everywhere the historic and harmonious setting of hall and palace and castle, scenes which the care and love of bygone centuries had hallowed which should have been left to us to link one generation with another. In its train came follies worse than those which provoked the satire of Addison. The garden was deprived first of its boundaries and then of its flowers; sham rivers, dead trees, and broken bridges were planted in appropriate positions, while over the countryside in the neighbourhood of the great houses there broke out a dreadful eruption of Gothic temples and Anglo-Saxon keeps, Corinthian arches and Druid amphitheatres, of classic urns, Chinese pagodas and Egyptian pyramids, all with inscriptions in Greek or black-letter appealing to the eye of taste and to the tear of sensibility.

It was understandable that

> . . . hedged in on every side by formalism, they [the landowners] grew weary of the silvery plash of the fountain and the bass murmur of the stepped cascade, of ordered bosquet, stiff canal and sanded parterre, of groves like green chests set upon poles, of smirking nymphs and leering satyrs and fine vases full of nothing. The long straight alleys seemed to them to be insipid, the evergreen hedges to be unfeeling; they hated the flower battalions which stood on parade in platoons of pinks and regiments of tulips and armies of asters, the stage scenery of box and turf and trellis which could not share in the hopes of spring or regrets of autumn, but was dead to all the music of the year.

The tragedy was the complete destruction of the craftsmanship, the artistry and the centuries of garden history. The scorned knots and parterres were carpeted over en masse with an anonymous green sward. There would be no going back.

However, the great Victorian era of plant discovery, breakthroughs in botany, marvels of engineering and the arrival of many literary garden writers was now on the horizon. They too would have their effect on garden history and they would bring – in time – a revival of topiary, knots and parterres.

OVERLEAF A painting of the English School, 1770–79, shows the great formal garden of Blenheim Palace wiped out and turfed over and 'contrived to pleasing effect' by 'Capability' Brown.

The Victorian Garden

England in the 19th century

I N THE NINETEENTH CENTURY the flood of exotic plants, trees and garden flowers arriving from the New World and the Orient took centre stage in the English garden. 'A flower garden has now become the appendage of every fashionable garden,' wrote Maria Elizabeth Jackson in the *Florist's Manual* of 1827.

Topiary and the parterre, however, remained in the doldrums until the Great Exhibition of 1851 at Crystal Palace. This vast and glittering edifice, a marvel of engineering, was constructed with 300,000 panes of the newly invented cast plate glass on an elegant skeleton of cast-iron columns. The gardens, which included such wonders as the *Horses of the Sun* from the Vatican, five life-sized sculpted dinosaurs and a glass fountain, also had a dramatic parterre decorated with urns and vases, planted out with some 50,000 scarlet pelargoniums.

OPPOSITE Crystal Palace, a wonder of the Industrial Revolution, designed by Joseph Paxton, 1851. The extravagant gardens fired the Victorian passion for bedding out and heralded the gradual return of the parterre.
BELOW The opening of the Great Exhibition at Crystal Palace, Hyde Park, 1851. Lithograph after Joseph Nash.

The demise of the old formal gardens had given the Victorians a fresh canvas. The newly rich industrialists, building grand mansions and important gardens to display their wealth, taste and horticultural knowledge, did not follow any particular dictates of fashion but took the freedom to choose whatever style they fancied. Buildings and their gardens now came in a wide range, including neo-Renaissance, neo-Palladian, neo-Romanesque, mock-Tudor, Second Empire, Gothic and Exotic.

The plant hunters

Imperial power, newly opened trade routes and missionaries travelling ever further afield had opened the way for the plant hunters. In 1804 the Horticultural Society had been founded with a prime objective of scouring the world for undiscovered flora. In 1859, Charles Darwin's *On the Origin of Species* was published and rocked the world.

A grand hero among the British plant hunters was Sir Joseph Banks (1743–1820), who, travelling with Captain Cook on HMS *Endeavour*, explored New Zealand, Botany Bay in Australia and the Great Barrier Reef. Joseph Dalton Hooker (1817–1911) returned from Sikkim (where he had been imprisoned) bearing many rhododendrons and rock plants from the icy fringes of the Himalayas. Robert Fortune (1812–1880) brought back from China new daphnes and jasmines, azaleas and magnolias (he also 'stole the secret of tea' for the East India Company), while Ernest 'Chinese' Wilson (1876–1930) introduced a staggering 3,356 Asian plants, 900 of which were new to Europe. David Douglas (1799–1834) met an early death when he was gored in a pit trap in Hawaii. But, before that, he had discovered many conifers in California and he left his indelible mark on European gardens with the 'Douglas' fir.

In an advertisement for seed in the *Horticultural Cabinet and Florist's Magazine* of 1836, 74 out of the 150 types of flower seed mentioned were recent introductions, largely from Chile, Mexico and California. In response to public demand, parks and botanical gardens opened to the public for the first time. Flower shows abounded. The latest fashion, for those who could afford it, was to gather entire collections of plants. 'Pinetums', 'arboretums', 'pomariums', 'stumperies', 'shrubberies', 'ferneries', 'rosariums', as well as rock gardens, heather gardens, grass gardens, willow collections and eerie 'rooteries', became the new essentials for fashionable garden owners.

By great good fortune, the invention of sheet glass coincided with the lifting of the glass tax in 1845. This coincidence opened up to people of relatively moderate means the possibility of propagating and growing tender plants in the northern hemisphere.

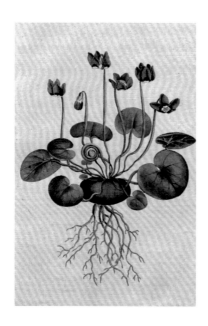

Gardening magazines

The proliferation of gardening magazines reflected the fascination with gardening, natural science and botany that had seized the country. The earliest of these periodicals was *The Botanical Magazine,* launched in 1787. Illustrated with hand-coloured engravings, it was dedicated entirely to foreign plants in cultivation. At its height it was a bestseller, with a circulation of 3000, despite costing a hefty four shillings a copy.

In 1826, John Claudius Loudon launched *The Gardener's Magazine.* Loudon (1783–1843), a giant among the many nineteenth-century horticulturists, was known as a botanist, town planner and landscape designer, but is best remembered for his prodigious literary output. His aim for *The Gardener's Magazine* was typically didactic: his intention was to 'enlighten the gardener' and to 'disseminate new and important information'. Opinionated, fearlessly critical and occasionally pontificating, the magazine kept up a lively discourse until Loudon's death in 1843.

Rivals soon included Joseph Paxton's *Horticultural Register and General Magazine*, founded in 1832. In 1833 Paxton's co-editor, Joseph Harrison, head gardener at Wortley Hall in Sheffield, brought out no fewer than three magazines, *The Gardener's and Forester's Record, The Floricultural Cabinet* and *The Florist's Magazine* (this last, at a reasonable sixpence a copy, scooped up a readership of 10,000). In 1837 the first gardening newspaper appeared in the form of *The Gardener's Gazette.*

However, it is the *Gardener's Chronicle* (also priced sixpence), edited by Paxton and the botanist John Lindley and launched in 1841, that is best remembered. It contained a mix of contributions from head gardeners, articles on natural history and garden botany, book reviews and news. The same year Loudon's wife, Jane, brought out the pioneering (but short-lived) *Lady's Magazine for Gardeners.*

In 1850, Thomas Moore, Curator of Chelsea Physic Garden, and William P. Ayres, a nurseryman, produced *The Gardener's Magazine of Botany*, with beautiful hand-coloured lithographs by the botanist and artist Henry Noel Humphreys. The end of the century saw William Robinson's *Gardening Illustrated* and *The Garden.* Shirley Hibberd's popular *Amateur Gardening* of 1884 catered for the cottager, while for the large estate owner *Country Life* was launched in 1897. Both are still in print today.

The 'picturesque' versus the 'gardenesque'

Lively discussion in the gardening periodicals included a heated debate about the 'picturesque' versus the 'gardenesque'. This dispute was, perhaps

Illustrations from *The Botanical Magazine; or Flower Garden Display'd* by William Curtis, 1790, showing *Helleborus niger* (top) and *Cyclamen coum* (bottom).

unintentionally, started by the Reverend William Gilpin, headmaster and vicar, who sketched landscapes on his holidays around Britain. In his *Observations* of 1792, he noted that gardens 'are never picturesque. They want the bold roughness of Nature . . . Only a scene as untame as a Scotch river with all its rough accompaniments could be the kind of beauty which might properly described as "picturesque".' As to the Palladian style, 'while it may be elegant to the last degree . . . should we wish to give it picturesque beauty . . . we must beat down one half of it, deface the other, and throw the mutilated members round in heaps.'

Sir Uvedale Price, a Herefordshire landowner, along with a group of like-minded friends – including the poet William Wordsworth – embraced the concept of the 'picturesque' and criticized 'Capability' Brown for being 'bland and tame'. His was the 'meagre genius of the bare and bald', his gardens lacking the desirable 'qualities of roughness and of sudden variation, joined to that of irregularity'. So, 'Among trees, it is not the smooth young beech, not the fresh and tender ash, but the rugged old oak and knotty wych elm that are the picturesque.'

The picturesque 'bold roughness of Nature' as portrayed by the Reverend William Gilpin, *c.*1792.

The View of Tintern Abbey on the River Wye, painted by Edward Dayes, 1799. The twelfth-century Cistercian monastery, torn down in the Dissolution, sets the mood for the picturesque.

Uvedale's neighbour, Richard Payne Knight, followed his convictions through to the extent of building Downton Castle, Herefordshire, on a precipitous rocky crag. It was a mock Gothic ruin surrounded by rough landscape. His poem entitled *The Landscape – a didactic poem in three books addressed to Uvedale Price Esq.* came out in the same year as Price's *Essay on the Picturesque, as Compared with the Sublime and the Beautiful* in 1794. He summed up the Brownian garden as

Spreading o'er its unprolific spawn
In never ending sheets of vapid lawn.

The transition from the Brown style is reflected in the career of Humphry Repton (1752–1818), the last of the great English landscape designers,

The Rosary Garden, from Humphry Repton's Red Book for the Earl of Bridgewater at Ashridge Park, Hertfordshire, 1813.

who, over his gardening lifetime, moved from the smoothness of the Brown landscape to the rough 'picturesque' (during his brief partnership with architect John Nash) and finally to a style that might be called 'gardenesque', as it embraced some formality around the house.

However, the expression 'gardenesque' first appeared in print many years after Repton's death, in an article by Loudon in the December 1832 edition of *The Gardener's Magazine*. Loudon had started out with designs in the 'picturesque' manner but, by 1822, in his *Encyclopaedia of Gardening*, he had come to prefer a degree of formality. In his introduction to the 1840 edition of Repton's *Landscape Gardening*, he described the 'picturesque' as the 'imitation of nature in a wild state, such as the painter delights to copy', whereas the 'gardenesque' was 'the imitation of nature, subjected to a certain degree of cultivation and improvement, suitable to the wants and wishes of man'.

Repton had retorted to his critics that while 'mouldering abbeys and the antiquated cottage with its chimneys smothered in ivy may be eminently appealing to the painter', he trusted that 'the good sense and the good taste of this country will never be led to despise the concept of a gravel walk, the delicious fragrance of a shrubbery, the soul expanding delight of a wide extended prospect, or a view down a steep hill, because they are all subjects incapable of being painted.'

Formalism and topiary were definitely making a comeback. By 1865 Robert Kerr, in *The Gentleman's House, or How to Plan English Residences*, was advocating a judicious mixture of the picturesque and the classic. 'A certain amount of symmetry is almost invariably adopted in the best examples for the immediate adjuncts of the House, whereas as regards the more remote arrangements the English style is now exclusively employed.'

Floriculture, the parterre and bedding out

The parterre returned as a frame for bedding out the new exotic plants. There was a variety of designs on offer. Loudon's 1822 *Encyclopaedia* presented five styles of planting flower borders. These were 'the general mingled' flower garden (a mixture which might include shrubs), the 'select' (for carefully chosen types of plants), the 'changeable' (where plants are kept in the wings ready to replace the old ones), the 'botanic', where 'plants are arranged according to botanical study', and the 'massed' flower garden or carpet bedding.

Though Victorian bedding out is now seen as garish and crude and is mostly restricted to parks and seaside 'clocks', it must have been an exciting novelty at the time. Never before had gardeners had at their fingertips a floral palette of brilliant primary colours.

The most popular bedding plants then (and arguably still now) were the reliable, easy-going, flowering-to-the-frost annuals and semi-hardies. Tried and tested performers included pelargoniums, verbenas and calceolarias, lobelias, petunias and *Salvia splendens*. The dahlia, introduced in 1789, had a special place in the heart of the Victorian gardener. For spring there would be tulips, daffodils, wallflowers and lobelias. Nurserymen busied themselves to perfect these plants for their new role. The geraniums were 'dwarfed' to make them more compact and less 'leggy', and new varieties soon appeared. These could be bought from nurserymen travelling to the market towns – so much more easily with the arrival of the railways – by mail order, and from new commercial nurseries like the giant Dutch-run Loddiges in Hackney.

Bed shapes

Released from the rigour of the classical parterres, a whole array of different designs for flower beds began to appear. The 'ribbon' style flanked each side of a straight or serpentine path but had the novelty of regular stripes of plants of different colours. Red, white and blue made a popular choice. The 'promenade' style demanded mirror-image planting each side of the path, whereas the borders of the 'wheel' style were arranged around a circular mound with showpiece planting.

'Pincushion' beds were in concentric circles designed to edge standards of 'curious shrubs' or 'eye-catchers' like floral pyramids or the 'flower basket'. This was a cake stand design, constructed of circular tiers of rustic woodwork or wire, with each layer planted with different bright bedding-out plants. *The Gardener's Magazine* suggested choosing further between 'Gothic', 'Elizabethan', 'Dutch' or 'French' patterns. Another idea was to make a cone out of rubble and poke in dwarf bedding plants, in the manner of today's mosaiculture, to get a topiary effect.

Joseph Paxton and the return of the classic

The Victorian era saw the rise of the head gardener to a position of influence. The most famous of these was undoubtedly Joseph Paxton (1803–1865). As a fifteen-year-old garden boy at the Horticultural Society's garden at Chiswick, he was spotted by the 6th Duke of Devonshire; by the age of twenty-three he had risen to be head gardener at Chatsworth. He went on to write many books, including his revered *Botanical Dictionary*, to edit five gardening magazines, including the *Gardener's Chronicle,* to finance plant expeditions and to become Liberal MP for Coventry. He designed the Crystal Palace, and was knighted by Queen Victoria. Contrary to the trend of the landscape school at the time, Paxton partially reinstated the baroque at Chatsworth. There he designed the gravity-fed Tsar's Fountain to reach twice the height of Nelson's Column and outdo the fountain at Peterhof – all for the amusement of the duke, who was expecting a visit from the tsar.)

Topiary gardens

Despite the fashionable antipathy to topiary at the time, some of the most famous English topiary gardens in existence today date from the nineteenth century.

Drummond Castle

Drummond Castle, in Perthshire, had been given an Italianate make-over in the eighteenth century, with fountains and other

waterworks, a grotto and statuary. In the 1820s and 1830s Lewis Kennedy, a nurseryman and former gardener to Empress Josephine at Malmaison, and his son George restored the parterres in heraldic fashion. The main parterre forms a St Andrew's Cross, with a sixteenth-century sundial in the centre. The surrounding beds were filled with rhododendrons and heathers, described as 'an immense Carpet of brilliant Colours'.

Levens Hall

Levens Hall, which miraculously survived the landscape movement, is treasured the world over for its aged yew topiaries. The original design was by a student of Le Nôtre, Guillaume Beaumont, who had previously been employed at Hampton Court. The owner was Colonel James Grahme, Keeper of the Privy Purse for James II and a Tory Jacobite, who had retired to his home in Westmoreland on William and Mary's accession.

OPPOSITE *Drummond Castle, Perthshire, seen from the Gardens*, painted by Jacob Thompson, 1847. The beautiful Italianate gardens at Drummond Castle, restored by Lewis Kennedy.
BELOW *Levens Hall*. An illustration from *Mansions of England in the Olden Time* by Joseph Nash, 1839–49.

It is probable that some of the existing yews were planted – and topiarized – when the garden was restored by Alexander Forbes, head gardener from 1810 to 1862. The topiary shapes include the affectionately named 'King and Queen', 'Judge's Wig', 'Howard Lion', 'Great Umbrellas', 'Queen Elizabeth and her Maids of Honour'. There is also a 'Jug of Morocco Ale', as well as peacocks and other entertaining shapes.

Packwood House

In the 1850s, at Packwood House, Warwickshire, yews were planted on the eighteenth-century mount. Forty years later, word had got round that they dated from the time of Cromwell and represented the Sermon on the Mount. A great single specimen yew known as the 'Master' stands on a mound. Twelve more yews allegedly represent the disciples towering over the 'multitude' of the scattered trees beneath.

Powis Castle

The topiary in the medieval castle of Powis in Wales was allowed to grow out during the landscape fashion of the eighteenth century. It was trimmed again in the Victorian era and the garden is now famous for its 30,000 feet/8,500 metres of gigantic yew hedging and some individual specimens that are 42 feet/13 metres high.

William Alexander Nesfield and the parterre

A key designer for the Victorian parterre was William Andrews Nesfield (1793–1881), a former army engineer and landscape painter who designed his parterres in almost any historical style to suit the house. When visiting clients, he carried a folder of designs including Dezallier's *parterres de broderie* and designs by Mollet and Boyceau as well as London and Wise. His commissions included the design of the parterre of the Palm House at Kew, work on Buckingham Palace and Regent's Park parterres for Prince Albert.

At Eaton Hall, Cheshire, a castellated Gothic brick mansion designed by John Vanbrugh, Nesfield put in a parterre of elegant scrollwork for the Duke of Westminster. One astonished visitor remarked that 'the scrolls are in many places, not six inches wide!! Nay, even less than that.' He became known for his emblematic designs and monograms, his mazes and, particularly, for his coloured 'gravel work'. At Eaton Hall, he painted the gravel on the parterres. By then, according to the *Gardener's Chronicle,* he was 'sought for by gentlemen of taste in every part of the country'.

Elvaston Castle

The landscape painter Edward Adveno Brooke toured the great Italianate gardens in Britain, talking to the owners and head gardeners. In his *The Gardens of England*, published in 1858, he left a useful record of a cross-section of some of the most fashionable gardens of the time, conjuring up the atmosphere in florid but lively terms, and providing detailed descriptions of the parterres. Among these the garden of Elvaston Castle shines out.

Elvaston Castle, owned by Charles Stanhope, 4th Earl of Harrington, inspired a topiary revival among the gardening elite. It took his head gardener, William Barron, twenty years to design and complete, with the help of ninety gardeners. It was intended to be a romantic and private retreat for Harrington and his young actress bride and was kept 'like a sealed book'.

Nesfield *broderie* parterres at Eaton Hall. From *The Gardens of England* by Edward Adveno Brooke, 1858.

Barron, who confessed to a 'passion for evergreens', enthused the earl, who treated him 'like a brother'. He became renowned in the horticultural world for his success in moving trees of immense size and age. A wonder of the garden was the 'extraordinary arbour, surmounted by singular decorations representing the birds of Paradise' constructed of a single tree, 'upward of a hundred years old', which was brought 'from a distance of twenty-five miles, twenty years ago' and 'the beauty of which would excite the wonder of the beholder'.

Some of the trees were planted in avenues several rows thick, arranged in tiers according to height. One such divided the pinetum (which contained every known species of European conifer) into spruces and firs, on the one hand, and pines on the other. There were rows of Irish yews, golden yews, monkey puzzles and deodars grafted on to cedars of Lebanon. The 11 miles of evergreen hedges were said to be 'shorn as smooth as an Axminster carpet'.

Edward Adveno Brooke notes 'Flora and Sylva – one or both may be found at all seasons'. He talks with enthusiasm about the 'columns,

The extensive and imaginative use of topiary and parterres at Elvaston Castle inspired a nineteenth-century topiary revival. The two illustrations shown here both come from E.A. Brooke's *Gardens of England*.
BELOW 'Garden of the Fair Star'
OPPOSITE 'Alhambra'

TOPIARY, KNOTS AND PARTERRES

minarets, interspersed with statuary', and 'gold yew trimmed into columns with crowns'.

In the 'Alhambra', architectural topiary mirrored that of the Moorish pavilion. In 'Mon Plaisir' a high yew tunnel was designed to be a cool retreat, with windows cut into it to give a view of the garden and the central monkey puzzle tree. In the 'Garden of the Fair Star', the topiary was clipped into columns surmounted with crowns. In 1899, *Country Life* commented: 'Among the many Regal Gardens of England, few are more remarkable than those of the Earl of Harrington at Elvaston in Derbyshire.'

Noel Humphreys and the new topiary

The effect of Elvaston, as word got round, was to bring many closet topiary admirers out into the open. In the 1850s, Noel Humphreys, a naturalist and artist who worked for *The Gardener's Magazine of Botany*, cautiously proposed 'a partial revival' of the formal garden and the despised topiary. His article 'The Effect of clip't Trees on decorative Gardening, and how far they are admissible' damns the old topiary, where

'trees were clipped into human figures, and these leafy monsters became a positive rage: the Yew, the Box, and other trees whose close growing foliage rendered them most suitable for torturing into those unnatural shapes, being cropped and sheared till it was supposed they resembled shepherds and shepherdesses, dogs and peacocks and other forms.' No, the 'partial revival' would be sourced from 'the best Italian gardens . . . with the best hints for the partial re-adoption of architectural and other simple and severe forms of foliage'.

Humphreys further criticized the contemporary flower garden for being flat, commenting that 'an Italian landscape without Cypresses, or an English one entirely without Poplars might be compared to the view of a city without steeples.' He recommends an 'amphitheatre of verdure', hedges and 'cropped limes' to make the garden more interesting than if it can be taken in with a single glance.

Trentham

At Trentham in Staffordshire, in the years 1834–40, Charles Barry designed a typically fanciful Italianate garden. His plan included transforming an islet into a version of the Isola Bella of the Italian Lakes, complete with a gondola and gondolier brought over from Venice.

Edward Arveno Brooke described an extensive parterre:

> . . . revelling in light and shade . . . with its smooth verdant carpet, broad walks and narrow pathways of fine gravel; its fountain urns and marble vases, of which there are four unique specimens rising from the centre of the principal angular compartments on large granite pedestals. The divisions between the beds – which are chiefly of an oblong, circular, and serpentine form – of these compartments consisted formerly of very light-coloured gravel, but the consequent glare and the heat of the sun's rays were found to be excessive, and detrimental to the effective outline of the plants. A fine mossy turf has lately been substituted and the result is most gratifying.
>
> A short time ago the plan of the outer borders underwent a change; it now presents a flowing chain pattern, distinctly formed by carefully kept box-edgings. In the centre of each link is a cypher filled with flowers, and from every fourth there also arises a tapering cypress. As a novelty in the arrangement, the narrow pathways and interstices running along the outer chain were laid down with different-coloured gravel, and the effect shows itself advantageously, especially from the Terrace.

Alton Towers

The garden at Alton Towers, also in Staffordshire, was designed by John Talbot, Earl of Shrewsbury. Known as 'Good Earl John' for his charity, he clearly also had a strong will and an independent spirit. He sought but ignored the best advice of the day and set about creating one of the largest formal gardens in England on his own. Thirteen thousand trees were planted in the landscaped park and a walker on the slope down to the river Churnet would pass a Dutch garden, a rock garden, a pagoda fountain and a Swiss cottage, a Gothic tower, a Greek temple, a Chinese pagoda, grottoes carved into the rock and a cottage for a 'blind harper' – not to forget a small 'Stonehenge'.

Brooke remarked on the use in the parterres of clay from the Staffordshire potteries nearby. He wrote that 'the interstices are filled with a material from the Potteries, called "Grog", which, when first laid down,

Charles Barry's design transposed Isola Bella – complete with gondola and gondolier – from the Italian Lakes to Trentham. From *The Gardens of England*.

The garden at Alton Towers was designed by its playful owner, the Earl of Shrewsbury, to include every fancy: a Chinese pagoda fountain, a Swiss cottage, a Gothic tower, a Greek temple, grottoes, a cottage for a 'blind harper' – even a small 'Stonehenge'. This illustration from *The Gardens of England* shows the colonnade.

is of a bright golden colour; the borders are composed of pounded brick, made with a highly-coloured description of clay, and broken into small fragments for the purpose. From a distance, the effect of this gay dress, illuminating the curves and lines of the dark green box, is quite novel, and, we believe, peculiar to these gardens.'

He was particularly taken with the S-shaped parterre for Shrewsbury. 'In front of the building is a beautifully designed monogram in box of the letter S, by Mr. Whitaker, who for several years has had the management of these gardens, and to whose skill and taste many of their attractions are due.'

The end of bedding out

Towards the end of the nineteenth century, good sense began to put paid to the huge expense of bedding out.

At the gardens at Shrubland Hall in Suffolk (designed by Repton with terraces laid out by Barry), the head gardener, a Mr Foggo, explained to Adveno Brooke that to 'maintain a large and brilliant display of bloom throughout the season, large reserves are always ready to fill up vacancies and preserve uninterrupted the display'. To achieve this he grew

80,000 geraniums, verbenas, lobelias '&c' annually, for turning out 'into numerous beds, borders, vases etc. and this independently of annuals raised from seed'. In the 1870s it is said that some two million plants were put in for the summer show in the London parks.

As to the womanly serpentine curves, they too were now losing their novelty and charm. The garden designer Shirley Hibberd (1825–1890) expressed the opinion that the C and S shapes, the half-moon, and the 'newt shaped' beds 'twisted like eels in misery'. Thomas James, author of 'An Essay on the Poetry of Gardening' in the *Quarterly Review* (1852), commented on the 'unmeaning flower beds that look like kidneys and tadpoles, and sausages and leeches, and commas'.

The elaborate parterres at Shrubland Hall, Suffolk, for which the gardeners had to grow 80,000 bedding-out plants every year. From *The Gardens of England*.

William Robinson

The reaction to the artificiality, showiness and pretension of the Victorians came in no uncertain terms in the form of William Robinson (1838–1935). He was a bombastic Irishman, an experienced, knowledgeable gardener and author of what is widely accepted as the most read and most influential gardening book ever written in the English language.

After a stormy youth in Ireland (during which time, some say, he set fire to his employer's greenhouse – though by other accounts the charge was merely that he opened the windows one frosty night), his considerable talents were recognized and he was recommended to the Royal Botanic Society's garden in Regent's Park, where he became an authority on wild flora. He went on to be awarded a grant to tour other botanic gardens and spent a year in France working as an agent to a large nursery and garden correspondent for *The Times*. Two books followed on French gardens.

He became garden editor for *The Field* and in 1870 *The Wild Garden* was published. In the same year, he founded *The Garden* magazine. Various other books followed. His undoubted masterpiece – with fifteen editions in his lifetime alone – was *The English Flower Garden* of 1883.

Robinson rightly saw much beauty in Britain's native flowers and trees. He favoured the English cottage garden, the wild garden, the rock garden and the alpine garden. In the herbaceous border he recommended that native flora could be extended with hardy naturalized plants.

His greatest bête noire was what he called 'Paxtonism' – bedding out and 'pastry work gardens'. He described bedding-out plants as 'tropical weeds that give a little showy colour for a few months' and the bedding-out gardener as one who tried to 'rival the tile or wallpaper man'. In *The English Flower Garden,* he described coming to London in 1861, when 'Crystal Palace, in its glory, was described by the Press . . . to be the most wonderful instance of modern gardening . . . all the theatrical gardening of Versailles reproduced in Surrey.'

He was shocked to find that the flower garden planting of the day was:

made up of a few kinds of flowers which people were proud to put out in thousands and tens of thousands and these patterns, more or less elaborate, were carried out in every garden save the very poorest cottage garden. It was not easy to get away from all this false and hideous 'art'. The genius of cretinism itself could hardly delight in anything more tasteless or ignoble that the absurd daubs of colour that every summer flare in the neighbourhood of nearly every country house in Western Europe.

And if Robinson hated bedding out and regimentation in the garden, he despised topiary even more. In his view, this was 'the most impudent outrage ever perpetrated on natural beauty in our gardens'. In *The English Flower Garden,* he writes that:

> The Yew Tree in its natural form is of good colour at various seasons; bronzy on some soils in winter, the flowering time, the fruiting time and in the Fall, full of fieldfares seeking food when driven from the North. It is only in old trees that we see its varied charm, always showing the stem so fine in colour; but as most of the gardens of our day only show, in the Yew, hard, dark lines, to give backgrounds, hence many miles of this forest tree in every home county, where all should be free and graceful.

He notes with distaste that 'some attempt has been made to make more popular this outrage to natural form.' He is furious to see endorsement for topiary in the *Observer*. In an article entitled 'Tree Sculpture', the paper had reported that:

> one may see trees – mostly Yew and Box – whose foliage ascends in spirals round their stems, like garlands twisted round so many Maypoles; trees cut into the shape of pillars and surmounted with leafy balls one on top of the other; trees in the form of birds, sitting, standing and flying; trees shaped like pyramids and even trees representing jugs and basins.

He says the work of 'disfiguring' is 'ignoble':

> What right have we to deform things so lovely in form? No cramming of Chinese feet into impossible shoes is half so foolish as the willful and brutal distortion of the beautiful form of trees . . . Topiarian effects appeal only to those blind to the grace and movement of the free, natural form.

Robinson failed to put gardeners off topiary. However, he revolutionized gardens for the twentieth century. The Robinson effect was to explode Victorian pretensions and breathe new life and common sense into a beautiful free style of planting. He had hit the perfect moment and spoke to a new anti-industrial generation – among others, the followers of the Arts and Crafts movement.

Two varieties of the native wood anemone, *Anemone nemorosa*, from a plate in *The Garden*. Robinson's favourite was the pale lilac *A.n.* 'Robinsoniana'.

228

The Arts and Crafts Movement

The late 19th and early 20th centuries

REACTION to the harsh realities of industrialization, shoddy manufactured products and the pretensions of the Victorians led to the flowering of the Arts and Crafts movement in the 1880s. The design philosophy was based on a return to simplicity, truth to materials and the preservation of traditional skills. And although most of its followers were members of the middle-class intelligentsia, or the 'reading classes', the Arts and Crafts movement also carried with it a strong anti-elitist message. It aimed to break down the divisions within society, between the 'fine' and the 'applied' arts and the professional and the amateur. It looked to make a brotherhood of artists.

The effect of the movement was far-reaching, not least in the shaping of modern garden design. It sowed the seeds of the garden that would come to be seen in the future as quintessentially 'English' – a formal structure set off by free, overflowing flower borders. A classic element would be garden architecture of clipped yew hedging, rather than stone, and there was a return to a little light-heartedness, a certain self-deprecating humour in the form of topiary birds, peacocks and the like.

The guiding spirit of the Arts and Crafts movement was John Ruskin (1819– 1900), author, art critic and lecturer, who was known for his high moral tone on the dignity of labour. He promoted the Pre-Raphaelite Brotherhood, which, like the Arts and Crafts movement, was both romantically inclined and actively concerned with social reform.

And the shining light of Arts and Crafts was the redoubtable William Morris (1834–1896). Poet, founder of the Socialist League and the Society for the Protection of Ancient Buildings, he is best known today for the elegant flowing and flowery fabrics and wallpapers and beautifully hand-crafted furniture produced by his company, Morris & Co.

The ideas of the movement spread across Europe and were taken up in America in the architecture of Frank Lloyd Wright and of Greene and Greene. It inspired other movements, including the Aesthetic movement, and guilds such as the Art Workers' Guild. Its ideals reached as far as Japan where the Mingei (Folk Crafts) movement flourished in the 1920s.

'Trellis', a woodblock printed wallpaper created by William Morris in 1864. It was inspired by the trellises in the garden of the Red House.

The Red House

In 1859, in preparation for his marriage to Jane Burden, muse of the Pre-Raphaelites, Morris invited the architect Philip Webb, who shared his ideals, to collaborate with him on the design of the Red House on Bexleyheath. It was Webb's practice, before laying a single brick, to make a careful study of the historic houses of the area, noting the particular stones, bricks and tiles used before seeking out and taking advice from the local traditional craftsmen and builders. He and Morris were united in their determination to give their architecture a sense of place and of time in the local history. They were passionate about preserving the finest traditions of English building, and Webb would later train many young architects to these unshakeable principles.

At the Red House, which was built on the site of an old orchard 'amid the rose-hung lanes of woody Kent', the garden plan was drawn up at the same time as that of the building. Later the Renaissance dictum that the architect should design house and garden as a unified whole was carried to a logical conclusion. The garden paths and walls were made of the same bricks and mortar as the house and the same proportions were scaled up.

The theme was mirrored in fabrics and furnishings, as were the *parterres de broderie* at Versailles, even down to the clothes that the court was required to wear (see pages 83–4). The Arts and Crafts women abandoned their stays and crinolines in favour of flowing medieval-style dress, causing something of a stir in the neighbourhood around the Red House. Morris remarked that when they rode out in his cart in their bright art fabrics the locals looked on them as 'if they were the advance guard of a travelling show'.

As the Pre-Raphaelites sought to achieve a purity in art which, in their view, had been lost since the late fifteenth century, so the Arts and Crafts also looked to medievalism, the Age of Chivalry and the legends of King Arthur. The Tudor garden with its heraldry, sundials and figurative topiary was another source of inspiration. At the Red House, the garden was designed along the lines of a *hortus conclusus*. Morris wanted it 'well fenced from the outer world'.

Georgiana Burne-Jones, who spent a lot of time at the Red House while her husband, Edward Burne-Jones, was, along with Rossetti, helping Morris to design the interior, noted that the garden comprised 'four little square gardens making a big square together, each of the smaller squares having a wattle fence around it, with roses growing thickly'. Another visitor remarked in 1863 that each of the squares 'hedged by sweet briar'

The Arts and Crafts Red House and the well in the garden, designed by Morris and Webb and built by craftsmen with traditional materials in 1859.

had 'its own particular show of flowers'. Lavender-bordered walks were laid out between the gnarled fruit trees of the old orchard.

Morris was a decade ahead of Robinson when he looked to traditional cottage garden plants and simple field flowers, those of the *millefleurs* tapestries and the illustrations from the old herbals, for his garden. These would flow through his wallpapers and fabrics as well in the stained glass windows that were a particular feature of the Arts and Crafts house. Morris and Webb dressed the garden walls luxuriantly with cottage garden climbers and sought out traditional old roses. The borders were filled with tall spires of great mullein (considered by most contemporaries to be a

weed), along with lilies, lavender, jasmine, hollyhocks, rosemary and –
a great favourite – sunflowers.

The cottage idyll

In an article written for *The Commonweal,* the socialist newspaper that
he edited, Morris expressed his delight in the cottage gardens of the
area around his next house, the Elizabethan manor of Kelmscott, in
Oxfordshire. These were 'bright with flowers, the cottages themselves
mostly models of architecture in their way. Above them towers here and
there the architecture proper of days bygone, when every craftsman was
an artist and brought definite intelligence to bear upon his work.'

The cottage, no longer *orné*, was becoming a practical proposition as
a home for the middle classes. The idea of the simple country life was
ever more alluring as an affordable escape from the smog and grime of
the industrial cities. Cottages were easy to come by as machinery and the
Enclosure Acts (which had reached their culmination by 1832) took their
toll on farm labourers, who abandoned their tied cottages as they headed
to the cities to find work.

Country Life, in October 1899, made the point in an article entitled
'Houses for people with hobbies', claiming that for 'men of moderate
means', 'prolonged town life is becoming more and more intolerable every
year', and that those 'who had long yearned for country houses on a small
scale, are beginning to realise their desires . . . some will keep the cottage
as their family home, while others . . . having taken their families for years
to poky and remote and expensive seaside lodgings, have discovered that
it is cheaper, healthier and infinitely more enjoyable to possess themselves
of an accessible house to which they may report for holiday or semi-
holiday purpose.'

The romanticism of simple country life and the garden also flowed
through children's literature, in the works of Lewis Carroll, Beatrix Potter,
Kate Greenaway and Frances Hodgson Burnett. The illustrator Helen
Allingham was the archetypal cottage romanticist, with her watercolours
of thatched cottages with roses round the door and a charming disorder of
hollyhocks and delphiniums peeping over the old garden walls, vegetables
growing among the flowers, fruit trees and topiary (the poor man's
sculpture) all adding up to a picture of rustic delight and fulfilment.

Running parallel with the cottage revival, there were serious concerns
about nature conservation, not least from Morris. He pointed out, in a
lecture on 'The Prospects of Architecture and Civilization' delivered to
the London Institution in 1880, that each new house took away 'a little

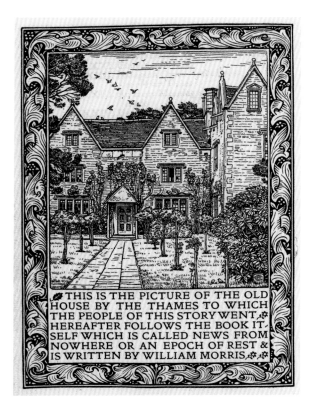

piece of the flowering green sward, a few yards of the teaming hedgerow'. In 1895, the National Trust was founded 'to preserve and protect historic places and spaces – for ever, for everyone'.

Gertrude Jekyll (1843–1932), the greatest plantswoman of her time, wrote in *Wood and Garden* in 1899 that she had 'learnt much from the little cottage gardens that help to make our English waysides the prettiest in the world. One can hardly go into the smallest cottage garden without learning or observing something new. It may be some two plants growing beautifully together by some happy chance, or a pretty tangle of mixed creepers or something that one always thought must have a south wall doing better on an east one.'

Owlpen Manor

One garden that caught Morris's imagination was Owlpen, a Tudor manor house near his Oxfordshire home at Kelmscott. Owlpen was a sleeping beauty, frozen in time since the death of its owner, Thomas Daunt IV, in 1749. The yew hedges were so huge and overgrown that the Victorian poet Charles Algernon Swinburne described it as 'the very finest & highest

ABOVE LEFT The frontispiece for William Morris's *News from Nowhere*, 1892. This illustration by Charles March Gere, engraved by W.H. Hooper, shows Morris's garden at Kelmscott Manor.

ABOVE RIGHT *Spring* by Helen Allingham, a painting of the 1890s: the cottage idyll complete with the poor man's sculpture – topiary.

Owlpen Manor today.

yew parlour in all England'. Avray Tipping wrote in *Country Life* in 1906 that by then it was 'a garden house more than anything else . . . making its brave fight against consuming Time'.

Rodmarton Manor

An Arts and Crafts house and garden that still shines out (though far from being a cottage in size) was Rodmarton Manor in Gloucestershire. In 1931, *Country Life* reported that it was what William Morris 'strenuously preached but never carried out with such completeness . . . Every stone and slate of Rodmarton has been quarried near by, brought to the site in farm carts, and then cut, shaped and laid by local masons.'

Started in 1909, it took twenty years to complete. Not only were works interrupted by the First World War, but also all forms of mechanization were firmly eschewed. The owners, Claud Biddulph, a stockbroker, and his wife, Margaret, took only a wing for themselves. Their large reception rooms were turned over to the village for classes in woodwork, embroidery, weaving and other crafts.

TOPIARY, KNOTS AND PARTERRES

Margaret Biddulph, who had before her marriage trained at Studley Horticultural College for Women, created an outstanding garden in the Arts and Crafts style. This garden was laid out in a formal fashion by her architect, but creatively planted by herself and her head gardener, William Scrubey.

The garden is divided into sections by high brick walls and yew or laurel hedges. A double avenue of pleached limes contrasts with the dark yew. A kitchen garden, a cherry orchard and specimen fruit trees provided for the needs of the house – 'productivity and self-sufficiency' being another key tenet of the Arts and Crafts movement. Mrs Biddulph even ground her own flour. Highlights of the garden include a (then novel) white garden and a 'troughery' of stone sinks, mounted on staddle stones. The garden – which has remained in the Biddulph family – is still known for the magnificent herbaceous borders. Also celebrated is the garden known as 'Topiary', situated by the long terrace the width of the house. Here the wide grass promenade is flanked by a row of box domes and tiered 'wedding cakes', with stepping stones leading into the distance.

Rodmarton Manor today: box domes and square shapes in the garden known as 'Topiary'.

At the manor house of Cleeve Prior, Warwickshire, 'The Twelve Apostles and the Four Evangelists' form a yew arcade with windows. A watercolour drawing by George S. Elgood, from *Some English Gardens* by George S. Elgood and Gertrude Jekyll, 1904.

Lutyens and Jekyll

The most famous partnership of the Arts and Crafts era was that of Gertrude Jekyll and Edwin Lutyens (1869–1944). Early in his career Lutyens made his name with his design for Jekyll's house at Munstead Wood, near Godalming in Surrey. He became noted as much for his domestic architecture as he was for his town plan for New Delhi (which, incidentally, included two life-sized topiary elephants in the viceroy's garden).

Gertrude Jekyll lifted planting schemes into the realm of an art form. Using a wide palette of plants, old favourites and new cultivars, she introduced to gardening the painterly concepts of playing with light effects, drifts of colour and contrasting textures and shapes. Lutyens's precise, hard-edged architecture, constructed out of the traditional materials of brick and stone and built by craftsmen in the best Arts and Crafts style, was set off and softened by Jekyll's graceful, impressionistic waves of plants.

From cottage to castle

It was only a small step from the rustic cottage to the even more romantic crumbling medieval castle. A landmark design was dreamt up by Robert Lorimer (1864–1929), future Arts and Crafts architect, when he was only sixteen. Robert's father, James Lorimer, was a professor at Edinburgh University, and the family spent their holidays at Kellie Castle in Fife. The teenage Robert envisaged the garden at Kellie Castle as a sanctuary, 'a chamber roofed by heaven'. He divided the space into different rooms, on a human scale, with mown grass, espalier apples and high box hedging. Robert's interest in topiary was already apparent as he put in a small garden with yew hedges 'shaped like birds'. His landmark planting was lavish and generous and would be a key to the future of garden design. *Country Life* described the roses as breaking like a 'wave over the summer garden'. Gertrude Jekyll spoke of the single hollyhocks that were planted in 'big free groups'.

In 1891, his first commission as a newly qualified architect was to restore Earlshall Castle, also in Fife, and create a new garden. As at Kellie, Lorimer allowed the park to come up to the castle walls on the windward

Lavish borders at Kellie Castle, designed by Robert Lorimer. A watercolour drawing by George S. Elgood, from *Some English Gardens*.

At Earlshall Castle, Fife, Robert Lorimer's free-standing yews form a St Andrew's Cross.

side and made a series of enclosed gardens on the leeward. He devised a pattern of small bays and straight walks, repairing the old walls where he could and replacing them with tall clipped yew or holly hedges where this was impossible.

As at Kellie, the planting was luxuriant and free. Rambling roses scrambled over the castle walls, spring bulbs were encouraged to naturalize into carpets under the trees, the herbaceous borders were spectacular and in the kitchen garden flowers were planted among the vegetables. Lorimer had pioneered a style of offsetting the formal with the wild that was to become a major trend in gardening.

He again broke new ground when he abandoned his planned classic parterre. The head gardener at Earlshall had the luck to be offered good money (£5 a tree) to remove some mature yews from a neighbour's garden, and Lorimer had the thirty-six yews collected by the gardener planted into the lawn in front of the castle in a saltire – the heraldic diagonal cross of St Andrew.

Gertude Jekyll was to write in *Some English Gardens* (1904) that Robert and his brother, John Henry Lorimer, were 'artists of the finest faculty'. In later life, Robert was to specialize in Scottish baronial architecture. He also brought the Glasgow School of Art to the Arts and Craft Exhibition in London's Regent Street in 1896.

Great Dixter

Word of the topiary lawn at Elvaston Castle (see pages 219–21) soon spread in gardening circles, and Nathaniel Lloyd, setting out to plan his garden in Sussex, asked Lutyens to include space for a topiary lawn of this type. In 1909, Lloyd (1867–1933) had retired from the printing business and had purchased Dixter, a medieval manor house with extensive land, farm buildings and the remains of a moat, but all so fallen down that it had been up for sale without any takers for a decade.

Lutyens, having seamlessly attached a rescued hall house to the old manor (now renamed 'Great' Dixter), pencilled in the outline of the garden with formal long straight walks and designed vistas. Nathaniel Lloyd – who later studied under Lutyens to became a Fellow of the Royal Institute of British Architects – took a particular interest in the tall architectural yew hedges that made the divisions, arches and entrances, saying that 'without enclosure, the feelings of protection, of peacefulness and of repose are altogether lacking.'

While his wife, Daisy, created the Robinsonian wild meadows and herbaceous borders which their son Christopher would later make famous, Nathaniel Lloyd put in the evergreen structure – including some very large topiary birds.

The topiary lawn at Great Dixter, in Sussex.

OVERLEAF The famous peacocks at Great Dixter, planted by Nathaniel Lloyd.

'Cutbush's Cut Bushes'. By the turn of the century topiary was making a grand comeback. Herbert James Cutbush's topiary nursery in Highgate had a royal warrant from King Edward VII and exhibited at shows including the RHS Chelsea Flower Show of 1913.

By 1925 his enthusiasm for topiary was such that he was inspired to write *Garden Craftsmanship in Yew and Box,* a practical work based on his experience of establishing yew and box topiary. He explained that he felt that the book would be useful, 'as there was no reliable treatise dealing with these matters and the art of topiary is jealously guarded by the professional gardener.' The book particularly enraged William Robinson, who described it as 'the poorest book that so far has disgraced the garden', adding that his 'vexation soon turned to pity that an artist, in any shape, should call his work, as shown in this book, art.'

However, despite Robinson's best efforts to discourage it, topiary was quietly having a renaissance. The church architect John Dando Sedding (1838–1891), part of the Morris clique (his office was next door to Morris & Co. in Oxford Street), made a spirited response to Robinson's views. In *Garden Craft Old and New* in 1891, he wrote defiantly:

It may be true, as I believe it is, that the natural form of a tree is the most beautiful possible for that tree, but it may happen that we do not want the most beautiful form, but one of our own designing, and expressive of our ingenuity . . .

I have no more scruple in using the scissors upon a tree or shrub where trimness is desirable, than I have in mowing the turf of the lawn that once represented a virgin world . . . And I would even introduce bizarreries on the principle of not leaving all that is wild and odd to Nature outside of the garden-paling; and in the formal part of the garden my yews should take the shape of pyramids or peacocks or cocked hats or ramping lions in Lincoln-green, or any other conceit I had a mind to, which vegetable sculpture can take.

Hidcote Manor

It was also in 1909 that Lawrence Johnston started to create his garden at Hidcote Manor, Gloucestershire. As at Great Dixter, Hidcote was divided by carefully judged axes into considered enclosures. Avray Tipping, Architectural Editor of *Country Life,* described the long Italianate prospects of Hidcote as composed of 'big structural lines' which give 'outlook and extent' and which stretch the length and width of the garden. On each side of these great walkways were 'adjuncts and dependencies', 'the small enclosures, differently treated and differently furnished, just as in a great house a central gallery, of which the pillared divisions do not hinder the end to end vista, may have, opening from it, a set of cabinets and closets for the display of duly selected and ordered objects of art and vertu'.

Johnston (1871–1958), an American born in Paris of wealthy parents (and related to two American presidents), had come to England with his mother, Gertrude Winthrop, in the early 1890s. After taking his degree at Trinity College, Cambridge, he went on to take British citizenship, enlist for the Boer War and fight in the First World War. Meanwhile, in 1907, Mrs Winthrop, who had hopes of turning her son into a country squire, had bought Hidcote, a seventeenth-century manor with 280 acres of land, a stone-built farmhouse and several cottages, at Chipping Camden, in the Cotswolds.

Hidcote had the additional draw for both of them of being within striking distance of an elite coterie at the Worcestershire village of Broadway. It was here that Johnston took tea, played tennis and cricket, and imbibed garden talk in the golden afternoons of the Edwardian era. Among the group was Alfred Parsons, the artist (and friend of William Robinson) who had designed for Henry James the garden at Lamb House, in Rye.

Johnston left no written records of the garden at Hidcote, but Vita Sackville-West, poet, novelist and garden-maker, who admired the garden (and fought hard later to get the National Trust to take it on), gave a picture of Hidcote as she saw it in 1949, the year after Johnston had left it and moved to the South of France.

She recognized that the garden's roots lay within the Arts and Crafts discipline, wondering whether 'it would be misleading to call it a cottage garden on the most glorified scale?' She pointed out that:

Clipped birds at Hidcote Manor,
described by Vita Sackville-West as
being in the cottage garden tradition
of 'smug broody hens, bumpy doves
and coy peacocks'.

. . . it did resemble a cottage garden, or, rather a series of cottage
gardens, in so far as the plants grow in a jumble, flowering shrubs
mingled with roses, herbaceous plants with bulbous subjects,
climbers scrambling over hedges, seedlings coming up wherever
they . . . sow themselves.

There is just enough topiary to carry out the cottage garden idea.
The topiary at Hidcote is in the country tradition of smug broody
hens, bumpy doves and coy peacocks twisting a fat neck towards a
fatter tail. It resembles all that our cottagers have done ever since the
Romans first came to Britain and cut our native Yew and Box with
their sharp shears . . . Major Johnston has used the old tradition
with taste and restraint and supplemented it with some arches of a
serene architectural value.

Nor must I forget the quincunx of pleached Hornbeam . . .
It gives a sudden little touch of France to this very English garden.
Neat and box-like, standing on flawlessly straight trunks, it has
always been so perfectly clipped and trained that not a leaf of it is
out of place.

Yew was also carved into columns, arches, porticoes and aerial hedges, while the clipped yew pillars in the Pillar Garden echoed the uprights of the sentinel cypresses of the Italian landscape. The carefree-looking borders were framed with military precision by sharply clipped box edging.

Vita described the great yew hedges, the 'tall, living barriers' which gave a feeling of 'luxuriance and secrecy', the 'harlequin of a hedge with five different things in it; Yew, Box, Holly, Beech and Hornbeam' which composed 'a green and black tartan', and the mixed hedge of yew and box which was 'an attractive combination with its two shades of green'. While the hedges of copper beech 'entirely redeem the Copper Beech from its suburban associations, as they may not inaptly be compared to an Isfahan carpet, with their depths of rose-madder and violet, and the tips of young growth as sanguine as a garden seen against the light.'[1]

Johnston also had a gifted planting ally in the socialite garden designer Norah Lindsay (1873–1948), who had a great natural flair for design and an unfailing eye for plant combinations. Her garden at Sutton Courtenay, in Oxfordshire, was freer and more daring than even Gertrude Jekyll could have conceived. The queen of (seeming) laissez-faire, she claimed in an article in

Norah Lindsay's astonishingly modern planting at Sutton Courtenay, Oxfordshire, captured by *Country Life*.

[1] From an article by Vita Sackville-West in the *Journal* of the Royal Horticultural Society, vol. LXXXIV, part II, November 1949.

The ancient walls of Cothay Manor, Somerset, set off an elegant Arts and Crafts cottage garden style of planting.

Country Life that 'in a garden where labour is scarce and the soil beneficent, all manner of tiny seedlings get overlooked and behold! A handsome clump has established itself in the most unlikely position, claiming squatter's rights and in nine cases out of ten succeeding in establishing its claim.'

Johnston's own interest in plants was so great that he sponsored and even joined (albeit accompanied by chauffeur and valet) some historic plant finding expeditions – to South Africa for Collingwood 'Cherry' Ingram and for George Forrest to Yunnan in south-west China. He even climbed Kilimanjaro and wrote a paper on 'Some Flowering Plants of Kilimanjaro'.

At Hidcote, each enclosure had a different story to tell and there were peaceful unadorned intervals between them. Little gardens off the axes included specialist areas like the Phlox Garden, the Fuchsia Garden and Mrs Winthrop's Garden (which had a yellow and blue theme). The architecture moved from rectangles to the round Circle and Bathing Pool gardens. The exciting Red Borders were described by Norah Lindsay's daughter, Nancy, as 'aflame with the vermilion and crimson and gold of oriental poppies, and African pokers, scarlet musk and orange Tiger Lily, Day Lily and Crown Imperials, amidst pyramids of copper-purple berberis, feathery clumps of the silver, russet and jade fox grass against a towering dark yew hedge'.

Cothay Manor

Many notable gardens were made during this period. Of particular interest is the garden created, in the 1920s, by Colonel Reginald Cooper (1885–1965) at the medieval Cothay Manor in Somerset.

Picking up on the medieval theme popular with the Arts and Crafts gardeners, Colonel Cooper created the silver and white Green Knight Garden, the Bishop's Room and the Walk of the Unicorn.

The Walk of the Unicorn, one of the many themed garden rooms at Cothay Manor.

Sissinghurst Castle

In 1930, Vita Sackville West (1892–1962), who had been brought up in the vast palace of Knole at Sevenoaks, and Harold Nicolson, diplomat and author, bought Sissinghurst Castle. Grandees in every area of their lives, including gardening, the Nicolsons were affiliated to the Bloomsbury group. Sissinghurst was a poetic ruin of a Tudor manor set in beautiful country in the Weald of Kent.

Harold took charge of the garden architecture and, despite the challenges of an irregular site, he held firmly to his belief that 'a garden scheme should have a backbone – a central idea beautifully phrased – and every wall, path, stone and flower bed has . . . a relative value to the central idea.' Looking out from the top of the Tower, and with the aid of lines and pegs and his sons waving flags at the end of vistas, he devised a scheme where the Lime Walk along the south side flowed into the Nuttery and the Herb Garden, while the outline of the Moat Walk (which set off at an angle) was cleverly blurred with plantings. The Rondel and the Rose Garden lead into the Yew Walk, a dark, narrow path of high yews that brings you to the light and airy White Garden.

Vita, meanwhile, was turning the borders at Sissinghurst into masterpieces of planting. She mixed flowering shrubs among roses and

A bird's-eye view of the White Garden from the Tower – the vantage point from which Harold Nicolson planned the layout of the garden.

bulbs among herbaceous plants, skilfully playing with kaleidoscopes of colour, shape and texture. Her single-colour and themed gardens became famous – from the cool White Garden set off with silver leaves to the scorching reds and oranges of the Cottage Garden with a central copper fading to verdigris surrounded by four sentinel yews. Her hundreds of roses were legendary, tumbling over walls and tied into frames. 'Why', she asked, 'plant one lily when six hundred will do?'

In 1937 Harold wrote to Vita at Sissinghurst with some jubilation, summing up their achievement, saying that they had got what they wanted to get, 'a perfect proportion between the classical and the romantic, between the element of expectation and the element of surprise. Thus the main axes are terminated in a way to satisfy expectation, yet they are in themselves so tricky they also cause surprise but the point of the garden

TOPIARY, KNOTS AND PARTERRES

will not be apparent until the hedges have grown up . . . But it is lovely, lovely, lovely – and you must be pleased with your work.'

One hopes that she was pleased, as the result of their combined talents would be to make Sissinghurst one of the most admired, and most influential, gardens of the twentieth century. Part of the charm of the flamboyant borders is that they are set against the plain dark architecture of Harold's topiary framework. The allure lies in the contrast – the tightly disciplined clipped hedges and the artistic extravagance, the nonchalance, a throwaway grace that gives the borders the appearance of a delightful accident. But as Vita perceptively observed – with regard to Hidcote but clearly speaking from her own experience – this 'haphazard luxuriance' was, 'of course, neither "hap" nor "hazard" at all'.

Arum lilies in Vita Sackville-West's much loved and copied parterre, the White Garden at Sissinghurst.

Summing Up

Into the 21st century

FROM THE VANTAGE POINT of the twenty-first century we are in a fine position to survey the full spectrum of topiary, knots and parterres through history. They come in many guises, from the grand and imposing to the humble and folksy, as well as, occasionally, the ludicrous. Many of the gardens mentioned in this book (and so many more that, regrettably, have had to be left out) are still in existence, with Levens Hall, Cumbria, the undisputed and queenly oldest. The garden is a rare survivor, laid out in the 1690s, overlooked by the eighteenth-century landscapers and beautifully maintained, without a break, by a succession of only ten gardeners over more than three centuries.

Modern restorations have unveiled the gardens of the masters of the Italian Renaissance and the fabled work of Le Nôtre, as well as many fascinating smaller gardens. Just one example is Kenilworth Castle in Warwickshire – the garden created at crippling cost by Sir Robert Dudley in a hopeless quest to woo his queen, Elizabeth I (another is Hatfield House, her childhood home). Many of the German princely gardens are now public parks – not least Princess Sophia's historic baroque garden at Herrenhausen. William and Mary's Privy Garden at Hampton Court and the Dutch palace of Het Loo are now in such authentic and mint condition that they look as if they were created yesterday.

The twentieth century saw a joyful resurgence of the topiary peacock and other such conceits, the arrival of the Japanese school of minimalism, the cult of the venerable sagging hedge, cloud pruning and the emergence of the cool crisp lines of modernism. German perennial planting, juxtaposed with sharply cut linear hedges, provides a clever solution to the twentieth-century requirements of high style, low maintenance, attention to the environment and to labour costs. Of late, a new type of formality that has emerged among designers and architects in landscape involves blankets of bespoke wild-looking 'prairie planting' set off by large-scale sculptural topiary.

The world's most venerated topiary garden at Levens Hall, Cumbria, still going strong after three hundred years.

Marqueyssac

One of the most surprising topiary gardens is at the Château de Marqueyssac in the Perigord region of France. Although it looks to be at the absolute cutting edge of today's design it was actually created in the nineteenth century, and not by a great architect, nor by a famous horticulturist,but by a retired local lawyer, Julien de Cerval. He devoted his latter years to creating the garden in his own way, maximizing the eagle's nest situation high in the mountains, with panoramic views over the Dordogne river. The garden is uncompromising, with barely a flower to be seen; nevertheless, it is now the most visited garden in the Périgord.

When Julien de Cerval arrived in 1861, the garden, which had been put in by Bertrand Vernet de Marqueyssac, Counsellor to Louis XIV, and barely changed in the intervening centuries, was in the classic Renaissance style. De Cerval swept it all away before planting one hundred and fifty *thousand* box trees. These were clipped into smooth sculptural and organic shapes like sea-worn boulders, reflecting the hills and dales of the surrounding mountains.

At Marqueyssac in the Dordogne, modernist organic abstract topiary, dating from the nineteenth century, reflects the curves of the surrounding mountains.

TOPIARY, KNOTS AND PARTERRES

Wherever you stand in the garden the perspective of the topiary changes, as each individual shape is different from all the others. To give a feeling of scale, Julien de Cerval added parasol pines to one side, and also a Judas tree and cypresses. He carpeted the existing holm oak woods with sheets of cyclamen brought in from Naples. And, as he planned to write poetry in his retirement, he put up a little stone hut, L'Asile du Poète.

Tulcán Cemetery, Ecuador

Another wonder among topiary gardens is in a cemetery on a hill close to the otherwise uneventful trading city of Tulcán, the highest city in Ecuador, on the border with Colombia.

The topiary was the creation of José María Franco Guerrero, head of the municipality of Tulcán parks, who was in charge of the new town cemetery when it opened in 1932. As is the custom in cemeteries, he planted the traditional trees of mourning, the 'graveyard' cypress, *Cupressus sempervirens* – hundreds of them, in straight lines over the new and bare 8-acre site.

The famous monumental topiary at the Tulcán Cemetery, Ecuador, started in the 1930s by the enterprising and imaginative head of parks.

The cypresses did well in the calcareous soil. We do not know how the idea came to him to start clipping, but, before long, interesting topiaries along the lines of pre-Columbian, Augustinian and Arabic figures began to appear. The visitors to the cemetery were delighted with his work, and so he continued.

There are now some three hundred immaculately clipped topiaries of animals, formalized birds – including parrots – monkeys, turtles, even a giant armadillo. In bas-relief on big hedges are cornucopias and more birds and symbols. There are many hugely impressive, monolithic giant heads and different architectural shapes, as well as arches and fancy hedging of every type.

The cemetery, now an international tourist destination, was declared to be a State Cultural Heritage Site and a Site of National Interest in 1984. When José María Franco Guerrero died the following year, the epitaph on his grave at the cemetery was: 'In Tulcán, [is] a cemetery so beautiful that it invites one to die!' His five sons have taken over the work of keeping up his legacy.

Château de Villandry, Loire Valley

The Château de Villandry in the Loire Valley has the most famous potager in the world. This forms only a small part of a less famous but magnificent and extensive series of French Renaissance parterres. Built in 1532 by François I's minister of finance, it had fallen into serious decline by 1906, when it was bought by Joachim Carvallo, a Spanish doctor, and Anne Coleman, his American heiress wife.

The Napoleonic land register, maps and Jacques Androuet du Cerceau's sixteenth-century *Les Plus Excellents Bâtiments de France* gave Carvallo the clues he needed to tackle the garden's restoration. From the height of the belvedere, the lacework of knots and parterres, each with a different theme, stretches almost as far as the eye can see. Carvallo himself designed the Garden of Music, with its parterre of box hedges clipped into musical symbols. Other parterres offer fans, butterflies, clubs, spades and scrolls; and in the Salon of Love there are hearts.

The potager follows the old traditions set by the medieval monks, who liked to plant their vegetable gardens in geometric patterns, so each square bed has a different pattern and is planted largely in a single colour –

Dr Joachim Carvallo's Garden of Music at the restored Renaissance garden at the Château de Villandry. The triangles represent lyres and there are harp shapes in the corners of the parterres.

OPPOSITE ABOVE Harvey S. Ladew's
hunting scene at Ladew Gardens,
Maryland, designed in the Roaring
Twenties.
OPPOSITE BELOW Characters from
a remarkable topiary interpretation
of Georges Seurat's painting
*A Sunday Afternoon on the Island
of La Grande Jatte* at the Old Deaf
School, Columbus, Ohio.

ornamental pink cabbages in one, blue leeks in the next, with some of the
beds around the edge filled with flowers.

Seen from above, the potager is a chequer-board of different-coloured
squares. Standard roses, symbol of the Virgin, are grown among the
vegetables, as they would have been by the monks for Marian worship
and for decorating the church. Local tradition has it that the lines of roses
represent the monks digging.

Figurative topiary

Some of the most famous examples of figurative topiary are in America.
One such is the celebrated hunting scene at Ladew Topiary Gardens, in
Maryland, designed by the playboy Harvey S. Ladew. He was born in New
York in 1887 to a life of ease, and, after serving in the First World War
as a liaison officer, he settled down to pursuing his passions – travelling,
partying, art and, above all, fox hunting. He even set a record by riding
to hounds on both sides of the Atlantic within seventy-two hours. *Tatler*
magazine summed him up as a 'gardener, sporting art patron and good
companion'. He must indeed have been a good companion, as counted
among his friends were Charlie Chaplin, Somerset Maugham, Clark
Gable, Colette, Noel Coward, T.E. Lawrence and Cole Porter.

In 1929 he bought Pleasant Valley Farm in Monkton, Maryland, right
next to the Elkridge-Harford Hunt Club. He had been greatly impressed
by the sight of a topiarized hunt, with fox and hounds in full cry, on the
top of a tall yew hedge surrounding an estate in England. He declared
at the time that he could 'never be happy if he could not reproduce this
marvellous piece of living sculpture in his garden'.

He went on to divide his derelict farm into fifteen exquisite garden
rooms, each themed on a single colour or for a single season – quite
the latest thing at the time in the cosmopolitan gardening world of the
Roaring Twenties. With admirable determination, he went about his
topiary single-handed, clipping over one hundred specimens. As well
as his fox and hounds, he crafted topiary swans on top of the hedge,
Churchill's top hat, a Chinese junk complete with sails, and a giraffe, as
well as abstract architectural shapes. Perhaps he did not take himself too
seriously, as he also converted a London theatre ticket booth, painted
pink, into a tea house – and there is a statue of Adam taking the apple
from Eve while holding two more behind his back.

Another famous American garden is the topiary park at the Old Deaf
School in Columbus, Ohio. When the school moved in 1953, its grounds
were opened as a public park. This is now the setting for a complete

topiary rendering of Seurat's picnic scene, *A Sunday Afternoon on the Island of La Grande Jatte*.

The idea came to an engineer and sculptor, James Mason, in 1978, while he was working for the Columbus Recreation and Parks Department, teaching at the Cultural Arts Center. He made bronze armatures for the figures (some of which are twelve feet tall). Different varieties of yew were trained to grow through and then clipped into shape.

In Longwood Gardens, Pennsylvania, there is another fine topiary garden, with smartly clipped animals, begun in 1936. The Green Animals Topiary Garden in Portsmouth, Rhode Island, has Thomas Brayton's extraordinary menagerie of life-sized topiary animals, started in the nineteenth century.

In Europe, also, you never know when you might come across a clipped topiary surprise. It could be on top of a hedge or by the gate, and sometimes you will come across a yew train or a boxwood car in a front garden. But for a really good show, look to the USA.

The resurgence of the maze

In the 1980s (the age of the Rubik Cube), a new generation of maze-makers began to produce complicated mathematical designs. Invention flowered in mirror mazes, landscape mazes, Japanese panel mazes, 'dark rides' and 'magic mansions'. There are mazes that lead down into grottoes and through underground passages; mazes with bridges, to provide a bird's-eye view for reorientation; inflatable mazes in funfairs; and – just to add to the disorientation – mazes with floors that revolve.

Adrian Fisher is a leader in the field of maze makers, with six entries in the *Guinness Book of Records*. He made history in 1993 with Don Frantz, a director of Walt Disney World, when together they invented the maize – or corn – maze in the shape of a giant stegosaurus, in Pennsylvania. Maize mazes have the mystical attraction of crop circles and appear in myriad shapes and forms in theme parks worldwide. Given sufficient land and a tractor, they can cover vast areas; they are even sometimes designed with the aid of GPS – Global Positioning Satellites.

However, despite competition, the hedge maze continues to hold its own. Two of the modern greats are at Longleat and Blenheim – gardens that have appeared in this book in various different guises and now carry on intrepidly as theme parks. At Longleat, in 1975, the future Marquess of Bath appointed a twenty-five-year-old prodigy called Greg Bright to make the largest hedge maze in the world – two miles of twisting paths, made up of sixteen thousand English yews, and with

six bridges to cross (for that important third dimension), leading to the central observation tower.

Adrian Fisher's Marlborough Maze at Blenheim celebrates the 1st Duke's triumph at the Battle of Blenheim in 1704. From the three bridges within the maze, the word 'Blenheim' can be seen spelled out in giant topiary letters around the centre, a topiary in the shape of the hub of a wheel of a cannon. Emanating from this are the artefacts of war recreated in topiary – flowing banners, trumpets, piles of cannon balls and spears. (Perhaps it is a relief for visitors to know that Google Earth is at hand on the mobile to help them find their way out if they get stuck.)

A detail of the Marlborough Maze at Blenheim Palace, showing the central wheel hub with the word 'Blenheim' spelled out in topiary.

The Renaissance revival. A classic terrace in England's most Italianate garden, at Iford Manor, Bradford-on-Avon.

The Italianate gardens of the early twentieth century

In the early twentieth century some remarkable gardens were created by a group of British architects and garden designers who were influenced by the Italian Renaissance, but scaled down the gardens to suit the British countryside and climate. Among them the most notable for topiary were Harold Peto, Bertram Clough Williams-Ellis and Russell Page.

Iford Manor in Wiltshire is one of the most romantic – and possibly the most genuinely Italianate – of twentieth-century English gardens. Harold Ainsworth Peto (1854–1933; his father was the builder who put up Nelson's Column in Trafalgar Square) retired early from the successful architectural practice of Ernest George and Peto (where Lutyens trained) and took to travel, collecting antiquities and garden design.

In 1899 he bought Iford, an elegant Elizabethan manor house with a Georgian façade. It was on a steeply wooded hillside which lent itself to theatrical Italianate garden terraces and flights of steps and – a key feature – offered from the top panoramic views out into the countryside

TOPIARY, KNOTS AND PARTERRES

across the river valley. Here, on the Great Terrace, he placed a loggia in the Tuscan style, with a colonnade supported by columns of pink Verona marble. Throughout the garden he designed places for his collection of sarcophagi, capitals, wellheads and columns and other treasures collected on his travels.

An essential green architecture of juniper, cypress and yew hedging, small parterres and sculptural clipped yew provides a framework, softened with roses scrambling over pergolas, delicate cherries and magnolias and masses of *Wisteria sinensis.*

Russell Page

Russell Page (1906–1985) was probably the most talented, and certainly the most influential, garden designer of the mid-twentieth century. He worked across the globe designing great parks and small gardens for European royalty and the beau monde in general. And he was author of possibly the most engaging garden design book ever written, *The Education of a Gardener* (1962).

Harold Peto's Roman columns originally framed a pair of yew cubes, but are now sympathetically clipped into the shape of the six hills of Siena with a cross at the top, symbolizing the ancient crest of the current owners.

TOPIARY, KNOTS AND PARTERRES

Sometimes described as a formalist in an informal age, Russell Page set the gardening tone in post-war Europe. This was a time when gardens were becomingly particularly shapeless and suburban, but he dismissed the arguments for and against 'formal' and 'informal', stating firmly that, whichever way you wanted to go, a garden needed a framework and declaring his passion for gardens with 'clear lines of composition' and 'good bones'. Like the great Renaissance architect Leon Battista Alberti, Page worked in patterns of simple squares, circles and rectangles. He enjoyed bringing in 'flavours of the past' as well as 'the geometry of the Renaissance, the secret feel of the medieval and cloister, the use of Arts and Crafts sequence garden rooms'.

The Russell Page parterre at Villa Silvio Pellico, near Turin, with hallmark geometry and pared down 'flavours of the past'.

The Japanese influence

Like many garden designers, Page was especially impressed by the garden art of Japan. He noted how a few years of neglect would reduce most gardens to a skeleton, yet Japanese artists, 'working with a few stones and sand four hundred years ago, achieved strangely lasting compositions.'

In 1853, Japan finally opened its doors to the West. *Japonisme* spread like wildfire, igniting the imaginations of – not least – the artists of the day. The prints of the exquisite seventeenth- and eighteenth-century *ukiyo-e* woodcuts by Japanese masters inspired Pierre Bonnard and Édouard Vuillard to take off-slant angles and perspectives and describe themselves as 'Nabis' – 'prophets of a new art'. Toulouse Lautrec adopted the theatrical facial expressions found in Kabuki theatre prints. Claude Monet went on to make at his home at Giverny in Normandy the celebrated water lily garden with the Japanese bridge. There was a gold rush among plant hunters for Japanese flora.

In Japan, gardening is seen as an art form on an equal footing with drama, painting or poetry. The arrangement of the garden is charged with cultural meaning, Shinto (the way of the gods) and Buddhist spirituality. Asymmetric and non-geometric forms are favoured. Symbolism lies in the vertical (*ten*, or heaven) and the horizontal (*chi*, or earth). The diagonal is *jin*, or man, with his feet in clay and eyes cast towards heaven. The simplicity, the minimalism and *feng shui*, the propitious placing of the stones, rocks, water and trees, are fundamental. All this was to have a lasting effect on garden design in the West.

Pruning is approached with much care and great skill. Trees (*niwaki*) are given formative pruning to capture and distil their intrinsic character. The trunks might be trained to bend to one side or to have double or multiple stems. Sometimes they are planted at an angle, or given a kink – as if hit by lightning – or restricted to a single branch on one side

An example of the influential Japanese style at the tea garden at Shofuen, Japan. Low-lying island shapes of topiary sculpted round large stones make a contemplative picture composed of a few carefully chosen elements.

only. The tops might be clipped into balls or 'steps'. To produce a good 'mophead' shape on a too-upright tree, branches are tied to splints.

As ancient rocks and *sabi* (stones with the patina of age) are treasured, so are trees. Sometimes they are 'aged' and weighed down to sag to give them a venerable appearance.

In imitation of this, in the West the ageing may be carried even further. A nearly instant billowing cloud hedge is sometimes created by planting yew or suitable shrubs out of line and, once they are established, carving into them with chainsaws. They look surprisingly authentic (at least in Western eyes) once they have put on more leaf.

The new traditionalists – Jacques Wirtz and a geometry of greens

The Japanese influence can be clearly seen in the simplicity and clarity of the work of the Belgian designer Jacques Wirtz (b.1924). His breakthrough came in 1970, when he won the competition to design the Belgian Pavilion for the Osako Expo. He was to set a garden design style which provided an elegant structure using a limited palette of repetitive patterns of grasses,

sculptural evergreens sometimes clipped into geometric shapes or planted as zigzag hedges, and trees which, alongside reflective water, were designed to complement the landscape and flow with it while being highly controlled.

He is quoted as saying that 'if a garden is not beautiful in winter, it is not a beautiful garden.' His partnership with his sons, Peter and Martin, Wirtz International, has an impressive portfolio which includes such flagship designs as the Carousel Garden – the park that links the Louvre with the Tuileries, originally designed by Le Nôtre – and Jubilee Park in London's Canary Wharf.

One of the most photographed of all his gardens, however, is that of his own home, a gardener's cottage on an eighteenth-century estate near Antwerp. He made garden history when, faced with a hedge that was on its last legs, rather than resorting to the normal practice of grubbing it out and starting afresh, he cut into the existing hedge and let it rejuvenate into soft blowsy mounds. This started – or at the very least accelerated – a fashion in Europe for the 'cloud hedge'. Of course cloudy hedges had always existed in old, untended gardens but never before had they been seen as a design statement.

Jacques Wirtz was possibly the first designer to make a sagging hedge into a design statement, when he clipped his own hedge – at his home near Antwerp – into billowing, cloud-shaped topiary.

OVERLEAF Clean lines and contrasting soft and hard textures of grasses and clipped hedging in the Lynn Garden, Ascott House, Buckinghamshire, designed by Wirtz International.

German perennial planting

One of the most exciting steps forward in wild planting style, following William Robinson's lead, was taken by German nurseryman Karl Foerster (1874–1970). In 1903, in his nursery in Berlin, he set out to reduce and refine his stock into those perennials that met his practical criteria of being beautiful, hardy, disease-resistant and long-lived. Even in winter, they should be sturdy, look good when massed together and need little maintenance. He focused on clumping grasses, an underused genus at the time, and, for example, was responsible for discovering and nurturing the now very popular feather reed grass, *Calamagrostis acutiflora* 'Karl Foerster'. The New German Style, a highly skilled form of meadow-style planting, particularly suitable to large spaces like parks, was developed.

The great Dutch landscape gardener Mien Ruys (1904–1999) did much to publicize Foerster's ideas. Her gardens set the style of using easy-going perennials and grasses in architectural clumps within a framework of clipped green architecture. From this evolved the 'Dutch Wave' among a group of designers and nurserymen that included Rob Leopold, Ton ter Linden, Henk Gerritsen, and – most famous of all – Piet Oudolf.

Piet Oudolf, a designer with a lifetime's grounding as a nurseryman, is quoted as saying that while his inspiration is nature, he has no desire to copy it, only to 'recreate the emotion'. The selected perennials are chosen

A geometric design of reflective water, yew columns and soft grasses designed by Mien Ruys.

and bred to perform a slow-burn succession of flowering, climaxing in late summer and having a beautiful frosted outline lit by low sunlight in their winter sleep. Once established they only need cutting down once a year, at the very end of winter, when they are ready to spring forth again for a repeat performance in spring.

Oudolf's works include several within the modern urban frame of the American city. Examples are the Lurie Garden in Chicago's Millennium Park and New York's High Line, one and a half miles of disused railway, now bordered with masses of perennials that provide an elegant, practical and low-cost solution to filling the space, greening the city, providing habitat for wildlife and brightening the day for pedestrians.

In the garden he designed at Scampston Hall in Yorkshire, Oudolf makes a play between the breezy forms of the soft grasses and the hard forms of sharp topiary – one parterre is composed of grasses and its counterpart is clipped hedging. It is 'the contrast and the tension between the two', he says, that fascinates him.

Piet Oudolf's own garden at Hummelo in the Netherlands. Wavy hedges and shaggy yew columns add structure and contrast to a mass planting of perennials.

In the garden created by Tom Stuart-Smith at Broughton Grange, in Oxfordshire, a rich carpet of perennials is defined by an angular pool and topiary punctuation.

The celebrated English garden designer Tom Stuart-Smith creates perennial meadows letting on to the wider landscape. They overflow with a sumptuous tapestry of colour, fade to a stark winter skeleton and are beautifully set off by the formality of topiary.

Across the Atlantic, landscape architects James van Sweden and Wolfgang Oehme pioneered the New American garden style of prairie planting in the 1960s. Their work on the gardens of many public buildings, embassies, universities and private homes, most notably in

Washington and New York, was highly influential. Their aim was to abolish the ubiquitous suburban lawn in favour of their interpretation of the wild beauty of the prairie. 'Think big,' van Sweden was reported as saying. 'Think huge leaves, enormous grasses and flowers big as dinner plates. The worst thing you can do is be ditsy.'[1]

[1] *Washington Post*, 1998

TOPIARY, KNOTS AND PARTERRES

The linear hedge

A trend among designers to give form and definition to 'wild' planting is the tightly clipped linear hedge. This can be like a silhouette against the grasses, offering solidity and contrast to the ephemeral forms. A popular conceit is to give it a freehand look, like a pencil line.

A 'pencil line' linear hedge among waving grasses at Le Jardin Plume, in Normandy.

Revelry in geometry

Ludwig Gerns, a Hanoverian born in 1948, creates an interesting imbalance in his gardens, with an asymmetrical tableau of hard and soft – tightly clipped box and yew hedging, contrasted with precision-cut angles and crescents in polished granite, glass and stainless steel. It is a revelry in geometry inspired by Russian early abstract artist Wassily Kandinsky (1886–1944).

Maximal minimalism

Another designer inspired by both Japanese gardens and abstract art is the architect and garden designer Christopher Bradley-Hole, author of *The Minimalist Garden* (1999) and *Making the Modern Garden* (2007). In 2013 he won a gold medal at the Chelsea Flower Show for a garden of asymmetrically placed clipped blocks of yew, box and hornbeam. Whereas the minimal is usually about 'form following function' and 'paring down to the essential', this garden is tightly packed for 'super density'.

Among the deliberately uneven blocks of hedging are pools of water and delicate grasses, wild meadow, woodland, heath and water margin flowers within a frame of charred oak (a Japanese technique) and green oak fencing. This thought-provoking garden, aiming to be viewed rather than entered, has echoes of the British countryside with its field patterns and ancient woodland, but has been composed to evoke a Zen calmness.

TOPIARY, KNOTS AND PARTERRES

Roberto Burle-Marx and the Copacabana parterre

Roberto Burle Marx (1909–1994), the Brazilian polymath – sculptor, designer, musician and botanist, but seeing himself above all as a painter – brought all his skills together in his exuberant garden design. He introduced Cubism in the vibrant patterns he created, not least the single vast arrangement of rhythmic swirling patterns for his parterres with palm trees covering the nearly three miles of Brazil's Copacabana beach promenade in Rio. His other great contribution to gardening was the seeking out of native Brazilian plants (previously considered to be of little interest for gardens) in professional plant finding expeditions, introducing them and incorporating them into his garden designs.

The wheat parterre

The great Spanish designer Fernando Caruncho is another who makes a point of using indigenous plants. In his Spanish gardens he works with a palette of native plants, and he includes echoes of Moorish history in his designs. The Japanese paring down to a few elements is another characteristic. Born in 1957, Caruncho studied philosophy at Madrid University before taking up garden design, and he brings to it a degree of spirituality.

His Mas de les Voltes (Wheat Garden), for a Catalan farmhouse is a breakthrough and utterly simple. It is composed of six parterres, on a grid that carries with it medieval associations. There are just three elements – grass and trees and (possibly a first from a garden designer) a crop of agricultural wheat planted for decorative purposes. The trees are alternately cypresses and the gnarled olive trees characteristic of the Mediterranean.

In a garden in Minorca, he has created a water parterre of sixteen squares. Some hold water but others are filled with mounds of clipped and shaped escallonia, a plant he prefers to box for clipping. He uses it again in the garden of his own home, near Madrid. Flowing waves of tightly clipped hedging provide a visual base for a pavilion – a single shot of red as the focal point in a predominantly green garden.

A few last thoughts on topiary

Arne Maynard, designer of some two hundred beautiful gardens, writes of the uses of topiary in the garden. Topiary with its 'weight and density', he says, 'is one of the simplest and most effective design tools for adding structure and drama to a garden. It can be used like signage to beckon you from one area of a garden to another. It is a way to connect architecture

OPPOSITE ABOVE The rhythmic parterre of mosaic at Copacabana beach promenade in Rio by Roberto Burle-Marx.
OPPOSITE BELOW Fernando Caruncho's Mas de les Voltes (Wheat Garden) in Catalonia.

to the landscape. It bridges the gap in scale between the mature trees and the less substantial plants in a garden.'

He likes its versatility, the different ways that – whether it be formal, informal or 'organic' – it can be made to hide a view or to frame one with a window, to provide visual axes through a garden or to divide up the space. Clipped greenery next to unclipped adds interest as a textural palette. With this in mind, he sometimes makes a topiary out of a single existing hawthorn or field maple within the hedgerow, to give it a 'naïve formality'.

He does not limit his topiary to yew and box but enjoys using hornbeam and particularly beech, for its colouring and because it hangs on to its leaves in winter. Hawthorn and field maple, he says, make 'naïve topiary forms, transparent and twiggy in winter and they look wonderful when they catch the low winter sun and cast shadows.' Pleached and pollarded trees offer a space-saving solution for marking pathways and they can screen views at eye level. A circle of pleached trees 'looks elegant in the centre of a garden and makes a light and airy intimate space.'

Topiary shapes clustered around Arne Maynard's house in Wales are 'like characters at a party or a dance'.

TOPIARY, KNOTS AND PARTERRES

At Allt-y-bela, his Elizabethan tower house in Wales, a single clipped beech just out of sight of the house signifies that it is around the corner.

On arrival visitors are met by a group of different-sized topiary shapes clustered around the house 'like characters at a party or a dance'. 'Some congregate in small groups and some stand alone, but all are sentinels at entrances or markers at particular points. A field tree has been shaped some distance away to give the appearance of 'a late guest arriving'. Tiered shapes stand out as individuals and some, dressed with 'flouncy skirts', look ready to break into an Elizabethan jig or gavotte.

So much fun can be had out of topiary, whether it is in taking 'leaves from the past', by adding a Tudor love knot in the front garden of a town house, or shaping a geometric castellated hedge, or a scalloped one or one formed into irregular waves. Topiary is also a folk art and here the possibilities are endless (though favourites tend towards the peacock or the cockerel). Garden design is like stage design, theatre in the round. Thanks to the invention of mechanical hedge trimmers and lightweight steps, we can all throw up backdrops, design an arena, bring in some wings, make arches or *berceaux*, verdant tunnels or aerial hedges. Even the faultless grandeur of the topiary at Versailles is within our reach, if that is what we fancy.

In the introduction to the 1995 edition of Nathaniel Lloyd's 1925 *Garden Craftsmanship in Yew and Box* the legendary plantsman Christopher Lloyd could not resist poking fun at his father. He wrote that Nathaniel had been frustrated in his love of 'precision . . . exact lines and precisely flat surfaces', because his hedges – which were intended to have 'the sternness of battlemented bastions' – relaxed in time to develop hilarious 'unintended swellings and obesity in unlooked-for directions'. His view is that topiary itself 'is a kind of fun, never intended to be taken too seriously, however cleverly executed'.

Serious or frivolous, topiary always has character and presence. While wonderfully impressive when it takes the form of an immaculate battlemented bastion, it has poetry and possibly even greater charm when it is overblown and blowsy with age. Either way, it will always be a win-win proposition.

OVERLEAF The 'battlemented bastions' at Great Dixter, today surrounded by free planting.

Garden glossary

Amphitheatre An open circular, semicircular or oval theatre with a central stage for plays or sporting events and tiered seating. Especially associated with the Greeks and Romans but taken up by the landscape movement of the eighteenth century, sometimes just made of turf.

Arbour A garden shelter, shady retreat or bower, a covered alley or walk, made of latticework covered in climbers, trained trees or topiary. Very popular in medieval gardens (in many an ingenious design) and continued ever since.

Baroque Derived from the Portuguese *barroco*, a misshapen pearl, 'baroque' was, at first, a derogatory term, applied to any form of art that did not aspire to the perfection of the Italian Renaissance. In gardens, it was later applied specifically to the extravagance epitomized in the formal gardens of Versailles and other great French gardens *c.*1600 to 1750.

Bedding out Carpet bedding, usually of annuals grown in the greenhouse and planted out en masse for a temporary display.

Belvedere From the Italian for 'beautiful to see'. A raised structure from which to admire the view.

Berceau From the French word for a cradle or crib: an arched arbour of trained trees or climbers over trellis, often used as the gateway to a garden in the woods or *bosquet*.

Bosco From the Italian for a wood, used in the Renaissance to describe a designed grove of trees (often of the same variety) with planned walks. Later became a *bosquet* in French and a *wilderness* in English.

Boulingrin A French term taken from the English 'bowling green', referring to a lawn (presumably kept to the same high standard as a bowling green), but with sloping banks around it and sometimes edged by parterres.

Cabinet de verdure A garden room defined by tall clipped hedges, like walls, often within a *bosquet* or a formal woodland.

Campagna Italian for the 'countryside', used particularly with reference to descriptions of the landscape by Pliny the Younger and to the wild classical landscapes of Nicolas Poussin and Claude Lorrain.

Cartouche A scroll shape, usually for an inscription.

Cascade A fall of water: the gardens of the Italian Renaissance provided many dramatic examples.

Chahar bagh A rectangulat garden divided into four smaller squares by walkways or flowing water, representing the Four Rivers of Paradise in the Islamic garden. The *quarters* used as a popular arrangement for the laying out of gardens ever since.

Clairvoie/clairvoyée An openwork gate, fence or grille providing a view. A characteristic of Dutch gardens of the seventeenth century.

Claude glass A slightly convex dark-tinted pocket mirror that gave a soft, painterly reflected image when held up by the viewer with his back to the view. Named after Claude Lorrain. Popular in the eighteenth century with artists and art and garden connoisseurs of the *Picturesque* school.

Colonnade A row of columns of any material, including clipped greens or trees.

Compartimento/compartiment A term used by the Italian and French Renaissance garden designers to describe the divisions of the space in the parterre design. Hence the *Parterre de compartiments*, a parterre divided into different spaces. In his book *Le Théâtre des plans et jardinage* of 1652, Claude Mollet claims to be the inventor of the *compartiments de broderie* (the French embroidery style).

Coquillage A display of shellwork often used in grottoes.

Entrelac The French term for a knot (as opposed to a *parterre*) where the patterns join up in interlacing bands without a break. Sometimes confusingly called an 'entrelac parterre'.

Espalier A method of training trees flat against a wall or support, an ornamental and space-saving method often used for growing fruit.

Exedra A semicircular recessed area in a garden, dating from ancient Greece, but especially popular for the display of orange trees in seventeenth-century Dutch gardens and for sculptures in eighteenth-century gardens such as that at Chiswick House.

Fabrique Fanciful garden buildings often with cultural associations. Popular in eighteenth-century landscape gardens as at Stowe or Stourhead.

Ferme ornée An ornamental farm, as Marie-Antoinette's le Hameau at Versailles, taken up by Switzer and Repton as a practical solution to providing a garden with an attractive working farm.

Finial The ornamental top of a pediment or a gate pier in stone, wood or topiary.

Flowery mead A meadow full of wild flowers, associated with courtly medieval literature and paintings.

Gardenesque A term invented by J.C. Loudon, in an article for the *Gardener's Magazine* in 1832. In accordance with his 'Principle of Recognition', trees and shrubs should be allowed to grow freely according to their natural habit within the ideal conditions of a garden.

Gazebo A garden pavilion or summer house providing a view.

Gazon coupé (cut work) A style of parterre cut out of the turf.

Giardino segreto The secret garden of the Italian Renaissance. See also *Hortus conclusus*.

Giochi d'acqua/jeux d'eau (water jokes) Practical jokes where water sprayed on unsuspecting visitors from hidden spouts. Particularly popular in the Renaissance Mannerist gardens.

Gothick Eighteenth-century revival of medieval architecture including, e.g., the pointed arch, the ribbed vault, the flying buttress. It later came back into fashion as the 'Victorian Gothic'.

Grotto A fantasy cave popular in gardens from the Renaissance, often decorated with shells or minerals, fake stalactites or mythical figures. Frequently part of a fountain or pool with allegorical statues, even automata of monsters and pagan gods. In the eighteenth century 'hermits' were hired to add to the atmosphere.

Ha-ha A sunken ditch, invisible to the eye from the house, or even from quite close, designed to keep livestock out of the garden while giving an uninterrupted view of the countryside beyond. Probably originally a military design.

Hortus conclusus An enclosed garden, with specific reference to the *Song of Solomon*, 'Hortus conclusus soror mea, sponsa' ('A garden enclosed is my sister, my spouse').

Interstices The gaps between the patterns in a *parterre* or *knot garden* which might be filled with flowers or inert material.

Knot garden A pattern on the ground that joins up like a knot.

Leadwork Cast lead statues and vases were popular with the Dutch and also in Britain in the late seventeenth century. Usually painted, sometimes to look like stone or bronze.

Locus amoenus A pleasant spot, the garden or the pastoral idyll.

Loggia A covered arcade open on one side, often attached to a house, e.g., Raphael's Loggia for Villa Madama near Rome.

Mosaiculture Used in the nineteenth century to describe carpet bedding that was arranged to make a picture. In modern times applied to a form of plant sculpture that is often mistaken for topiary, although the technique is entirely different: plants are placed within a 3D framework (which often includes a watering system).

Mount A man-made hillock built to provide a prospect or a view over the garden – particularly popular with the Tudors.

Nymphaeum From ancient Greece and Rome where a temple, a shrine or a natural cave or grotto, with water in some form, was consecrated to a nymph or nymphs, especially the nymphs of springs. Taken up in the Renaissance and beyond.

Palissade From the French: a severe hedge clipped straight, sheer and tall like a wall.

Parterre Takes various forms: *parterre en broderie* (embroidery parterre of swirling patterns); *parterre de pièces coupées* (where the patterns were cut into the turf on simpler lines) and the *parterre à l'anglaise* or 'plat', which was a much plainer style.

Patte d'oie From the French for 'goose foot': radiating paths meeting at one point.

Physic garden A garden set aside for medicinal plants.

Picturesque Describes the eighteenth-century movement in garden design to imitate the landscapes of the Italian *campagna* as painted by Claude and Poussin.

Pinetum An area laid aside for a collection of conifers.

Plate-bande A flower border within or alongside a parterre.

Pleaching Making a hedge on stilts by cutting off the lower branches of a line of trees and joining the branches in an aerial flat screen.

Pleasance A medieval term for a pleasure garden or for a park for games or hunting.

Pleasure ground A cultivated garden for pleasure and walking as opposed to the less cultivated park designed for hunting or to be viewed from a carriage.

Quarters and rounds Square beds divided into quarters and circular beds.

Quincunx An arrangement of four dots on the corners of a square and one in the middle, like the 'five' on a dice. A pattern much used in tree planting from the Renaissance onwards.

Rococo From the French *rocaille* (pebblework) and *coquille* (shell). A playful, light-hearted style taken up in the late eighteenth century with fanciful and exotic buildings, grottoes and other notions.

Rosarium A formal rose garden.

Rosary A devotional rose garden.

Rotunda A circular building, often open, with a dome supported by columns, sometimes attached to a temple.

Salle de verdure A garden room within a designed *wilderness* or *bosquet*.

Sharawadgi The word used by Sir William Temple in his essay *Upon the Gardens of Epicurus* (1692) to describe a doctrine of asymmetry in Chinese garden design. (However, it is not a Chinese word.)

Star or *étoile* A circus or meeting point for paths, usually associated with rides through the *wilderness* of a large estate or park.

Stove A hothouse, so called as in the seventeenth century greenhouses were heated by Dutch stoves.

Topiarius A Roman slave gardener with particular responsibility for the topiary.

Treillage Elaborate and highly skilled trelliswork made by a *treillageur* (as at Versailles). Traditionally made of chestnut wood and often painted. Known as 'carpenter's work' in England.

Trompe l'œil Cheating the eye – the art of illusion. Much practised in gardens.

Wilderness An ornamental woodland or grove.

Further reading

Adams, William Howard, *Nature Perfected – Gardens through History,* Abbeville Press, 1991

Benes, Mirka and Dianne Suzette Harris, *Villas and Gardens in Early Modern Italy and France,* Cambridge University Press, 2001

Brix, Michael, *The Baroque Landscape: André Le Nôtre and Vaux-le-Vicomte,* Rizzoli, 2004

Brown, Jane, *Vita's Other World: A Gardening Biography of Vita Sackville-West,* Viking, 1985

Bruton-Seal, Julie and Matthew Seal, *The Herbalist's Bible: John Parkinson's Lost Classic Rediscovered,* Merlin Unwin, 2014

Burnett, David, *Longleat: The Story of an English Country House,* Collins, 1978

Castell, Robert, *The Villas of the Ancients,* Garland Press, 1982

Coffin, David R., *Gardens and Gardening in Papal Rome,* Princeton University Press, 1991

Colonna, Francesco, *Hypnerotomachia Poliphili: The Strife of Love in a Dream,* Thames and Hudson, 1999

Conan, Michael (ed.), *Baroque Garden Culture: Emulation, Sublimation, Subversion,* Dumbarton Oaks, 2005

Crisp, Frank and Catherine Childs Crisp Paterson, *Mediaeval Gardens: Flowery Medes and other Arrangements of Herbs, Flowers, and Shrubs grown in the Middle Ages, with some Account of Tudor, Elizabethan, and Stuart Gardens,* Hacker Art Books, 1966

De Caus, Salomon, *Le Jardin Palatin: Hortus Palatinus,* Editions du Moniteur, 1981

Du Prey, Pierre de la Ruffinière, *The Villas of Pliny from Antiquity to Posterity,* University of Chicago Press, 1994

Elliott, Brent, *Victorian Gardens,* Timber Press, 1986

Farrar, Linda, *Ancient Roman Gardens,* Sutton Publishers, 1998

Green, David, *Gardener to Queen Anne: Henry Wise, 1653–1738, and the Formal Garden,* Oxford University Press, 1956

Hadfield, Miles, *A History of British Gardening,* John Murray, 1979

Harvey, John, *Mediaeval Gardens,* Batsford, 1981

Hazlehurst, Franklin Hamilton, *Jacques Boyceau and the French Formal Garden,* University of Georgia Press, 1966

Hill, Thomas, *The Gardener's Labyrinth,* edited by Richard Mabey, Oxford University Press, 1987

Hitchmough, Wendy, *Arts and Crafts Gardens,* V&A Publications, 2005

Hunt, John Dixon, *The Anglo-Dutch Garden in the Age of William and Mary,* Taylor and Francis, 1988

— *The Dutch Garden in the Seventeenth Century,* Harvard University Press, 1990

— *The Picturesque Garden in Europe,* Thames and Hudson, 2002

— *William Kent, Landscape Garden Designer,* Zwemmer, 1987

Jacques, David, *Georgian Gardens: The Reign of Nature,* Batsford, 1983

Jacques, David and Arend Jan van der Horst, *William and Mary,* Christopher Helm, 1968

James, John, *The Theory and Practice of Gardening,* Gregg International Publishers, 1969

Jardine, Lisa, *Going Dutch,* Harper Collins, 2008

Jennings, Anne, *Georgian Gardens,* English Heritage, 2005

Kern, Hermann, *Through the Labyrinth: Designs and Meanings over 5000 Years* Prestel, 2000

Littlewood, Antony Robert, Henry Maguire and Joachim Wolschke-Bulmahn (eds), *Byzantine Garden Culture,* Harvard University Press, 2002

Lloyd, Nathaniel, *Garden Craftsmanship in Yew and Box,* E. Benn Ltd, 1925

Macdougall, Elizabeth B., *John Claudius Loudon and the Early Nineteenth Century in Great Britain,* Dumbarton Oaks, 1980

— (ed.), *Medieval Gardens,* Harvard University Press, 1986

Mayer, Laura, *Humphry Repton,* Shire Publications, 2014

Morgan, Luke, *Nature as a Model: Salomon de Caus and Early Seventeenth Century Landscape Design,* University of Pennsylvania Press, 2007

Page, Russell, *The Education of a Gardener,* Penguin Books, 1962

Parkinson, Anna, *Nature's Alchemist: John Parkinson, Herbalist to Charles I,* Frances Lincoln, 2007

Pennick, Nigel, *Mazes and Labyrinths,* Robert Hale, 1990

Pliny the Younger, *The Letters of the Younger Pliny,* Penguin Books, 1969

Richardson, Tim, *The Arcadian Friends: Inventing the English Landscape Garden,* Bantam Press, 2007

Rutherford, Sarah, *The Arts and Craft Garden,* Shire Publications, 2013

Sedding, John Dando, *Garden Craft Old and New,* J. Lane, 1901

Strong, Roy, *The Renaissance Garden in England,* Thames and Hudson, 1979

Turner, Roger, *Capability Brown and the Eighteenth-Century English Landscape,* Rizzoli, 1985

Walpole, Horace, *History of the Modern Taste in Gardening,* Ursus, 1995

Weiss, Allen S., *Mirrors of Infinity: the French Formal Garden & 17th-Century Metaphysics,* Princeton Architectural Press, 1995

Whaley, Robin and Anne Jennings, *Knot Gardens and Parterres,* Barn Elms, 1996

Index

Acknowledgments

Author's acknowledgments

Working with Pimpernel Press on this book has been a great pleasure and a privilege. My thanks to my kind and erudite editor, Jo Christian; to Sue Gladstone, the masterly and wise picture editor; and to Anne Wilson, the designer with the magician's touch. My sincerest thanks also go to the European Boxwood and Topiary Society for their generous support and encouragement.

Picture credits

With the exception of those listed here, all the images in this book are in private collections or in the public domain. The publishers have made every effort to contact holders of copyright works. Any copyright holders we have been unable to reach are invited to contact the publishers so that a full acknowledgment may be given in subsequent editions. For permission to reproduce the images below, the publishers would like to thank the following:

By courtesy of G. Ajmone-Marsan: 262

Akg-images: 100/101, 134/5, 139 (photo Jérôme da Cunha)

Alamy Stock Photo: 235 (©David Humphreys); 244, 248 & 249 (©The National Trust Photo Library)

Bridgeman Images: 6 & 97 (Château de Grand Trianon, Versailles); 15 (Biblioteca Marciana, Venice); 26 (Sant' Apollinaire in Classe, Ravenna/Cameraphoto Arte Veneziana); 28/9, 60/61, 99, 162/3 (De Agostini Picture Library/A. Dagli Orti); 34 (Städelsches Kunstinstitut, Frankfurt-am-Main); 38 (British Library London/©British Library Board); 44 (Musée de l'Île de France, Sceaux); 72, 130, 169 (Private Collection/The Stapleton Collection); 74 (Château de Versailles); 93 (Bibliothèque Nationale, Paris); 108 (Royal Collection Trust ©Her Majesty Queen Elizabeth II, 2016); 113 (Hatfield House, Hertfordshire); 164 (British Library, London); 166 (Hanbury Hall, Worcestershire/National Trust Photographic Library); 173 (©Collection of the Earl of Pembroke, Wilton House, Wiltshire); 177 (Private Collection/photo ©Christie's Images); 190 (Biblioteca Estense, Modena); 192 (Collection of the Duke of Devonshire, Chatsworth); 198/9 (Stourhead, Wiltshire/National Trust Photographic Library); 201 (Hartwell House, Aylesbury, Buckinghamshire/National Trust Photographic Library); 204/5 (Chartwell, Kent/National Trust Photographic Library/Derrick E. Witty); 206 (London Metropolitan Archives, City of London); 209 (Bibliothèque des Arts Décoratifs, Paris); 216 (Private Collection); 233 right (Private Collection)

Danièle Canay: 265

By courtesy of Fernando Caruncho: 276 below (photo Loraint Toussaint)

Carol Casselden: 239, 240/41, 280/81

©Country Life: 245

Chris Crowder: half-title page, title page, 250/51

Diego Delso: 8 right & 253 (Wikimedia Commons , Licence (C-BY-SA4.O)

Ethan Doyle White: 231 (Wikimedia Commons)

©Fishbourne Roman Palace/Sussex Archaeological Society: 18

Caroline Foley: 7 above right, 7 below left, 9 above left, 12, 234

Courtesy of Ludwig Gerns: 274

Getty Images: 46 (DEA/G. Dagli Orti); 95 (Science & Society Picture Library); 259 (Jason Hawkes); 264 (John S. Lander); 268 (Cora Niele)

Digital image courtesy of the Getty's Open Content Program: 76, 94, 158/9, 185

Roger Last: opposite contents page, 272/3

Andrew Lawson: 246, 247, 254/5, 260, 266/7, 269 (designer Piet Oudolf), 270/71 (designer Tom Stuart-Smith), 275 (designer Christopher Bradley-Hole)

Reproduced with the kind permission of His Grace the Duke of Marlborough, Blenheim Palace Image Library: 179

By courtesy of Arne Maynard: 278 (photo William Collinson)

The Metropolitan Museum of Art/www.metmuseum.org: 148 & 149 (Gift of Edith Neuman de Végvár, in honor of her husband, Charles Neuman de Végvár, 1964)

The Metropolitan Museum of Art/www.metmuseum.org: 183 (Bequest of W. Gedney Beaty, 1941)

The Metropolitan Museum of Art/www.metmuseum.org: 196 (Harris Brisbane Dick Fund, 1942)

The Metropolitan Museum of Art/www.metmuseum.org: 228 (Purchase, Edward C. Moore Jr. Gift, 1923)

Yan Monel: 13

Neosnaps/flickr: 261

Private Collection: 111

Richard Raworth: 252

RIBApix: 67

Royal Collection Trust/©Her Majesty Queen Elizabeth II, 2016: 114/5, 156/7

Shutterstock: 276 above

Christine Ternynk: 257 above

www.turkisharchery.com: 31

Tylers Museum, Haarlem, The Netherlands: 151

By courtesy of Paul Veenhuijzen: 238

©Victoria and Albert Museum, London: 40, 83, 84

Wellcome Library, London/Wellcome Images: 32